Dear Theophilus:

Two Letters from Luke

by John W. Wade

You may obtain a 64-page leader's guide to accompany this paperback. Order number 41037 from Standard Publishing or your local supplier.

A Division of Standard Publishing
Cincinnati, Ohio 45231
No. 41036

© 1985 the STANDARD PUBLISHING CO.,
Division of STANDEX INTERNATIONAL CORP.

Library of Congress Cataloging in Publication Data

Wade, John William, 1924-
  Dear Theophilus.

  1. Bible. N. T. Luke—Commentaries 2. Bible.
N. T. Acts—Commentaries. I. Title.
BS2589.W33 1985   226'.407   85-9728
ISBN 0-87239-968-0 (pbk.)

Printed in U.S.A.

1985

TABLE OF CONTENTS

Chronological Charts

Maps

Chronology of Luke

Luke tells when John the Baptist began his work (Luke 3:1-3), but after that he gives little indication of the passing of time. John, however, mentions enough special days to show that Jesus' ministry continued more than three years and included four Passover feasts. This outline shows how chapters 1—18 of this book fit into the three years of Jesus' ministry.

Chapter in this book	Reference in Luke	Notes of time
1. The Silence Is Broken	1:5-25	
2. Announcement of Jesus' Birth	1:26-38	
3. Visit of Mary and Birth of John	1:39-80	
4. The Birth of Jesus	2:1-40	
5. Jesus' Baptism and Temptation	3:1—4:13	Jesus about thirty Luke 3:23
At this point Luke omits events of about nine months that are recorded in John 1:29—4:42. The first Passover of Jesus' ministry was early in that period.		Passover A.D. 27 John 2:13
6. Jesus' Early Ministry in Galilee	4:14-44	

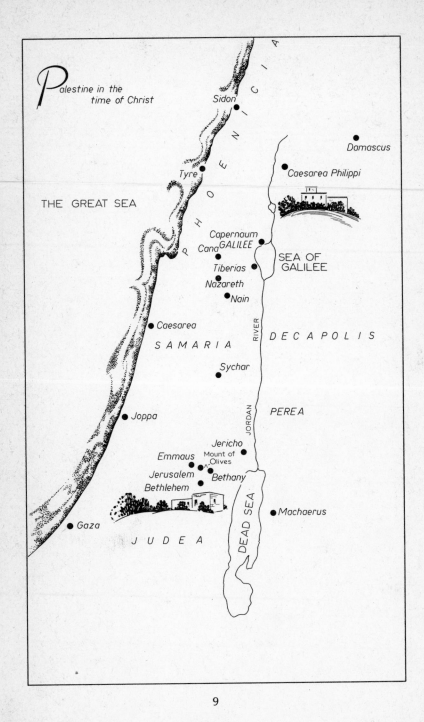

Palestine in the time of Christ

THE GREAT SEA

PHOENICIA

Sidon

Damascus

Tyre

Caesarea Philippi

Capernaum
Cana GALILEE
Tiberias
Nazareth
Nain

SEA OF GALILEE

Caesarea

SAMARIA

JORDAN RIVER

DECAPOLIS

Sychar

Joppa

PEREA

Jericho
Emmaus Mount of Olives
Jerusalem Bethany
Bethlehem

Gaza

JUDEA

DEAD SEA

Machaerus

9

Introduction

Luke 1:1-4

The editors have chosen to combine this study of the Gospel of Luke and the book of Acts into one book. This makes good sense because both Biblical books were written by the same man, addressed to the same reader, and together give a continuing story. The two books might fittingly be called First Luke and Second Luke. In First Luke (the Gospel) we read of Jesus' teachings in preparation for the church, and in Second Luke (Acts) we see the beginning, growth, and spread of the church.

Of all the writers of the Bible, perhaps about forty altogether, Luke is unique in at least one respect. He is the only Gentile among them. Beyond this we know little about him. We do know that he accompanied Paul on many of his travels. We are told that he was a physician (Colossians 4:14), and this fact is evidenced by his more specific and detailed discussions of diseases mentioned in his Gospel. But we don't know where his home was originally, although some have suggested either Macedonia, Asia Minor, or Antioch of Syria. And we don't even know the circumstances that led to his becoming a Christian.

Luke addresses both his Gospel and the book of Acts to a certain Theophilus. The form of address, "most excellent," suggests that the addressee was a person of prominence, possibly even a Roman official. The two works were written to inform the man about Christianity, concerning which he had already been taught (Luke 1:4). If Theophilus was a Christian, these books would make him a more knowledgeable Christian. If not, the aim was to persuade him to become a Christian or at least to look upon Christianity more favorably.

Both books are written in excellent Greek, perhaps the most literary Greek in the New Testament. Luke writes as one using his own language rather than as a person who is writing in a second language.

Luke's Gospel has been called the "universal Gospel," for it shows an interest that goes beyond narrow Jewish provincialism. For example, Luke traces Jesus' lineage not to Abraham but to Adam (Luke 3:23-38). It is Luke alone who gives us the parable of the good Samaritan (Luke 10:30-37). He also mentions that the one grateful leper was a Samaritan (Luke 17:11-19). Luke seems to give more attention to the poor, the sinner, the outcast. Women also have a prominent place in his Gospel. He tells the story of Jesus' birth from the viewpoint of Mary (Luke 1, 2), and it is he who gives us the fascinating picture of Mary and Martha in their home (Luke 10:38-42).

Unlike Matthew and John, Luke was not an eyewitness of the events recorded in his Gospel. However, he compensated for this by carefully examining the sources—writings by others and testimonies of eyewitnesses (Luke 1:1-4). In Second Luke (the book of Acts) he records many events of which he was an eyewitness. Evidently the other records in Acts, like those in the Gospel, are the result of careful investigation.

In this study we have chosen to use the New International Version for most of our discussion. This is an accurate version that has put the Word of God into a readable, modern form. This fact, along with its wide acceptance, makes it a convenient version to use.

Our prayers are with you as you use this brief study. After two thousand years, we are convinced that Luke's writings can still do what they did in the first century—bring men to Christ and inspire them to grow in Him.

The Silence Is Broken

Luke 1:5-25

In a symphonic movement a composer on occasion inserts what is called a grand pause. At that point in the concert every instrument is stilled. As the echoes of the musical strains and the murmuring of the audience are absorbed in the vastness of the concert hall, one can almost hear his own heartbeat. Every eye is riveted on the conductor as every listener in breathless anticipation awaits the next chord. Thus the grand pause serves in a dramatic way to concentrate attention on what is to follow.

In a somewhat similar fashion, God wrote a grand pause into the score of His plan for human redemption. For hundreds of years He had spoken to the Jewish "forefathers through the prophets at many times and in various ways" (Hebrews 1:1). But most of the Jews had not been listening. They had been too busy, drawn away by the temptations of the world. Because they were not listening, God ceased His revelation through the prophets for more than four hundred years. Malachi, the last of the prophets, carried out his ministry around 430 B.C. He closed with a message of God's continuing concern for His people. God would send Elijah to them before that "great and dreadful day of the Lord" (Malachi 4:5).

No one knew when that day would be. No doubt many seers arose who claimed to be able to understand Scriptural prophecies and to read the signs of the times. Their claims all proved false. But even though God did not speak during this period, He was busy preparing the people to receive His next and most important revelation. He allowed them to pass from the control of the Persians to the control of the Greeks. Then when the empire of Alexander broke up, He allowed them to become a political football between Egypt and Syria. Eventually, after a heroic struggle, they were led to their independence by the Maccabees. But before long, their own leaders became every bit as corrupt and oppressive as the foreign rulers they replaced. Finally God permitted them to be conquered by the Romans, who governed the land through wicked Herod.

During these long years through which God was silent but active, many became discouraged and abandoned their hope that He would ever send them a Messiah. Others found a way to live with the present, selling their convictions for a mess of worldly pottage. But some, refusing either to give up hope or compromise their faith, clung stubbornly to the belief that someday God would break His silence and send them His Savior. As time wore on, this Messianic expectancy became ever more intense, building almost to a fever pitch by the time Luke's narration begins. Because the people were so eager for the Messiah to come, some of them were easy victims of false and selfish leaders (Acts 5:35-37). But when the real Messiah came, many were disappointed because He would not lead a violent revolt against Roman rule.

The Channel of God's New Revelation
Luke 1:5-7

During the long centuries of His silence, God had been at work preparing Israel to receive His new revelation. Now under the reign of Herod the Great "the time had fully come" (Galatians 4:4). God was ready to speak. God has never been limited in the channels He has used to bring His message to man. The Old Testament revelation came through shepherds and kings, princes and paupers, the learned and the humble. It should not, then, surprise us that God chose a priest through whom to sound the first note of His new revelation.

This marvelous revelation came near the end of the reign of that Herod whom we have come to call the Great. He ruled from 37 to 4 B.C. An Idumean rather than a Jew, he was placed on the throne by the Romans. Through his clever political maneuvering and his cruelty, he managed to keep his throne even during the civil war between Octavian and Antony. He attempted to endear himself to the

Jews by completely remodeling and enlarging the temple, but they still held him in contempt. He died only a few years after the incident related here, and his death was unlamented.

The channel God chose for His new revelation was not the one that man might have chosen. Man would have been inclined to choose the powerful, the prestigious, the showy. God, on the other hand, chose poor and humble people for His channel. Yet in spite of their humble status, or perhaps because of it, they were pious people who were receptive to the call of God.

In those troubled times lived a priest named Zechariah. His name, which means "Jehovah has remembered," seems most appropriate for one who was to receive words from a God who had not forgotten His people.

As early as the reign of David, the priests were so numerous that they had to take turns serving in the sanctuary. For this purpose they were divided into twenty-four divisions or courses, with each division serving a week at a time. Zechariah belonged to the division named for Abijah, head of the priestly family in David's time (1 Chronicles 24:10). His wife, Elizabeth, was a descendant of Aaron, so she also was of priestly lineage.

First, let's see the good news about this couple. Luke says they were "upright in the sight of God." He then goes on to specify in what ways they were upright: they observed "all the Lord's commandments and regulations blamelessly" (1:6). The picture is of a pious, faithful couple. But now comes the bad news: "They had no children." The impact of this tragedy is lost on people in our day, for whom childlessness is frequently considered a blessing. By contrast, in Biblical times children were considered one of God's richest blessings, and childlessness was a disgrace. We see this dramatically illustrated in the case of Rachel, who cried out, "Give me children, or I'll die!" (Genesis 30:1). Zechariah and his wife were both well advanced in years, and so there was little likelihood that they would ever have children.

The Condition of God's New Revelation
Luke 1:8-11
The burning of incense was a part of the daily worship service in the temple. It occurred twice daily, once in the morning and once in the evening. Ordinarily a priest had the privilege of conducting this service only once in a lifetime. The priests were selected for this service by lot, and on this occasion the lot fell to Zechariah. This

experience must have been one of the highest and holiest of the old priest's life, and no doubt he entered the sanctuary with no little fear and trembling. But in spite of his intense emotions, he could scarcely have anticipated the dramatic experience that was to follow.

We have no way of knowing why God chose that moment to reveal His message to Zechariah. But it did come at a time when the old priest was experiencing intense religious emotions, a time when he would be most receptive to a word from God. Those who criticize institutionalized religious activities need to be reminded that significant religious experience can occur within a most formal setting. Instead of abandoning our regular meetings, we need to make them vital and meaningful. It does not take a special revelation to make worship real.

The Content of God's New Revelation
Luke 1:12-20

Even as Zechariah concluded his service of making the incense offering, an angel stood by the right side of the altar. We are later informed that the angel was Gabriel. The name *Gabriel* means "man of God" or "hero of God." He is first mentioned in the Old Testament, which records that he brought a message to Daniel (Daniel 8:16; 9:21). Later he appeared also to Mary in Nazareth to announce that she was to become the mother of the Messiah (Luke 1:26, 27).

Zechariah responded as most of us would under similar circumstances—he was afraid. Gabriel's first action was to quiet his fears and reassure him. Then came the message, so unexpected and yet so joyous! Zechariah's prayer would be answered—Elizabeth would bear him a son, who would be named John, which means "the Lord has been gracious."

Gabriel gave further information about John. He would be a source of joy and delight. He was never to drink wine or other fermented beverage, and he would be filled with the Holy Spirit. In the spirit and power of the ancient prophet Elijah, he would turn the people back to God. This prophecy was fulfilled years later when John's call for repentance brought people to respond by the hundreds.

But the last bit of information brought by the angel was the most important. John's greatest task was "to make ready a people prepared for the Lord" (Luke 1:17). Clearly this has reference to John's special function in preparing the way for the coming of the Messiah.

16

Zechariah was hardly capable at the time of comprehending the meaning of this prophecy. Nor, it would seem, did he live long enough to witness John's ministry as the forerunner for Christ.

Zechariah responded with disbelief. After many years of fruitless praying, how could he expect to become a father in his old age? As a sign that his word was dependable, Gabriel gave a prophecy that would be fulfilled at once. It was not a pleasant sign, for it was both a sign and a punishment for Zechariah's lack of faith. He would not be able to speak until the prophecy was fulfilled in the birth of his son. Through the months, this would be a constant reminder that God's word is to be trusted.

It is easy enough for us to criticize Zechariah for his lack of faith. But we are likely to be a bit more temperate in our criticism of his failure when we carefully examine our own weaknesses. His mind was closed to God's revelation because neither he nor his fellow priests had ever experienced a revelation like that before, and because childless couples who have grown old do not then begin to produce children. Do we not also on occasion close our minds to the teachings of God's Word because, well, we have never thought of it before or we have never done it that way before?

The Conclusion of God's Revelation
Luke 1:21-25

As Zechariah tarried in the temple, somewhat dazed by his experience, the crowd of worshipers outside became a bit restless. They were rather like a modern church full of worshipers when the preacher goes five minutes over his allotted time. When the old priest finally appeared, the people immediately sensed that something was wrong. He stood mute before them, unable to pronounce the usual benediction. Instead he signaled with his hands, indicating that he could not speak. Apparently by these signs he was able to communicate enough so that the people understood he had seen some kind of vision. His pious behavior and reputation convinced them of the sincerity of his claims.

One might suppose that Zechariah's handicap would have prevented his further service in the temple, but such was not the case. He continued his ministry until his obligation for the week had been fulfilled. Then he and Elizabeth returned home, which we learn from verse 39 was "in the hill country of Judah." We have no way of locating exactly where this was, but apparently it lay somewhere in the rather barren hills south of Jerusalem.

After they returned, Elizabeth conceived as Gabriel had promised. We can readily imagine both her joy and her eagerness to share the good news that her reproach was taken away. We can only speculate about why she went into seclusion. Perhaps it was to meditate and to praise God that her disgrace of barrenness was removed. Perhaps, on the other hand, God's timetable required that her pregnancy not be made public until the coming birth of Jesus had been announced to Mary.

Announcement of Jesus' Birth

Luke 1:26-38

Suppose that in the year 4 B.C. you were put in charge of a committee to design publicity to promote the virtues of Nazareth. A tough assignment? Right. Nothing about the little village distinguished it from a hundred other dreary, dusty hamlets nestled in the Galilean hills. Nazareth was not famous for any article of trade produced there; no historic event of any significance had ever happened there; no famous person had ever lived there—or even visited there, for that matter. So write it off and forget it.

Write it off and forget it? Well, not just yet. By human standards there wasn't anything outstanding about the village, but God had different standards. He saw there a young maiden who by her virtue had won God's approval. Perhaps her outstanding qualities had not gone unnoticed by her family and neighbors, but apparently there was nothing about her that called special attention to her.

Nazareth
Luke 1:26

For all we know, Mary was born and had grown up in Nazareth. Though Nazareth was a small village in Bible times, it was not totally isolated from events that occurred in that part of Palestine. The town itself is in a depression surrounded by hills. Over the ridge to the south lies the Plain of Esdraelon, the site of several Old

Testament battles. From a hill to the north of town one can see Mount Carmel fifteen miles to the west. Between Mount Carmel and Nazareth passed a major road that connected Egypt with the empires to the north and east. Fifteen miles to the east in a deep depression nestles the Sea of Galilee. Far to the north one can see Mount Hermon, snow-covered most of the year. Today Nazareth is a city of ten thousand or more, many of whom seem to make their living by selling souvenirs to tourists or by displaying various holy places to them.

It was here that God chose to intervene once more into human history and take one more step in His plan for man's redemption. Once again Gabriel was the agent God used to carry His message. Six months earlier he had appeared to Zechariah in the sanctuary to announce the birth of John. Now he appeared to Mary to announce the birth of Jesus.

Mary and Joseph
Luke 1:27

This Mary is to be distinguished from several other women in the New Testament who bore the same name: Mary Magdalene, Mary the sister of Lazarus, Mary the wife of Clopas and also the mother of James the less and Joses, and Mary the mother of John Mark. Luke gives us several bits of information about Mary of Nazareth.

She was a virgin. This fact has been the source of much controversy, but Luke leaves no doubt about it. The Greek word he uses means virgin (1:27). Mary's reference to herself further underscores this fact (1:34). (The *King James Version* translates this more literally: "seeing I know not a man.") It is strange that some have found the doctrine of the virgin conception a barrier to their faith. If one can believe that God created the physical universe and the laws that govern it, why is it hard to believe that He could on this occasion set aside the laws that ordinarily govern conception?

Mary was betrothed or engaged to Joseph. In that culture, betrothal was a solemn matter. Ordinarily it could be set aside only by a bill of divorcement. Infidelity during the betrothal period was looked upon as adultery (Deuteronomy 22:23, 24). A betrothal was sometimes entered into when a girl was as young as twelve years old. This leads us to suppose that Mary was quite young at this time, perhaps only sixteen or seventeen. This supposition is based only on the customs of the time and place, however. The Bible has no statement of Mary's age.

20

Joseph, the man to whom Mary was betrothed, was a descendant of David, and thus from the tribe of Judah. Matthew traces Jesus' lineage back through Joseph to David and on back to Abraham (Matthew 1:2-16). Although Joseph was not Jesus' physical father, he would be counted as such legally for the purpose of genealogy.

Message From Heaven
Luke 1:28-33

Mary was alone and apparently indoors when Gabriel appeared to her. His first word was "greetings," or "hail," as the *King James Version* has it. However, it is likely that he spoke in Hebrew or Aramaic, and thus the greeting actually used was the familiar "Shalom." Mary was then addressed as "highly favored." This exalted salutation was appropriate, since she had been selected to become the mother of the Messiah. Gabriel then reassured her by affirming that God was with her.

Though Gabriel attempted by his greeting to assure her, Mary's initial response was one of shock and fright. To understand this reaction, we need only to imagine what our own mental state would be if a Heavenly being would suddenly appear before us. But her concern went beyond this first shock. In her mind she tried to discover a reason why she, a humble peasant girl, should be so honored. Her humility was certainly one of the reasons that such great honor came to her.

Gabriel's response was intended to calm Mary's fears and reassure her: "Do not be afraid." He had used the same words when he had approached Zechariah (1:13). Mary did not have to be afraid, because in spite of her humble origin she had found favor with God.

These words may have eased some of her fears, but Gabriel's words that followed must have puzzled her more than ever. She would conceive and bear a son. He would be named Jesus, which was the equivalent to the Hebrew name Joshua. The Hebrew name meant "Yahweh is salvation," a name that appropriately points out Jesus' mission to the world: "he will save his people from their sins" (Matthew 1:21).

Gabriel then began to describe the role that Jesus would play in God's eternal plan. "He will be great." This brief statement, sublime in its simplicity, understates His greatness. He will be not just great, but the greatest. Of course Mary could not comprehend the full implications of this statement. How does one measure greatness? By accumulated wealth? By power? By public acclaim? Jesus in His earthly ministry would have failed all of these tests that are considered so important in our modern world. His greatness would lie in who He was—the Son of God—and in what He would accomplish—the salvation of His people.

Gabriel emphasized who Jesus was. He would be called "the Son of the Most High." This term *Most High* is used in the Old Testament to refer to God (Numbers 24:16; Deuteronomy 32:8; 2 Samuel 22:14; Psalm 7:17; Hosea 7:16). Jesus is uniquely the Son of God, a fact that is reaffirmed in verse 35. Jesus' followers are sons of God in a different sense (John 1:12), but only Jesus was literally and physically conceived by the influence of the Holy Spirit. The *King James Version* describes this special relationship by calling Jesus God's "only begotten Son" (John 3:16). God has other sons (1 John 3:2a), but no other of the same kind, no other begotten in the same way.

This divine Son would be given the throne of His father David, said Gabriel. On the human side He would be a direct descendant of David, and in this verse we see a fulfillment of the prophecy in 2 Samuel 7:11b-16, a promise that the sons of David would occupy the throne of Israel forever. Jesus has no successor on that throne. His own personal rule is eternal.

Mary must have been overwhelmed by the promise that her Son, not yet conceived, would someday be ruler over the house of Jacob. Like most Jews of her day, when she thought of the kingdom of David she undoubtedly thought in terms of a physical kingdom. In her time, rulers for such a kingdom did not come from humble peasant stock. But the kingdom of the Messiah is more than just an extension of the dynasty established by David. It is a spiritual kingdom that will last forever. During His ministry Jesus spoke often of His kingdom (Mark 1:14, 15). He brought in a new era in which the spiritual ultimately triumphs over the physical. History bears ample testimony to this. All that remains of the great empires of Egypt, Babylonia, Assyria, Greece, and Rome are but a few relics that hint of their past glory. The kingdom of the Messiah, on the other hand, continues to expand and grow in power. What a source of strength it is to realize that we serve a king who will reign into eternity!

Pregnancy by Miracle
Luke 1:34-38

The implications of Gabriel's statement were overwhelming. We can hardly suppose Mary comprehended them fully. But she did raise one practical problem. How could she become a mother without having sexual relations with a man? Her question was different from that raised by Zechariah (1:18). In doubt he asked, "How can I know it will be as you say?" He was punished for his lack of faith. Not in doubt but in wonder Mary asked, "How can such a marvelous thing happen?" To that Gabriel gave a simple answer.

Mary would become pregnant, not through sexual relations with a man, but through the miraculous power of the Holy Spirit. Some reject the Biblical account of the virgin birth, claiming that it is but a reflection of ancient myths that tell of pagan gods who have sexual relations with human beings and beget demigods. But how different is the Bible record! In Grecian myths, for example, the gods assume human form and lustfully, often violently, engage in physical sex relations. The Biblical account contains nothing like this. There are no physical relations, no lust, and no violence. The conception occurs in a supernatural manner without any physical contact.

As further assurance, Gabriel then announced that Elizabeth was already six months pregnant. During those months she had withdrawn from public life to keep her happy secret, so the angel's message came as a complete surprise to Mary. Like anyone else, Mary would have supposed it was impossible for Elizabeth to have a baby. But the angel met that supposition squarely: "Nothing is impossible with God!" God could intervene miraculously to cause aged Elizabeth to become pregnant.

If Mary had any trouble believing Gabriel, the narrative does not indicate it. Her attitude was one of complete and humble submission: "I am the Lord's servant." Literally, the word that Mary used to describe herself is "slave," but in modern thinking that word has such negative connotations that most translators have softened it to "handmaid" or "servant." Still the more lowly name of slave is appropriate. Mary's humility put no limit on her duty. She was God's possession, to be used as He wished.

When he had delivered his message and Mary had submitted to the will of God, Gabriel quickly departed. His mission was accomplished, and in beautiful simplicity this scene drew to a close.

The Significance of the Virgin Birth

The account we are considering, along with the birth of Jesus as recorded in Matthew 2 and Luke 2, is one of the most beautiful and moving passages in the whole Bible. It is unfortunate that it has become the source of controversy. Some students, conditioned by the skepticism of our scientific age, reject out of hand the possibility

23

of a virgin conception. According to this kind of thinking, nothing can be accepted unless it is supported by data limited by scientific criteria. Such a narrow view of reality must lead ultimately to the rejection of a Creator God who can intervene in human affairs. If we believe in the Almighty, we can hardly question the word of the angel: "Nothing is impossible with God" (Luke 1:37).

Others reject the virgin birth by taking the position that it is not adequately supported by Scripture. One wonders how much more explicit an explanation could be than that set forth in Luke's account. Matthew does not report Gabriel's visit to Mary, but he does tell of the visit of the angel of the Lord to Joseph with the same message. Indeed, Matthew quotes Isaiah 7:14 as further evidence of the virgin birth: "The virgin will be with child and will give birth to a son."

Mark, since he begins his Gospel with the beginning of John's ministry, does not mention the virgin birth. But of course, he doesn't mention the birth of Jesus at all. Nor does the Gospel of John contain the birth narrative, but in his prologue John sets forth the pre-existence of Christ in such a dramatic way that the virgin birth seems most appropriate.

In view of the incarnation, Jesus Christ is divine, but He is also human. It seems entirely logical that the divine entrance into humanity should occur in a unique fashion. Thus the virgin birth makes quite good sense. Only once in history has God come into the world to live the life of a human being. Only once in history has the Holy Spirit miraculously intervened so that a virgin bears a child. All agree that Jesus' life and ministry were unique. Why should it be hard to believe that His birth was also unique?

The Status of Mary

All will agree that Mary was the best qualified woman in the world to become the mother of our Lord. She was qualified by her training, by her virtue, by her humility, and by her complete submission to the will of God. Thus she deserves the loving respect of every Christian. To accord her any less would be to display both ignorance and ingratitude.

Unfortunately, some believers have gone far beyond this. Mary has been elevated to a position almost equal with that of Christ—man's co-redemptrix, she is called. People are encouraged to bow before her image in adoration and to pray to her. They are told that she was a perpetual virgin, that she was conceived without sin, and that both her body and her soul ascended into Heaven. In some places Mary has for all practical purposes replaced Jesus Christ as our Redeemer. Needless to say, none of these teachings have support in the Scriptures. After the birth accounts, Mary is mentioned only infrequently in the Gospels and the remainder of the New Testament. These references provide no basis whatever for the elaborate theologies that have developed about her.

If the Bible is to be the basis of our faith, then we must say no to these exaggerated teachings. But in our rejection of them, let us not be guilty of denying Mary all the honor and respect that is due her.

Visit of Mary
and Birth of John
Luke 1:39-80

Luke's background as an educated Greek especially equipped him to be sensitive to lyric poetry. It is no surprise that it is he who records for us several hymns of praise to God by Mary, Zechariah, Simeon, and the angels at Jesus' birth. Luke, guided by the Holy Spirit, strongly suggests that the coming of our Lord was a joyous occasion, one that was appropriately accompanied by songs. The last half of Luke 1 records an important part of that glorious chain of events.

Mary's Visit to Elizabeth
Luke 1:39-45

Gabriel did not specifically order Mary to visit Elizabeth, and yet the suggestion was strong. A visit to Elizabeth would confirm the angel's word that she was pregnant. This, in turn, would strengthen Mary's faith in his prophecy that she was to become the mother of the Messiah.

Within a few days after Gabriel's visit, Mary left Nazareth and hastened to the town in the hill country where Elizabeth lived. This town has never been identified, but it may have been in the vicinity of Hebron. By the most direct route, this would involve traveling ninety to a hundred miles. But many Jews, seeking to avoid all contact with the despised Samaritans, would take a longer route down the east side of the Jordan River. This would add another thirty miles to the journey. Such a trip would take at least a week.

It is difficult to imagine how Mary's parents or Joseph could have been persuaded to allow a teenage girl to make such a trip. And on top of that, she apparently went alone; at least no mention is made of a traveling companion. This may suggest that the highways were a lot safer then than they are now. It also suggests that God providentially arranged for her to go and watched over her as she traveled.

When Mary arrived at her destination, she greeted Elizabeth. At the sound of Mary's voice, the baby leaped in Elizabeth's womb. Movement of a six-month-old fetus is quite normal, a fact that Luke, a physician, surely was aware of. Apparently this movement was so different that both Elizabeth and Luke recognized it as extraordinary. The word here translated "leaped" sometimes conveys the idea of leaping for joy (Luke 6:23), but in this case Elizabeth added another word to declare that the unborn baby's leap was a joyous one (verse 44).

Elizabeth herself was immediately filled with the Holy Spirit. Under His guidance she was able not only to understand the meaning of her baby's movement, but also to recognize Mary as the mother of the promised Messiah. Joyfully and loudly she acclaimed that fact in words that were structured like much of the Hebrew poetry from the Old Testament.

Her next response was one of humility. She felt that she had been honored by Mary's visit. Since there is nothing in the text to indicate that Mary up to that point had mentioned to anyone that she was to become the mother of the Lord, we must conclude that the Holy Spirit revealed this to Elizabeth.

Mary was blessed because she was to bear the Christ, but she was also blessed because of her faith. When the angel announced to her that she was to become the mother of the Messiah, she believed without any hesitation. Her actions stood in contrast to those of Zechariah, who in similar circumstances doubted (Luke 1:18-20).

Mary's Hymn of Praise
Luke 1:46-56

Mary's response was a joyous hymn of praise that is sometimes called the Magnificat. This name is the first word in the Latin Vulgate version of this hymn. Like Elizabeth's words of praise, Mary's hymn reflects the terminology, the cadences, and the literary devices of

Old Testament poetry. In many ways it reminds us of Hannah's hymn lifted up under similar circumstances (1 Samuel 2:1-10). This should not surprise us, because as a Jewish girl Mary from childhood was steeped in the literature of the Old Testament.

In verses 46-49, Mary poured forth her pent-up emotions, emotions that she had been holding back since Gabriel's announcement. Now that Elizabeth shared her great secret, she was free to give full expression to her joy. Her major emphasis was praise of God for honoring one so lowly as she.

In the verses that follow, her song turns from her personal joy and honor to sing of God's action in general. It sings of bringing down the mighty and lifting up the humble. Marx rejected Christianity as "the opiate of the masses." On the other hand, E. Stanley Jones observed that these verses form "The most revolutionary document in the world." Barclay points out that the Magnificat speaks of three revolutions.

In the first revolution (verses 50, 51) God shows mercy upon those who fear Him, but He scatters the proud. This is a moral revolution through which a person comes to value people rather than things and comes to honor others more than himself. When God scatters the proud, it certainly will be revolutionary in our materialistic, self-centered generation.

The second revolution is a social revolution (verse 52). God casts down the rulers and exalts the humble. But how different this revolution is from the countless revolutions that have racked the twentieth century! These revolutions, many of them Marxist inspired, have promised to elevate the humble. But once in power, the revolutionaries have often become more oppressive than the tyrants they displaced. Only God's revolution will bring lasting and desirable social changes.

The third revolution is economic (verse 53). The hungry are filled with good things while the rich go away hungry. We live in a world filled with hunger; a third of the world goes to bed hungry every night. Overpopulation, natural disasters, and human greed have all contributed to this want. To compound the tragedy, no one really knows how to go about solving the problem. Christians may sincerely want to help, but they find themselves frustrated and discouraged at the size of the task and the meager results of their efforts. But we can rest assured that God's revolution finally will bring about the real economic changes that He desires.

Verses 54 and 55 conclude the hymn with a reference to history.

Though Israel had often been disobedient and wayward, God had not forgotten His promise to Abraham and his descendants. His mercy had not abandoned them through their many trials.

Mary's visit lasted about three months. During this period she and Elizabeth no doubt had many long discussions about what had happened to them and what the future held in store. Since Mary came in the sixth month of Elizabeth's pregnancy, her three-month visit ended close to the time when Elizabeth's baby was born. It may seem surprising that Mary did not remain until after the birth. Possibly she wished to avoid the crowd of visitors that would be present then. On the other hand, it is possible that she did stay for a short time after the birth. Luke does not necessarily record all events in the order they happened. Perhaps he chose to finish the account of Mary's visit, and then go back to tell of the birth that happened a little while before the visit ended. Either before or after Elizabeth's baby was born, Mary went home to Nazareth to face the criticism that surely would come when her pregnancy was known.

The Birth of John
Luke 1:57-66

Luke now gives his attention to Zechariah and Elizabeth. God's promise of a son was fulfilled. John's birth was the occasion for rejoicing by neighbors and relatives. Even a normal birth would have brought many visitors into the home, but this unusual birth was especially a source of joy and thanksgiving. The parents must have looked back and thought how dramatically their lives had been changed.

According to the law, all male children were to be circumcised on the eighth day (Leviticus 12:3). As a priest, Zechariah would be especially careful about observing this ritual that marked the baby as one of God's people according to His covenant. It seems that circumcision was the occasion for a party to which relatives and friends were invited.

Apparently the practice was to name the child at this ceremony. A boy did not necessarily take his father's name, but the visitors thought it would be appropriate to call the child Zechariah. The old priest had waited a long time for a son, and he was not likely to have another. What would be more natural than to have his name carried into the next generation? Elizabeth, however, indicated that such was not to be the case. This boy's name was to be John. This was a popular name at the time. The New Testament mentions five different men who wore it. But the relatives protested that no one in the family had ever borne this name before.

Unwilling to accept Elizabeth's declaration, they appealed to Zechariah. At this time he was still unable to speak or hear (Luke 1:20). By signs they made known to him their problem, but to communicate with them he had to resort to writing. The tablet he used may have been made of wood covered with a thin coating of wax. One wrote upon it with a stylus of wood or metal. To their amazement, Zechariah wrote, "His name is John." In effect, Zechariah was saying that the baby already had a name that had been given by God (Luke 1:13).

At this moment Zechariah's tongue was loosed, and he was able to speak just as Gabriel had predicted (Luke 1:20). His first words were words of praise to God for His wonderful blessings. The months of silence had given him ample opportunity to meditate upon these blessings, and now his praise was poured forth abundantly in the hymn recorded in verses 67-79.

The unusual events surrounding the conception and birth of John were the talk of the town and the surrounding countryside. Many people were wondering what the future might hold for a baby born under such unusual circumstances. Undoubtedly they had high hopes for him. Luke adds, "For the Lord's hand was with him." The Lord's hand with anyone means the Lord's help, bringing success. (Compare Acts 11:21.) The Lord's hand against anyone means defeat and disaster (Acts 13:11). To the child John, the Lord's hand brought good health and proper growth (Luke 1:80).

Zechariah's Song
Luke 1:67-79

Once he was able to speak again, Zechariah's lips poured forth a stream of joyous praise. We are not told precisely when he lifted up this song. It may have been immediately after he regained his voice, for his first words were words of praise (verse 64). Or he may have voiced this great song a little later. His words came as a result of his being filled with the Holy Spirit. This song is sometimes called the Benedictus, from its first word in the Latin version.

Mary's song has often been compared to Hannah's song in the Old Testament. Zechariah's song more closely resembles some of the prophetic writings of the Old Testament. The theme of his song is God's mercy, a theme that is also expressed in John's name, which means "Jehovah is gracious."

In verses 68-70 Zechariah praised God for the salvation He had already begun to provide. Since Mary's visit, Zechariah knew that she was to become the mother of the Messiah. It is evident that in these verses he was speaking of Jesus rather than John, for John was from the tribe of Levi, and thus not a descendant of David. The word *horn* is often used in the Old Testament to symbolize either strength or honor. In this situation, both would be appropriate.

When Zechariah spoke of salvation, did he have in mind political salvation or spiritual salvation? Was he thinking of freeing Israel from the tyranny of Rome or Herod, or did he have something more in mind? Verses 71 and 74 may seem to have reference to political enemies, but verses 77-79 clearly refer to spiritual salvation. We may question how Zechariah came to speak about a spiritual salvation when others all about seemed to understand salvation in physical and political terms. It is doubtful that Zechariah came to his conclusion through his own thought processes. We need to keep in mind that he was "filled with the Holy Spirit," who led him into new truths.

In verses 72-75 Zechariah continued the salvation theme. By terms of the covenant He had made with Abraham, God promised to protect His people from their enemies. But because of their rebellion, God had permitted them to come under persecution. Now, however, rescue is at hand. But the emphasis is on spiritual blessings rather than on physical ones. They are to be rescued from their enemies, not that they may enjoy riches and comfort, but that they may be free to serve Him without fear.

One cannot help thinking of the faith of our Pilgrim fathers, who gave up all of their comforts and most of their physical possessions to find religious freedom. Contrast this with the prevalent attitudes today. Many would readily surrender their freedom to worship in order to gain pleasure and wealth. Like the ancient Israelites, we may yet find that in trading our faith for possessions we lose both.

Having sung of the wonderful salvation God is offering, Zechariah in verses 76 and 77 turned to the part his son would play in all this. Though the people had long looked for the coming Messiah, it turned out that Jesus would not be the kind of Messiah they had hoped for. His would be a spiritual kingdom, and to prepare the people for such a kingdom it was necessary for someone to go before Him. It was John, Zechariah's son, who would have this crucial task.

Zechariah closed his song (verses 78, 79) with a striking figure comparing the Messiah to the rising of a new day. ("The dayspring from on high" is the way the *King James Version* phrases it.) The image depicts persons, perhaps travelers, who have lost their way in the darkness. As they cower in fear of death, the light of Christ bursts upon them, showing them the path of peace.

John's Years to Maturity
Luke 1:80

The conclusion of Luke 1 briefly sums up the life of John until his ministry began. After the dramatic events of his birth and the incidents that preceded it, this summary seems anticlimactic. We would like to know much more about those years. What happened to Zechariah and Elizabeth? What kind of education did John receive? Where did he spend his youth? But the Holy Spirit has chosen not to satisfy our curiosity in these matters. It is commonly believed that Zechariah and Elizabeth, both advanced in years, died before John reached maturity. This led some to speculate that John was raised by members of the Qumran community, located near the Dead Sea, but the many differences between their message and John's seem to minimize that possibility. John's habitat during the years until he was about thirty was the desolate area west of the Dead Sea. Here he had opportunity to prepare himself for the great work God had for him.

The Birth of Jesus
Luke 2:1-40

"When the time had fully come, God sent his Son, born of a woman, born under the law" (Galatians 4:4). In this brief statement Paul sets forth the fact that God had for centuries been working toward this one great event. Luke, too, is quite conscious that God's actions were not whimsical but carefully planned. The incarnation is a fact rooted firmly in history, and Luke stresses this by giving us its specific historical context. Jesus' birth was not some mythological event that supposedly took place somewhere in the misty past. It was something that happened in history, and since Luke wrote only about sixty years after the event, it could readily be confirmed by records and witnesses.

The Birth in Bethlehem
Luke 2:1-7

Caesar Augustus was the emperor of the Roman Empire that by the end of the first century B.C. ruled the Mediterranean basin. Augustus, whose name was actually Octavius, came to power along with Antony during the turmoil following the assassination of Julius Caesar. But Octavius and Antony soon had a falling out. Octavius defeated Antony in the Battle of Actium in 31 B.C. and took complete control of the Empire. In 27 B.C., the Senate conferred upon him the title Augustus. The reign of Augustus was a benevolent one, especially when one compares it with that of most rulers of that period. His reign ushered in the Pax Romana, a time of relative peace throughout the Empire. This was an important feature in making the time right for the coming of the Messiah. Peace would make it much easier for His messengers to carry His story and His call all over the Empire. Thus God was using even the heathen to bring about what He had planned.

About 8 B.C. Augustus issued a decree that a census of the whole Empire be taken. While other records make no specific reference to this census, other censuses were taken at fourteen-year intervals beginning at A.D. 6. The *King James Version* calls this a "taxing," but the word really means a census. However, the purpose of the census probably was to provide a basis for levying taxes. This census took place when Quirinius (or Cyrenius) was governor of Syria. Quirinius became the civil governor of Syria at a later time, but he was a military ruler in the area at this time. The Greek word for *governor* can properly describe him in either position. Primarily it means leader.

Just why the people were required to go to their own towns to register we are not told. Many students suppose the official family records were kept there, and the registration there helped to keep them up to date. Traveling to a distant town to register laid a heavy burden on the people, but imperial Rome rarely worried about the inconvenience of her subjects. Apparently Joseph originally came from Bethlehem. Some have speculated that he even owned a house in Bethlehem, making him taxable there. They base their theory on the fact that he later moved from the stable to a house there (Matthew 2:11). But there is no other basis for this theory, and he may have rented a house.

On a larger scale, we can see the hand of God intervening to bring about the fulfillment of a prophecy that the Messiah would be born in Bethlehem (Micah 5:2). When the "time had fully come," God providentially moved Augustus to decree a census. This decree required each Jew to return to his ancestral town, which in Joseph's case was Bethlehem. The timing was such that Mary and Joseph were in Bethlehem when Jesus was born. Yet in all of this God acted in such a way that none of the participants were aware of how they were fulfilling prophecy.

The trip from Nazareth to Bethlehem was about eighty miles by the most direct route and would have taken several days to complete. With Mary's pregnancy almost full term, this would hardly have been a pleasant experience. It may also have occurred during the cold, rainy season, adding further to the discomfort of the travelers. We really have no information about the time of year.

Within a short time of their arrival, the baby was born. It is quite possible that the exertion of the trip hastened the birth. The newborn baby was wrapped in "swaddling clothes" *(King James Version)*. These were strips of cloth that were wrapped around the baby. It is likely that Mary had brought these in preparation for the birth. Lacking a bed or cradle, the parents laid the baby in an animal feeding trough. This has given rise to the belief that the birth occurred in a stable, though of course such a trough could be in a corral or field with no roof over it.

"There was no room for them in the inn." How loaded with meaning is that statement! It seems symbolic of events later in Jesus' life, when men had no room for Him in their hearts. Only on the cross and in the tomb was there room.

The accommodations available in Bethlehem were hardly up to Holiday Inn standards. The word here translated "inn" refers to a lodging place, not a luxury hotel. These stopping places are sometimes called khans or caravansaries. They provided shelter for travelers and their animals, but little else. Usually the shelter was built about an open court that might contain a well. Some were two stories tall, with shelter for animals on the first floor and guest rooms on the second. In others, the stables were separated from the inns. When an inn was crowded, travelers might find shelter with the animals. With the presence of many extra visitors in Bethlehem for the census, the inn was full.

An ancient tradition places the stable in a cave. Visitors to Bethlehem today are shown a cave that reputedly is the birthplace of Jesus. While animals were sometimes sheltered in caves, there is no way that one can prove that Jesus was born in a cave, much less that He was born in the cave now shown. Even though we do not know the exact spot where He was born, it is clear that it was a humble place, not a royal palace. How different things would have been had we been making the arrangements!

Announcement to the Shepherds
Luke 2:8-20

Just as Jesus was born in a humble place, so the first announcement of His birth came to humble men. Shepherds, because they could not observe all the ceremonial laws, were considered the

most lowly of men and were often looked down upon by the orthodox Jews. Some have suggested that the flock over which they
watched was one kept especially for temple sacrifices. If so, how
interesting it is that those who guarded the sacrificial lambs should
be the first to hear of the birth of the Lamb of God!

The presence of the shepherds near Bethlehem at the time of
Jesus' birth has been the basis of many efforts to date the birth. But
the evidence is not strong enough either to prove or disprove De-
cember 25. How ironic that the holiday most widely observed by
Christians in the West cannot be precisely dated! Who knows? Perhaps God intended not to emphasize the date but the event.

The presentation of the news was dramatic—an angel of the Lord
appeared to them and God's glory surrounded them. Little wonder
that they were overwhelmed by fear. Once the angel had reassured
them, he gave them his message. The newborn baby is called Savior,
a term that the Gospel accounts do not often use. This Savior is also
Christ the Lord. Among the Jews the word *Lord* was used instead of
Jehovah, the personal name of God. So the angel may have been
saying that the long-awaited Christ or Messiah is God as well as
Savior.

So the shepherds would be able to find the Christ child, they were
given a sign. He would be wrapped in strips of cloth or swaddling
clothes and lying in a manger. There may have been other babies in
Bethlehem wrapped in swaddling clothes, but it is highly unlikely
that any of them was lying in a manger.

Before the shepherds could go into Bethlehem to seek the baby,
they were treated to a Heavenly concert. Some students protest that
we should not speak of a concert or a choir, since the record says the
angels were saying, not singing. But saying can be done in song, and
what the angels said sounds like lyrical poetry. It seems quite probable that the angels sang.

This angelic choir was described as a "host," a term that often
means an army or strong military force. It is noteworthy that the
Heavenly army came not with clashing of swords but with a song
extolling peace. The choir first of all sang praises to God, not just
here on earth, but in the highest. We often speak of this song as the
"Gloria in Excelsis," a phrase taken from the Latin text. The rest of
the song promised peace on earth. One may argue that this promised peace has never been achieved. But if we notice carefully what
the angels said, we will see that they did not promise peace to all
men. As enjoyable as universal peace would be, the world will

never experience it as long as sin reigns in men's lives. The angels' song promised peace on earth only to "men on whom his favor rests." The *King James Version* says, "On earth peace, good will toward men," but more modern translations reject this because it is based on later manuscripts.

The *New American Standard* is perhaps clearest at this point: "On earth peace among men with whom He is pleased." The angels promised peace only to those who pleased God by walking in His ways. We need to understand also that this was a promise of internal peace, not necessarily a promise of a life free of strife and conflict. Near the end of His earthly ministry, Jesus made a similar promise to His disciples: "My peace I give you" (John 14:27). Then He quickly added, "I do not give to you as the world gives," for they would have many trials in this world. The peace that the angels and Jesus promised was the "peace that passeth understanding," the calm assurance we can know when we place our lives in Jesus' keeping. Storms may rage about us, persecutions may engulf us, yet we can be at peace because we trust in Him.

Once the echoes of the angelic choir had died away among the Judean hills, the shepherds eagerly turned to Bethlehem to find the child. Whether they paused long enough to make arrangements for some of their number to care for their sheep we are not told. It seems altogether likely that in their haste to seek out the babe, they forgot all about the sheep. After all, who would want to stay behind and watch sheep when such an exciting mission lay before them?

How long it took them to find Jesus and Mary we do not know. However, Bethlehem was then a small village, and their search could not have consumed much time. In our Christmas plays we seem always to portray their arrival while it was still night, and probably rightly so. They must have been struck by the sharp contrast between the glorious announcement of His birth and the humble circumstance of the actual event.

Once the shepherds had seen the child, they spread the word of their experience to others. It is not difficult to imagine their excitement as they later shared their story with their families and friends. Undoubtedly some were skeptical. The skeptics seem always present to dampen the enthusiasm of those who have exciting good news to share. Many, though, would believe them, for theirs was an age of faith, not an age of cold, scientific skepticism. Pious Jews had no doubt that God watched over them and on occasion intervened in their activities in miraculous ways. For generations they had anticipated the coming of the Messiah, and this anticipation would make them ready to believe such a story as the shepherds told.

Once the shepherds had found the Christ child as the angels had promised, they returned to their flock, rejoicing and praising God. We wonder what happened after that. As the days grew into weeks and then into months, did their memories of that glorious night begin to grow dim? We would like to believe that their enthusiasm never waned, that they continued to remember and give thanks. But if they were like most of us, their joy over the events of that night would begin to fade, especially if there were no further experiences to reinforce their faith. The inspiration of a brief moment is rarely enough to sustain us for a whole lifetime. We need to be reminded regularly and frequently of all that God has done for us. That's why He has provided opportunities for us on the first day of each week to meet together and commune with Him.

Regardless of what the shepherds did after that night, we know that Mary remembered. We can understand how her life had been in turmoil after the appearance of Gabriel with the dramatic announcement that she was to be the mother of the Messiah. Though her faith sustained her, she no doubt had questions about the whole thing. As the story continued to unfold, she was able to fit each new bit of information into the picture. The words the shepherds brought found a place in her heart because they fit and made the whole picture a bit more understandable. In the years that followed she undoubtedly had many occasions to recall the shepherds' report both as a source of joy and a support to her faith. Brief insights like this into the life of Mary, recorded only in Luke, have led many to feel that Luke had an opportunity to interview her before he wrote his Gospel.

Observing the Rituals
Luke 2:21-24

Joseph, like all devout Jews, was careful to observe the details of the law. Every male was to be circumcised on the eighth day following his birth (Leviticus 12:3). This marked him as coming under the covenant. It was customary at this time to give him a name, and so Mary and Joseph officially gave the baby the name God had already given Him—Jesus, meaning "Savior."

According to the Mosaic law, a new mother was considered ceremonially unclean for forty days after the birth of a son (Leviticus 12:4). During that period she was not allowed to enter the temple.

At the end of the forty days she went to the temple and completed the purification rite by offering a sacrifice. The sacrifice was to be a yearling lamb and a pigeon or turtle dove (Leviticus 12:6). However, if the woman was poor, she could substitute two doves or two pigeons (Leviticus 12:8). The fact that Mary offered a poor person's sacrifice is another indication that Jesus was born into relative poverty.

This occasion also offered Mary and Joseph the opportunity to present Jesus to the Lord. This practice also reflects the law of Moses (Exodus 13:1, 2), which stated that every firstborn male belonged to God. The idea behind this goes back to the time of the Exodus, when the firstborn were slain in Egypt. No firstborn were spared except those of the Israelites who had properly applied blood to the doorposts and lintels. They had been redeemed by the blood (Exodus 12:21-23). From this came the practice of requiring every firstborn to be redeemed (Exodus 13:11-13). The redemption price was five shekels of silver (Numbers 3:44-47). While this was not a large sum by our standards, it represented a sizable sum of money then.

The Encounter With Simeon
Luke 2:25-35

We know nothing about Simeon except what we read here. There is no indication that he was a priest or had any official duties in the temple. Apparently he was a pious Jew who frequently came to the temple to pray. He was waiting for "the consolation of Israel" that would come with the Messiah.

The prophets of gloom had much to complain about. The Jewish nation had lost its independence to Rome; and an insane tyrant, Herod, kept the people in constant terror. Corruption was rampant in high places, including the temple. The Pharisees who originally set out to purify the religious life of the people had fallen into a narrow legalism that squeezed the life out of religion. While they zealously taught God's law, in their own living they were far from doing God's will (Matthew 23:1-3).

And yet in the midst of this, God had a man (He always does, one way or another) who had faith, who never lost hope. In the midst of darkness old Simeon could see a little gleam of light. The Holy Spirit had revealed to him that before his death he would see the Messiah. Such a revelation may have come by a dream, a vision, a voice, or in some other way. The revelation was so distinct that Simeon never had any doubt about its authenticity.

When Mary and Joseph brought Jesus into the temple, the Spirit moved the old man at that very moment also to enter the temple. Simeon took the child in his arms and raised his voice in a hymn of praise that is often referred to by its Latin title, *Nunc Dimittis*. In the first couplet he praised God that he could depart in peace because God had fulfilled His promise. In the second couplet he identified that blessing—God's salvation. In the third couplet he indicated the scope of that blessing—to both the Gentiles and the Jews.

He described it as "a light for revelation to the Gentiles" because, lacking the fuller revelation God had given the Jews, they needed further light to understand God's purpose for them. That same salvation would be "glory" to the Jews. Though the Jews had been blessed by God through the centuries, their greatest glory would come finally through the Christ.

Simeon's statement that salvation would be available to the Gentiles seems quite surprising in view of the Jews' exclusiveness. In their narrow nationalism, they were quite certain that God's special blessings were reserved for them alone. Yet at the very beginning of Jesus' earthly life, Simeon's statement made it very clear that God's message of salvation would no longer be confined to one nation.

Joseph and Mary were amazed by Simeon's words. Was it just the fact that Simeon appeared so suddenly before them that caused them to marvel? Or was it the content of his message? He said God would offer salvation to the Gentiles through their Son. Certainly this would startle them, for there is no reason to doubt that they were typically Jewish in their attitude toward the Gentiles.

After he blessed them, Simeon brought words that must have cast a somber pall over their joy. This innocent child, said Simeon, would "cause the falling and rising of many." It was not that He would make many fall and then rise; but some would fall into condemnation by rejecting Him, and others would rise to eternal life by believing in Him.

This child would also become a sign pointing men to God, but this sign would be rejected and spoken against. How true this was in His ministry when His very name aroused some to blind rage! It was equally true during the early days of the church when people everywhere were talking against the Christians (Acts 28:22). In rejecting Christ, people revealed what kind of persons they really were.

Simeon's final words were for Mary. Though Jesus would grow up to become the perfect Son, He was destined to bring anguish into her life. While His childhood days as He grew up in Nazareth

40

would be peaceful ones for Mary, yet the day would come when anguish and sorrow would become her lot. During His ministry, but especially at His death on the cross, she would feel the full brunt of this prophecy. Artists in every age have depicted her in her suffering at the cross. Nowhere is this better seen than in Michelangelo's famous sculpture, the *Pieta*. There chiseled in stone for all ages to see is the pent-up anguish of a brokenhearted mother holding the lifeless body of her Son.

Greeting of Anna the Prophetess
Luke 2:36-38

Joseph and Mary had yet another unusual encounter when they met Anna. All that we know about her is contained in these three verses. She was a prophetess, but about her prophetic gift we are told no more than we see here. She was of the tribe of Asher, one of the so-called "ten lost tribes" of Israel. Obviously not all of the tribe of Asher had been lost. Further, tribal records were evidently still being kept when Luke wrote his Gospel. Anna was a very old woman. The *New International Version* indicates that she was eighty-four, but the *King James Version* can be taken to mean that she was a widow for eighty-four years and therefore was more than a hundred years old. She was a very devout woman, spending her time in the temple by day and by night to fast and pray. Her dedicated life illustrates that a person may continue to serve God even in the days of declining strength and productivity.

Anna approached the holy family just as Simeon concluded his prophetic statement. Led also by the Spirit, she gave thanks to God, pointing to the child as the one through whom God would redeem Israel. Her testimony, added to that of Simeon, must have made a double impact on her hearers. Perhaps she continued her prophetic testimony for some time after Joseph and Mary had left the temple with Jesus.

The Return to Nazareth
Luke 2:39, 40

If one were to read only Luke's account at this point, he might believe that Joseph and Mary returned to Nazareth immediately after Jesus' dedication and Mary's purification in the temple. But if we read Matthew's account, it is obvious that some time, perhaps two years or more, elapsed before they made this trip. Matthew tells of the visit of the Magi (Matthew 2:1-12). This certainly had to come

41

after Jesus' dedication in the temple; for when the Magi left, Joseph immediately took the family to Egypt (Matthew 2:13-15). There they remained until after Herod's death (4 B.C.).

After these events they returned to Nazareth. Here Jesus grew and matured as any normal child would. Since He was completely human as well as completely divine, there is no reason to believe that His childhood experiences were greatly different from those of other children in His village. He did, of course, have the blessing of living in a home with devout parents, who must have done everything within their power to provide an ideal home for Him. Further, we are told that the "grace of God was upon Him."

Jesus' Baptism and Temptation

Luke 3:1—4:13

After Jesus' birth, flight to Egypt, and eventual return to Nazareth, the years are passed over in silence except for one brief episode. When Jesus was twelve years old, He journeyed to Jerusalem with Joseph and Mary for the Passover. There in the temple He engaged the teachers in some serious theological discussion. His penetrating questions and the depth of His understanding of the issues brought amazement to the scholars.

After this one incident, which provided one more thing for Mary to ponder in her heart, Jesus remained obedient to Joseph and Mary. It would appear that Joseph died some time after this. In the accounts of Jesus' ministry he is never mentioned along with Jesus' mother and brothers. As the oldest son, Jesus probably assumed the responsibility for supporting His mother and His younger brothers and sisters until the brothers were grown. His neighbors knew Him as a carpenter (Mark 6:3).

The Ministry of John the Baptist
Luke 3:1-6

At the beginning of the second chapter, Luke dates Jesus' birth at the time of the first census taken when Quirinius was governor of Syria. Likewise he begins the third chapter by nailing down the time of the events that follow. John the Baptist and Jesus were not legendary figures who lived at some vague time in the dim past. They were historic persons whose lives could be dated by relating them to the Roman and Herodian rulers who were their contemporaries.

Most scholars agree that John's ministry began in A.D. 26. Jesus, who was born in 5 B.C., was then about thirty years old (Luke 3:23). Turbulent times had followed the death of Herod the Great in 4 B.C. He had left his kingdom to three of his sons. One son, Archelaus, was given Judea, Samaria, and Idumea, the desert area to the south of Judea. A brother of Archelaus, Herod Antipas, ruled over Galilee and Perea. Philip, a half-brother, was ruler over Iturea and Trachonitis, areas to the east and north of the Sea of Galilee. Lysanias, no relation to the Herods, was tetrarch of Abilene, a territory north and west of Damascus. Archelaus, who had been given the greater part of the domain of Herod the Great, proved to be as cruel as his father and much less capable. He was removed by the Romans in A.D. 6. Rome then appointed governors over this area. Pontius Pilate was the fifth such governor.

Luke also gives us information about the religious leaders at the time. Annas had actually been high priest at an earlier date but, becoming embroiled in politics, he had been removed from office by the Roman authorities. Eventually his son-in-law, Caiaphas, had gained the office. According to Jewish custom, a high priest served as long as he lived. Many of the Jews therefore continued to regard Annas as the rightful high priest. While Caiaphas was officially the high priest, Annas still exercised considerable influence. Luke quite properly regards the two as holding the office jointly.

This was the setting when "the word of God came to John." That expression reminds us of the call of the prophets in the Old Testament. At the time God's word came, John was living in the desert around the Dead Sea. Upon receiving his call, he went into the country along the Jordan, where he was more likely to find an audience for his message. Like the prophets of old, he thundered out a message of repentance. Those who heeded the message and repented were led into the waters of baptism for the remission of their sins.

There was something new and startling about this message. Judaism of that day had taught that forgiveness of sins came by making the proper sacrifice and observing the proper rituals. In contrast, John demanded a radical change of heart. Without this, nothing else mattered. Even baptism, unless it was preceded by repentance, could not bring about the remission of sins.

To authenticate his ministry before the people, John pointed to the prophet Isaiah. More than seven hundred years earlier, Isaiah (40:3-5) had predicted that before the coming of the Messiah, God would send a forerunner to prepare the way. "The forerunner is here," John now proclaimed, "and I am he!" What an audacious claim for one who had little formal education and who had spent most of his life in the desert, far from the centers of power!

The words of Isaiah referred initially to the return of the Jews from the Babylonian captivity. A way was to be prepared for God to lead His people back home. But in its fuller sense the prophecy referred to the one who would come as a forerunner of the Messiah. The people must be made spiritually ready for His coming. They needed to be prepared morally, but they also needed to have many of their false ideas about the Messiah corrected. Most of the Jews wanted and expected a Messiah who would lead them in a military campaign to throw off the Roman yoke and establish once again an independent Jewish kingdom. Part of John's mission was to lead the people to see their need for moral regeneration. This would prepare them to think in terms of a spiritual rather than a physical kingdom.

John's Message
Luke 3:7-14

John's greeting to those who came out to hear him indicated that he had not read *How to Win Friends and Influence People*. To call them a "brood of vipers" was hardly the most tactful way to welcome them. Yet the rough language of this rough prophet from the desert did not alienate them. It seemed to attract them all the more. No doubt many came out of curiosity to hear this unusual preacher in the wilderness. It was to those especially that John's strong language was aimed. In that age as in this, there were shallow curiosity seekers who had little real interest in religion. Only shocking language could jar them out of their worldly concerns.

Some men can be reached by a message of gentle love. Others must be frightened by the threat of impending judgment. It was these that John addressed. The "coming wrath" may have referred either to the coming destruction of Jerusalem or to God's Judgment Day. Either reference had the potential of capturing and holding their attention. John demanded repentance: not just lip service, but a changed life that gave clear evidence of a changed heart.

John anticipated the argument they would make based upon their Jewish ancestry. After all, they were children of Abraham. For centu-

45

ries God had blessed them and cared for them. Why should they have to repent? Nationalistic pride had blinded them to much of their history. True, they were God's chosen, but often in the past He had brought judgment upon them when they had strayed from the paths He had set before them. He had even permitted them to be carried off into a long and painful captivity. It may surprise us that they did not realize that their special status alone would not save them. Yet we do not have to hunt far today to find many who feel that the piety of godly parents or even grandparents will somehow save them also.

John's response to this kind of thinking was just as pointed as was his greeting. God, if He so chose, could create physical children of Abraham from the rocks that littered the riverbank. John's call was for them to become true spiritual descendants of that great patriarch. God does not judge a person on the basis of who his father or his grandfather was. He judges, instead, on the commitments one makes for his own life.

In a vivid figure John urged them to act, for the hour of judgment was at hand. The ax already lay at the root of the tree. In Palestine, trees that produced fruit were very valuable. But it was so much work to water, trim, and fertilize a tree that an unproductive one was quickly cut down to save precious water and other resources. Since fuel was in short supply, such a tree was quickly consigned to the flames. John's hearers had no trouble catching the point he was making.

Perhaps some rejected John's message, but many were cut to their hearts and cried out, just as men did later on Pentecost (Acts 2:37), asking what they must do. John's answer was not some high-flown theological theory, but several practical suggestions. Note first of all that John did not ask them to give up their work and family life and join him in the ascetic life of the desert. John's life and ministry were unique, and he did not suggest that others ought to imitate him in all he did.

It seems that three different kinds of people questioned John: ordinary people who made up most of the crowd, tax collectors, and soldiers. All seemed to have a sense of guilt about their lives and sought guidance from John. To the first group, John made the practical suggestion that they share their possessions and their food. In Palestine in that day there were many who lived a hand-to-mouth existence, and so there were always those close at hand who needed help. The tunic John mentioned is called a coat in the *King*

James Version, but the word *tunic* describes it better. It was a garment worn next to the skin and under the outer cloak or robe. In colder weather one might wear an extra tunic for additional warmth. John asked only that a person give up one of these. But nothing is said to indicate that the food they were asked to share was extra. John seemed to suggest that they should surrender some of their sustenance, truly a sacrificial act.

In every age there have been many who have suffered from hunger and nakedness. But for the most part they have lived out of sight in remote corners of the globe or in slums seldom visited by more affluent people. The mass media have changed all of that, and now none of us can plead ignorance. Our consciences have been touched by pictures on our TV screen of starving children and disease-ridden adults.

Yet even as our consciences prick our hearts to do something to help, we feel a sense of frustration as we seek to find where and how we can help. Many international relief organizations have done commendable work in providing relief for the needy. Our government has spent untold billions in foreign aid and welfare. Still, in spite of all these efforts, the problem seems only to become larger. At the present rate of population growth, it can only become more serious. It is estimated that world population will exceed five billion by the end of the decade and six billion by the year 2000. The critical shortage of food, clothing, and shelter for such a burgeoning population is almost certain at some point to erupt in violence.

John's advice to the people of his day is still appropriate. But the question remains: How can we use our limited resources to do the greatest possible good? We have learned from previous efforts that even with the purest of intentions we sometimes succeed only in making the problems worse. In offering a steady supply of handouts, we have often destroyed men's dignity and encouraged them to become professional paupers.

It was simpler in the first century. One saw a person in need and helped him in whatever way he could. Now our best minds have not been able to devise methods that will help the needy without ultimately harming them. Yet with prayer and concern we must keep trying to find answers.

John's second bit of advice went to the tax collectors. In ancient Palestine, tax collectors, often called publicans in the *King James Version,* would not have won any popularity contests. Tax collectors have a bad reputation in every society, but that was especially true

47

among the Jews. Not only did they collect taxes, they did so for the Romans, the despised enemy.

The method of collecting taxes had built-in possibilities of fraud and excess. Rome sold the right to collect taxes in a province to a wealthy person. He in turn would subdivide the province and farm out collection rights to smaller areas within it. This practice was carried out right down to the local towns and villages. In the process, every person in the system managed to make a profit. To insure his profits, a tax collector could always coerce his victims by calling in Roman soldiers, who were never far away. Given such an opportunity, human greed feels few constraints.

Yet in spite of the graft and extortion that certainly must have been a part of the system, not every tax collector was the evil-hearted villain his neighbors thought him to be. The fact that some of them came to hear John indicates that they were not completely lacking in moral discernment. The examples of Matthew Levi (Luke 5:27) and Zacchaeus (Luke 19:2-10) further illustrate this fact.

In view of their opportunities for extortion and the unpopularity of their profession, we might have expected John to tell the tax collectors to seek other employment. Surprisingly, he didn't. He urged them to remain at their posts, but to resist the temptation to collect more than the arrangement required them to.

The soldiers who came probably were Jews rather than pagan Romans. They may have been in the service of Herod Antipas, King of Galilee, though possibly some Jews even joined the Roman army. As a part of the establishment allied with Rome, they too were unpopular; and like the tax collectors, they had opportunities for graft and extortion. Again, John did not require them to leave their profession. Rather, he insisted that they conduct themselves honestly. Then he added another requirement, that they not complain about their wages, a universal complaint among soldiers. Other wage earners also have been known to grumble.

Is This the Messiah?
Luke 3:15-20

Both the content of John's message and the authority with which he proclaimed it made a profound impression upon the people. With their hopes running high that Christ was soon to appear, it is not surprising that many took John to be the promised Messiah. John quickly corrected this false notion. The coming Messiah was more powerful than he. Indeed, John asserted that he was not even worthy

48

to untie the Messiah's sandals. John was baptizing in water, but the Messiah would baptize far more dramatically with the Holy Spirit and fire. This looked forward to Christ's ministry and Pentecost, when the apostles were baptized in the Holy Spirit (Acts 1:5; 2:1-4).

John's prophetic vision carried him beyond Jesus' earthly life to His return in judgment. The threshing floor provided a dramatic figure to describe that judgment. In Palestine a threshing floor was a bare rock or an earthen surface leveled and packed hard. It was located where a strong breeze would blow across it. The sheaves of grain were laid out on this and a heavy sledge was pulled over them by oxen. Sometimes threshers would further beat upon the grain with flails. With winnowing forks they then would throw the grain and chaff into the air. The grain would fall to the threshing floor, but the chaff would be blown away. The grain could then be gathered and stored, but the chaff was burned. So God's people will be gathered into His city forever, but those who reject Him will be baptized in unquenchable fire (Revelation 21:7, 8).

Standing alone, the doctrine of judgment hardly qualified as good news. The good news that John preached was that God had provided a way of escape from the terrors of judgment.

It was nearly a year later when John was put in prison, but Luke records it here to finish the story of his public preaching.

The Baptism of Jesus
Luke 3:21, 22

Even though John disappointed many of the people when he informed them that he was not the Messiah, they continued to flock to hear him and to respond to his message by submitting to baptism.

Matthew 3:14 tells us that John at first refused to baptize Jesus. We do not know how well acquainted the two men were. Their mothers were relatives (Luke 1:36), and probably they had met in Jerusalem at the annual feasts. Possibly John had been told about the angel's prediction before Jesus was born (Luke 1:32, 33). John's baptism was "a baptism of repentance for the forgiveness of sins," and apparently John knew that Jesus was without sin. Jesus, however, insisted that He be baptized. His baptism was not for the forgiveness of sins, but "to fulfill all righteousness," to set an example of obedience.

Jesus' baptism provided an opportunity for God to give His stamp of approval to His Son. As Jesus offered up a prayer following His baptism, the heavens were opened and the Holy Spirit in the form of a dove descended upon Him. We are not told why the dove was chosen as a symbol of the Holy Spirit. But a dove does show qualities of purity and innocence, qualities most appropriate to the Spirit's nature. The descent of the Spirit should not be taken to suggest that Jesus did not enjoy the blessings of the Spirit until that moment. It is best to understand this event as marking the beginning of Jesus' public ministry. We know that John saw the dove and recognized it as marking Jesus as the Son of God (John 1:32-34). We are not told that others saw it, or if they did, that they recognized its significance.

After the dove had descended on Jesus, the voice from Heaven gave approval to Jesus: "You are my Son, whom I love; with you I am well pleased." Something similar happened on two other occasions. One occurred on the mount of transfiguration (Matthew 17:5; Mark 9:7); the other was during the last week of His ministry, as the shadow of the cross loomed large (John 12:28). Each time marked a significant point in Jesus' life. At His baptism it confirmed the beginning of His ministry; on the mount of transfiguration it marked a crucial turning toward Jerusalem and the cross; in the final week it prepared Him for the agony of the cross.

The Ancestors of Jesus
Luke 3:23-38

Prophecies in the Old Testament made it plain that the Savior was to be a descendant of Abraham, of the tribe of Judah, and of the family of David. Luke interrupts his story to list Jesus' ancestors, showing that Jesus is of the proper family line to be the Messiah. Luke goes beyond Abraham, however, and traces the line all the way back to creation.

It is puzzling to see that the list is not like the one in the first chapter of Matthew. The explanation may be that Luke lists the ancestors of Mary, though he uses the name of Joseph, son-in-law of Heli. Matthew traces the line of Joseph. He was Jesus' father legally, though not actually. Through him, Jesus was legal heir to the throne of David. Through Mary, he was literally a descendant of David.

The Temptation of Jesus
Luke 4:1-13

Following His baptism, Jesus was led by the Spirit into the desert, where He was tempted by Satan. Three of those temptations are described for us, but it is not likely that these were the only temptations Jesus had to face during that period. These are presented as typical examples of the others.

Jesus' temptations pose a serious theological problem. Since He is God and God cannot be tempted, some have taken the position that the temptations were not real but a kind of charade that Jesus went through to show us how to meet similar temptations. True, Christ is God; but He is also human, and as a human being He certainly could be tempted. That's exactly the point the writer of the Hebrew epistle made: "For we do not have a high priest who is unable to sympathize with our weaknesses, but we have one who has been tempted in every way, just as we are—yet was without sin" (Hebrews 4:15). The temptations were every bit as real as the ones we have to face, and Jesus had to resist just as we should.

For forty days the devil kept tempting Jesus, but his greatest effort came at the end of that period, when Jesus was the weakest from His long fast. The first temptation was aimed at this physical weakness. There was nothing inherently wrong in satisfying His physical needs, but the devil suggested doing it in a wrong way. Some see here a temptation for Jesus to doubt that He really was the Son of God, a subtle effort to get Him to deny what God had said a few weeks before at His baptism. More plainly, it was an effort to get Jesus to use His miraculous powers to satisfy His own needs. Jesus answered Satan's temptation by quoting Scripture (Deuteronomy 8:3). He would live by God's word first of all, and apparently He had word from God that His miraculous power was to be used for others.

Jesus' answer was appropriate for that occasion, and it is appropriate in every age. Spiritual things are more important than physical things, a truth that our materialistic age has been slow to grasp. Too many of us have made the instant gratification of our appetites the ultimate goal of our existence.

In another temptation Satan took Jesus to a high place where he showed Him all the kingdoms of the world in an instant. Of course no mountain is high enough to allow such a view of even the Roman Empire by natural sight, let alone the kingdoms on the far side of the globe. Probably it is best to think of this as an experience that happened in a vision rather than physically. The catch was that Jesus had to bow down and worship the devil in order to receive the promised kingdoms. This was a temptation to power, especially significant for the Messiah, who would be expected to wield great power in carrying out His work.

The quest for power has been a virulent temptation in every civilization. It has come in different forms, but the desire for a person to control others seems ever present. We see it displayed by bloody tyrants like Hitler and Stalin. We see it in more subtle forms in those who manipulate us through advertising to purchase their goods. Whether through raw power or clever persuasion, some men seem always desirous of controlling others. In its most subtle forms men are led to use improper means to accomplish what are good and noble causes. In the course of history we can see that men have resorted to tyranny in the name of spreading God's kingdom.

We need to note further that Satan offered as a bribe that which he really didn't own. While Satan does have great temporary control over the world, it was not really his to give. In the same way, the devil today offers us fancy baubles that he knows don't belong to him and that he also knows will quickly pass away.

As in the first temptation, Jesus answered Satan's offer by quoting Scripture. This time He quoted the essence of Deuteronomy 6:13. Again and again during His later ministry Jesus quoted Scripture as His authority. If our Lord held the Scriptures in such high esteem, should not we as His followers share that view?

Another temptation took place in the temple area in Jerusalem. Satan had Jesus stand on one of the highest peaks, then challenged Him to fling himself down. In order to make his offer look more enticing, he tried to substantiate it by quoting Scripture. The devil is clever, no question about that. Once more he insinuated his disbelief: "If you are the Son of God." Then he urged Jesus to make a spectacle of himself by flinging himself down. "After all," he said, "God will not allow any harm to come to you."

In this temptation Satan hoped to get Jesus to test God in an arbitrary fashion. It was a temptation to take a shortcut to success, a way that avoided the cross. By making a cheap spectacle of himself, He could gain a quick following. But Jesus refused to take the easy way. He did not attempt to argue with Satan, but a third time quoted Scripture.

This third temptation is recorded second by Matthew, and the one Luke records second is put in third place. Probably Luke records them in geographical order—two temptations in the wilderness and one in Jerusalem—while Matthew puts them in the order in which they occurred. The final one, the climax, was the temptation to worship the devil in order to gain the world. Then it was that Jesus drove the devil away (Matthew 4:10).

Thwarted in these three attempts, the devil left Jesus. But his departure was only temporary, for Luke tells us that he left "until an

52

opportune time." On several occasions during Jesus' ministry, Satan returned to set other traps for Him. Whatever else we may say about the devil, we have to admit he is persistent.

In these temptations Jesus demonstrated His power over Satan and his wiles. He also showed us how to resist the evil one—quote Scripture. Wise indeed is the Christian who has followed the injunction to hide the Word in his heart that he may not sin against God (Psalm 119:11).

Jesus' Early Ministry in Galilee

Luke 4:14-44

In developing his Gospel narrative, Luke makes no attempt to record all the events of Jesus' ministry. Matthew, Mark, and Luke give only passing references to the early months of it. The Gospel of John supplies considerable information that they omit. This covers several months, during which John the Baptist and Jesus both were teaching. John's public ministry ended when he was imprisoned by Herod Antipas because some of his preaching condemned that wicked king. Luke mentions this but does not indicate exactly when it occurred (Luke 3:19, 20).

Following His baptism, the Gospel of John reports that Jesus went back to the place where John was teaching. John the Baptist introduced Him to some of his own disciples as "the Lamb of God, who takes away the sin of the world!" (John 1:29, 35, 36). As a result, some of these men left John and began to follow Jesus. Among these were Andrew (who recruited his brother, Peter), Philip and Nathanael, and probably James and John, the sons of Zebedee (John 1:35-51).

After this, Jesus and His disciples returned to Galilee, where He performed His first recorded miracle at a wedding feast in Cana. Jesus and His mother and brothers then left for Capernaum. After a short time there, He, along with His disciples, left for the feast of the Passover in Jerusalem. A number of exciting events occurred during that visit to Jerusalem, among them the cleansing of the temple and the dialogue with Nicodemus (John 2:1—3:36). After several months of teaching in Judea, Jesus returned to Galilee (John 4), where Luke's account once more takes up the story.

The Rejection at Nazareth
Luke 4:14-30

Jesus' ministry in Galilee met with wide success. The power of the Spirit was upon Him, enhancing and magnifying His work. The news of Him spread rapidly through the area. At this point in His ministry His popularity was on the rise, and the synagogues of the region were open to Him. It seems that there was as yet no serious opposition to Him in Galilee, though the authorities in Jerusalem certainly were annoyed by His cleansing of the temple.

Jesus' growing reputation preceded Him as He returned to Nazareth. No doubt the local citizens were quite pleased that one of their own had received such acclaim, and they probably accorded Him an enthusiastic welcome when He arrived. After all, it wasn't too often that one from their obscure village had such honors heaped upon him. On the Sabbath, Jesus went to the synagogue to worship, "as was his custom."

The Old Testament did not specifically require that a Jew attend the synagogue worship each Sabbath. In fact, the Old Testament does not even mention the synagogue unless it be in Psalm 74:8. There some versions speak of the destruction of synagogues, but other versions interpret the Hebrew word as holy places, meeting places, or places where God is worshiped. It is generally thought that synagogues began during the Babylonian captivity and developed in the time between the Old Testament and the New.

Across the years the synagogue became the center of religious life in the towns and villages. Each Sabbath the people gathered there to study the Scriptures and to worship. At other times, the synagogue was used as a school and for community meetings. Since Jesus was reared in a pious Jewish family, we would expect Him to attend the service every Sabbath. In this, as in so many other ways, Jesus' life serves as an example for us.

Probably the synagogue service in the first century began with a recitation of the *Shema* from Deuteronomy 6:4-9. This passage begins, "Hear, O Israel: the Lord our God, the Lord is one." This was followed by a prayer and by the reading of a selection from the Pentateuch, the first five books of the Old Testament. These readings followed a schedule that allowed the Pentateuch to be read in its entirety over a three-year period. Then a selection from the Prophets was read. Since the Scriptures were in Hebrew, a language most Jews of the first century no longer understood, these readings were followed by a translation into Aramaic, the vernacular language at the time. Both the reader and the audience stood as the Scriptures were being read.

In the absence of a priest or rabbi, the men of the synagogue ordinarily took turns reading and expounding the Scriptures. It was not unusual for a visiting teacher or other distinguished guest to lead in this part of the service. Thus Jesus was given the opportunity to speak on this occasion. The Scriptures were in scroll form rather than a book. The scrolls were kept in a cabinet at the front of the synagogue. As Jesus arose to read, He was handed a scroll containing the book of Isaiah. Whether the passage He read was the one scheduled for that day or whether He selected one appropriate for the message He planned to deliver, we are not told. In any case, it did fit the message Jesus gave.

The passage He read was Isaiah 61:1, 2, one of the many rich Messianic passages found in Isaiah. Probably He read it first in Hebrew and then translated it into Aramaic. While this passage may have looked to its first fulfillment in the return of the captives from Babylon, there is no doubt that its greater fulfillment was in the life of Christ.

The Spirit of the Lord was on Jesus in the sense that the Spirit enpowered Him, gave Him direction, and authenticated His ministry. In the Old Testament, prophets, priests, and kings were ceremonially anointed as they were installed in office. In Jesus' case the anointing was not literal, but the term was used in a figurative sense to indicate God's approval of His ministry. His ministry was to be to the poor, the prisoners, the blind, and the oppressed. It may very well be that the primary reference is to the spiritually poor, the spiritual prisoners, the spiritually blind, and the spiritually oppressed, but Jesus' later ministry gives many examples that show that He was also concerned with people's physical needs.

Once Jesus had completed the reading of the Isaiah passage, He rolled up the scroll and handed it to the attendant. Then He sat down, as was the custom, to deliver His message. Every eye was upon Him in eager anticipation of the teaching He was about to bring. Luke has given us only a little of the sermon He preached, but Jesus' opening words may have been quoted verbatim.

"Today this scripture is fulfilled in your hearing!" The very audacity of these words must have so shocked the hearers that they missed their full import. The people's initial response was one of approval. Jesus did not speak of some golden age in the past whose glory had long since disappeared. Neither did He describe in glowing terms some utopia far in the future. Rather He spoke of the now, the present. Even as they listened to Him, the prophecy of Isaiah was being realized.

As they began to have second thoughts, however, their mood began to change. They were amazed that such words spoken with such authority could come from one who, so far as they knew, had limited formal education. They certainly knew of His life. After all, He had lived among them for almost thirty years. While the Scriptures tell us very little about Him during those years, Luke does state that He "grew in wisdom and stature, and in favor with God and men" (2:52). This certainly indicates that His life met with the approval of His friends and neighbors in Nazareth.

The thing that they couldn't quite accept was that one of such humble origins—"Joseph's son"—could have such insights into Scripture. Their acceptance of Him as only "Joseph's son" is the key to their attitude. It seems quite evident that the villagers did not know about His divine origin. All they knew was that Joseph had reared Him in his own household as his own son. There is probably another factor at work in this situation also—jealousy. Some people have such petty minds that they find it difficult to believe that one of their own number has made good. The people at first liked the idea that a great Messianic prophecy was being fulfilled in their day. The thing that upset them was that Jesus claimed to be the instrument by which these things would come to pass.

Because He was able to read their hearts, He anticipated their objections. "Physician, heal yourself!" must have been a common proverb in that day. While it did not precisely fit the situation, people seeking support in an argument are not always too careful about their arguments. The point that they were making was that since Jesus had performed miracles in other cities, He ought to perform miracles in Nazareth, indeed, right there in the synagogue.

Jesus responded to the proverb with what must also have been a widely quoted saying: "No prophet is accepted in his home town." Then, as He often did in disputes, Jesus turned to the Scriptures for support. He recalled to their memory the example of Elijah. A severe famine caused by a prolonged drought brought much suffering to

57

the land. There were certainly many widows among the Israelites who were worthy of help, yet Elijah provided only for a widow of Zarephath who lived near Sidon in the land of Phoenicia (1 Kings 17:7-16). In the same way, though there must have been many lepers in the land of Israel, the only one that Elisha healed was Naaman from a hostile neighboring nation, Aram or Syria (2 Kings 5:1-14).

As Jesus gave these two examples, perhaps the thing that most infuriated the people of Nazareth was that both persons who were helped were Gentiles. Popular among the Jews was a narrow nationalism that would limit God's blessings to them alone. Anyone who challenged this view was certain to feel their ire. There was simply no room in their thinking for the grace of God to extend beyond Israel. Unfortunately, such narrow, selfish views are still widely held, and they pose serious barriers to the worldwide spread of the gospel.

It is difficult for us to understand how the people of Nazareth so quickly changed their mood from one of approval and amazement at His gracious words to one of blind fury. To us who have grown to cherish religious toleration, it seems strange indeed that their religion should drive them into such a rage. We have become more openminded, we feel, and thus do not hold such narrow views. But if the truth were known, we are probably no more tolerant than they were. What we often take for religious toleration is really religious indifference. One doesn't become outraged over things that aren't important to him. But men still become furious and are willing to fight about such things as race and politics. These things have replaced religion at the center of many lives. We cannot justify the attitudes and actions of the people of Nazareth, but we moderns are hardly in a position to point a finger of accusation at them.

The people's anger turned the house of worship into a place of violence and bedlam. Forcing Jesus out of the synagogue, they drove Him out of the town and to the brow of a cliff. Apparently Jesus offered no resistance as they pushed Him along. Physical resistance would have been futile and would have served only to infuriate them all the more. There was no legal basis for their actions. Years later Jesus was accused of blasphemy because He claimed to be God's Son (Matthew 26:63-66), but that accusation was not made here. Neither was there any proper judicial proceedings. Those who would kill Jesus were not a judge and jury. They were a lynch mob.

Several locations have been suggested as the spot where this scene came to a climax, but it cannot today be identified with certainty. Just as they were about to carry out their wicked deed, Jesus turned upon them and walked through their midst unharmed. Some hold that a miracle occurred at this point, that His divine majesty was so evidenced that the people were rendered powerless. It may be, however, that at the last moment the people came to their senses and realized that they had almost shed innocent blood. They fell back in embarrassment at the terrible thing they were about to do. Whether His escape was miraculous or providential, it prevented His death from coming prematurely. His time had not come, and God would not allow men to upset His timetable.

This must have been a heartbreaking experience for Jesus—rejected by those who knew Him best and should have loved Him most. Familiarity did indeed breed contempt. But Jesus' anguish over His rejection was matched by their loss. Other towns in the area knew the excitement of Jesus' miracles and the blessing of His teaching, but not Nazareth.

Teaching and Miracles
Luke 4:31-37

Since He could no longer work in His home community, Jesus quickly left for Capernaum, located on the northwest shore of the Sea of Galilee. This town became the center of His Galilean ministry. The attitude of the citizens was more receptive, and as a result He performed many miracles there.

On the Sabbath, perhaps a week after His trying experience in Nazareth, Jesus was once more in a synagogue, this time in Capernaum. The attitude of His hearers and the results that followed were quite different from those in His hometown. The people were amazed by His words because He spoke as one having authority. This contrasted sharply with the way the scribes taught. They hesitated to assert anything on their own, preferring rather to quote others to bolster their position. Further, they often engaged in hair-splitting debates over issues that were quite remote from the real needs of the people. Jesus' popularity stemmed in no small part from the fact that He touched on the heartfelt needs of His hearers. Modern sermonizers may well learn a lesson from that example.

As remarkable as His teaching was, the incident that followed was even more startling. A man possessed by an evil spirit had come into the synagogue. Under the influence of the demon, he cried out with a loud voice, interrupting Jesus. It was a cry of anguish, a cry from a being who knew himself to be doomed. The demon knew that he could not withstand the power of Christ, and he knew that Jesus was the Son of God. We know so little about the demon world that we can only speculate about how the demon came to this knowledge. It is clear that he knew things that most of Jesus' human companions had not yet come to understand.

Jesus immediately silenced him. Though the demon publicly acknowledged Jesus as the "Holy One of God," this was not exactly the kind of testimony Jesus wanted. The credibility of any witness depends very largely upon his character. Obviously the testimony of a demon would not be helpful but would be detrimental to Jesus.

Jesus' next words were to call the demon out of the man. The demon was not going to surrender without a struggle, and he violently threw the man to the ground. But these final efforts proved vain before the power of Jesus, and so the man was set free.

The crowd stood in amazement at what happened. They were familiar with the efforts of exorcists among them to cast out demons. They knew that these men often used elaborate rituals and mysterious incantations to accomplish their purpose, and did not always succeed. Yet Jesus did no such thing. A few spoken words were adequate to banish the evil spirit. The people were amazed not only because He cast out demons, but because He did it with such obvious authority and power. The surrounding area was soon buzzing with excitement over this miracle.

The question of demon possession raises some problems for moderns. Some reject the whole idea. The phenomena that the Bible ascribes to demons, they explain as the activities of persons suffering from serious mental problems. It is true that some of the behavior of these persons does resemble the actions of psychotics, yet this will not explain all of their actions. In Jesus' day some may have ascribed all manner of illnesses to demon possession, but the Gospel writers carefully distinguish between demon possession and ordinary diseases.

The Old Testament has little to say about demon possession or evil spirits, and yet the problem seems to arise on every hand during Jesus' ministry. Many believe that Satan and his cohorts made an all-out effort to thwart Jesus' work, and the many demon possessions reported in the Gospels were but one example of this attack.

Recent movies and television programs have brought demon possession to the attention to the public. While some of these programs have left people with distorted ideas and inordinate fears of demon possession, they have at least conveyed to us some idea of the evil and hideous powers that belong to Satan. Whatever conclusions we may come to about demon possession today, we cannot escape the realization that Satan and his allies are a force that must be reckoned with.

Additional Miracles in Capernaum
Luke 4:38-41

Luke at this point mentions Simon Peter for the first time. He gives no explanation about who Peter was, for that disciple was well known among the churches and evidently was known to Theophilus, to whom Luke addressed his Gospel (Luke 1:3). During this period of His ministry Jesus made His headquarters in Capernaum, and He must have been a frequent visitor in the home of Peter. On this Sabbath Day, it seems, He went home with Peter after the meeting at the synagogue.

Peter's mother-in-law was suffering from "a high fever." Matthew and Mark say only "a fever"; but Luke, who was a physician, often describes diseases in a more detailed way or in more technical terms than do the other Gospel writers. Jesus responded to the request to help her by bending over her and rebuking the fever. The cure was instantaneous and complete, so complete that she arose and began to wait on them.

Word of this healing and the casting out of the demon must have spread rapidly about the town. When evening came, people suffering all kinds of illnesses made their way to Peter's home. Since many of these had to be carried, their friends and families waited until evening and the end of the Sabbath to bring them. To carry a person any distance would have been considered a violation of the Sabbath. Along with the miracles of healing, Jesus also cast out many demons. As was the case earlier in the day, He refused to allow them to proclaim to the world that He was the Son of God.

Jesus Proclaims the Priority of the Gospel
Luke 4:42-44

After this exciting day, a day that brought many healings and also confrontations with the forces of the evil one, Jesus went out early the next morning to a quiet place to pray and meditate. In so doing He set an example for us who live in a pressure-cooker culture. All of us occasionally need to stand aside from the busy rush of life about us and find a place of solitude where our spiritual batteries may be recharged.

Those who had witnessed the great day of miracles were not inclined to let Jesus enjoy even this brief respite. After all, He offered a service better than Medicare and a lot less expensive, and so they were not going to let Him get away. If they could just keep Him in Capernaum, their hometown would soon become the medical center of Palestine.

But Jesus wasted no time in straightening them out about His priorities. Physical healings occupied a prominent place in His ministry, yet the proclamation of the good news came first. Christians still debate these same issues. Some, especially the advocates of the social gospel, insist that we must first minister to men's physical needs. Others, following Jesus' example in this case, argue for the priority of preaching the gospel. Jesus left no doubt about which should come first. But in placing the greater emphasis on preaching the good news, He has not given us license to neglect ministering to men's physical needs.

Jesus' Growing Ministry in Galilee

Luke 5:1—6:16

The Gospels give us only a very abbreviated account of Jesus' life. Along the way we are told of a busy day here, or a series of activities there, or now and then a very crucial event in His life. But many interesting incidents occurred at other times, and we get only tantalizing hints of these. For example, we read nothing about the twelve disciples in the early chapters of Luke. Simon Peter is first mentioned without any introduction in connection with the healing of his mother-in-law. In all likelihood, Luke did not give a detailed introduction to Peter because the audience for which he was writing was already quite familiar with him. Luke's writing was directed to Theophilus, who had been taught about Jesus (Luke 1:3, 4); but we do not know just what he had been taught.

Followers and Foes
Luke 5

In the fifth chapter, Luke tells us several interesting events in Jesus' ministry. Peter, James, and John were challenged to leave their nets and follow Jesus to become fishers of men (Luke 5:1-11). Andrew is not mentioned in this passage, but undoubtedly he was included (Matthew 4:18, 19). Jesus healed a leper. As a result, crowds swarmed to Him for healing, forcing Him to withdraw to isolated places for prayer (Luke 5:12-16). When He healed a paralytic, He claimed the power to forgive sins. This sparked a controversy with the Pharisees and lawyers who had come from all over the country to check on His teaching. They would have charged Him with blasphemy, but the power Jesus displayed in performing the miracle silenced them (5:17-26).

After this, Jesus met Levi, a tax collector, who was busy at his tax booth. (We know him also as Matthew.) Jesus challenged him also to become a disciple. The amazing thing is that he left everything and followed Jesus. To celebrate his new vocation, Levi gave a banquet for many of his tax-collector friends. Thwarted in their efforts to charge Jesus with blasphemy, the Pharisees seized upon His presence at the banquet to criticize. Since the publicans were generally held in disrepute, the critics hoped to discredit Jesus by making Him appear to condone their notorious practices—the old guilt-by-association ploy. In a classic bit of satire, Jesus turned their charge back upon them: "It is not the healthy who need a doctor, but the sick. I have not come to call the righteous, but sinners to repentance" (Luke 5:27-32).

One thing we must say about Jesus' enemies—they were persistent. They next sought to attack Him with the help of some disciples of John the Baptist. John lived a rather austere life, eating a simple diet and fasting often. Since Jesus and His disciples did not follow such ascetic practices, they tried to make Jesus look more worldly and less spiritual by contrast. Once more Jesus thrust aside their attack. He compared himself to a bridegroom. It was certainly inappropriate to fast while the bridegroom was present. Since Jesus was the true bridegroom of the church, then it was absurd for His disciples to fast during His presence (Luke 5:33-35). There would be time enough for fasting when the bridegroom was taken from them by His death on the cross.

Jesus concluded this discussion by issuing a most profound statement in the form of a parable. The old era was about to pass away; a new age was dawning. The fact that the Pharisees refused to accept this would prove destructive to them (Luke 5:36-39).

Lord of the Sabbath
Luke 6:1-5

The Pharisees were never more zealous than when they were defending the sanctity of the Sabbath. Moses had set forth its sanctity in the fourth Commandment: "Remember the Sabbath day by keeping it holy" (Exodus 20:8). Keeping the Sabbath holy, Moses went on to say, meant the cessation of labor. Some specific examples of labor that were forbidden were later given. They included such things as kindling a fire (Exodus 35:3) and gathering wood (Numbers 15:32-36).

The Old Testament gave only a few such examples, and so a precise definition of what constituted labor left some room for differences of opinion. For example, would feeding one's livestock or milking a cow be considered labor? In terms of energy expended, it would certainly be more strenuous than merely kindling a fire. However, these activities of caring for one's animals were permissible both because they were necessary and because they were considered acts of mercy.

Men with a legal bent of mind could not tolerate much vagueness about such an important matter. In the centuries following the close of the Old Testament the scribes and Pharisees had busied themselves compiling an ever-lengthening list of activities forbidden on the Sabbath. Their efforts to undermine Jesus' popularity with the people had thus far been thwarted, but now Jesus' activities on the Sabbath afforded them another opportunity to attack Him.

One occasion arose when Jesus and His disciples were passing through the grainfields on the Sabbath. Apparently some time had elapsed since their last meal, for Matthew tells us they were hungry (Matthew 12:1). We gather also that they were some distance from home and could not return home in time for a meal.

The wheat fields were usually quite small by our standards. Paths through the fields not only provided access to them, but also served to divide one man's field from another's. As the men walked along these paths, the grain would be within easy reach. Since the grain was beginning to ripen, we know that it was the spring of the year, probably May. At this stage, the grain is still soft enough to be eaten without further preparation after separating it from the husk.

In plucking a few heads of grain and threshing them in their hands, the disciples were not guilty of stealing the grain, and they were not so charged. The Old Testament permitted one to pluck kernels with his hands from a neighbor's field, but he was not allowed to use a sickle to cut the grain (Deuteronomy 23:25).

The Pharisees charged Jesus' disciples, rather, with violating the Sabbath by working. "Why are you doing what is unlawful on the Sabbath?" they asked. Jesus might have answered their charge by pointing out that what the disciples were doing did not violate the law, but violated only their regulations. In the meaning of the law,

65

what the disciples were doing was not work. However, such a defense might have led to a long-drawn-out session of nitpicking over legal definitions and technicalities.

Jesus chose a completely different defense. He turned as He often did to the Old Testament and cited an example from the life of David (1 Samuel 21:1-6). Jesus chided them for professing to be authorities in the law and yet not understanding its real meaning. The incident Jesus mentioned occurred when David was fleeing from King Saul. Lacking provisions, David went to Nob where the ark of the covenant was temporarily located before it was taken to Jerusalem. He asked for bread and received from Ahimelech, the priest, the consecrated bread, which had been on the table in the tabernacle. It seems clear that both David and the priest thought the rule could be suspended in an emergency, even though it was established by divine law.

In the tabernacle the table of showbread stood in the Holy Place. Each Sabbath twelve fresh loaves were placed on the table and the old loaves were eaten by the priests (Leviticus 24:9). The Scriptures make it clear that this bread was reserved for the priests, and no one else was to eat it. Yet it was given to David, who shared it with his men. Clearly, what David did violated the ceremonial law. Since the Pharisees did not condemn him, it was clear that they thought that in some cases human need is more important than ceremonial law. Mark records that Jesus expressed the same principle in this way: "The Sabbath was made for man, not man for the Sabbath" (Mark 2:27). The Sabbath was intended to give comfort and strength to man. To make it the cause of discomfort and hunger was to abuse it, not to keep it.

Jesus then took the argument a step further before they could even raise the point that He was not David. David, though he was God's anointed, was still a man. If he could in time of need be given the holy bread, why should the Pharisees challenge Jesus' disciples for breaking a man-made law? It was God who said man should not work on the Sabbath, but they were men who said rubbing out a few handfuls of grain was forbidden work. After all, "the Son of Man is Lord of the Sabbath!" He who was given all authority certainly had complete authority over the Sabbath. Jesus did not at this point formally abolish the Sabbath observances; rather, He claimed that He could apply the Sabbath law better than the Pharisees could.

We may wonder why the Pharisees did not challenge such a bold claim. We can only conclude that they were so bested in the argument that they missed the full impact of what He was saying. The claim that He was Lord of the Sabbath would have sounded like blasphemy to them if they had really understood what He said.

Healing on the Sabbath
Luke 6:6-11

The tension between Jesus and His opponents continued to mount. In the previous incident, the Pharisees challenged the actions of the disciples. Now on a later Sabbath they were ready to challenge Jesus.

As was His custom, Jesus was in the synagogue on the Sabbath. We are not told where this synagogue was. It may have been in Capernaum, but it may just as well have been in one of the other towns around the Sea of Galilee. Among those in attendance at the synagogue were Pharisees and teachers of the law. Unfortunately their motives were less than noble. They had not come to worship, but to find some basis for accusing Jesus.

Also present in the audience was a man with a shriveled right hand. There is nothing to indicate that the man came seeking to be healed, but the Pharisees saw in his presence the opportunity to trap Jesus into a violation of the Sabbath regulations. While the Mosaic law says nothing about healing on the Sabbath, the teachers of Jesus' day generally held that healing on the Sabbath was permissible only when one's life was in danger. No such emergency existed in this case, and there was no good medical reason why his healing could not have been postponed until another day.

Jesus had one advantage in this encounter. He knew exactly what His enemies were thinking. Knowing their thoughts, He could have postponed the healing and avoided a confrontation with the Pharisees. There are certainly times when avoiding a conflict is appropriate, but this was not one of them. Jesus saw in this situation an opportunity to expose the wickedness of His enemies and show how baseless were their man-made laws.

In order that none could miss what He was going to do, Jesus asked the man to stand up in front of the people. He wanted to make sure that none could accuse Him of working in a dark corner. Perhaps Jesus also wanted to arouse sympathy for the man and show how completely lacking in mercy were the Jewish lawyers. The man obeyed Jesus without question. According to Matthew 12:10 the Pharisees sensed what Jesus was about to do and asked, "Is it lawful to heal on the Sabbath?"

Jesus then turned their question back on them in the form of a dilemma: "I ask you, which is lawful on the Sabbath: to do good or to do evil, to save life or to destroy it?" If they had answered to do good, then Jesus would have had justification for performing the good deed of healing the man, and their narrow interpretation of the law would have been swept away. If, on the other hand, they had said to do evil, they would have stood condemned in the eyes of the people who naturally would have been sympathetic toward the crippled man.

Mark tells us that, faced with this dilemma, the Pharisees remained silent (Mark 3:4). Their silence announced their hypocrisy to the whole audience. Jesus' question also had an added barb which they could scarcely have missed. Jesus was proposing to do good by healing on the Sabbath. By contrast, they were doing evil by seeking some way to discredit Him and destroy Him.

This is one of the occasions when the Scriptures tell us that Jesus became angry, moved by righteous indignation at the hardness of their hearts (Mark 3:5). Jesus gave them an opportunity to look at themselves and repent of their wickedness, but they silently and stubbornly rejected this opportunity. Jesus would offer them similar opportunities in the months ahead, but most of them would reject these opportunities and grow ever more adamant in their opposition to Him.

Men have not changed greatly over the centuries. When they make up their minds to reject truth, every encounter with truth only further hardens their hearts. Sin has a way of feeding on itself and growing ever more intense in the process. We need to watch ourselves. Can we be steadfast in holding the truth, but not too stubborn to see our errors?

Jesus' attention was now turned to the man. "Stretch out your hand," He commanded. The man quickly obeyed. Imagine his joy when he saw that his shriveled hand was whole again. The healing was instantaneous and complete, without any intermediate steps.

Jesus had not even touched the man, nor had He required the man to do any more than lift his hand. Even the most legalistic Pharisees could hardly argue that there was any work here that violated the Sabbath. Since the Sabbath had not been desecrated and a mighty miracle had been performed, one would expect the Pharisees to be elated. Quite the opposite was the case. They were furious—"filled with madness" is the way the *King James Version* expresses it. They were angry because this miracle further enhanced Jesus' reputation among the people. Thwarted in their efforts to defeat Him, they withdrew and began to plot what they might next try against Him. Mark tells us they "went out and began to plot with the Herodians how they might kill Jesus" (Mark 3:6). The Herodians were partisans of Herod, Rome's puppet king in Galilee. Normally the Pharisees regarded them as enemies. Their willingness to consort with those enemies shows how desperate and depraved the Pharisees had become.

Calling of the Twelve
Luke 6:12-16

The growing opposition of the religious leaders brought Jesus' ministry to a critical point. As His popularity with the people grew, the leaders' hatred became more intense. At first they raised questions about His teaching; then they began to openly challenge Him; now they were plotting to kill Him. He knew very well that this opposition would not stop until His teaching ceased, either by His withdrawing from the public scene or by His death at their hands.

He could not abandon His work, and so the other option—the cross—cast its ominous shadow across His ministry. He began to take steps that would ensure the continuation of His work after His death. His method of doing this was to draw around Him a group of men whom He could train for this task. As we examine the twelve whom He chose, several things come to our attention.

First of all, they were chosen only after Jesus had spent the night in prayer. Jesus had withdrawn from His disciples, the crowd, and His enemies and had gone out alone "into the hills" to pray. While Luke does not tell us specifically that He prayed about the matter of choosing the twelve, yet it is certainly a safe assumption that He did.

We may raise a question about why the Son of God found it necessary to pray to the Heavenly Father. If He is divine, one with the Father, why was such communication necessary? In our limited understanding there is no adequate answer to this. We can only conclude that the answer to this question is hidden in the mystery of the incarnation. But the fact that Jesus prayed does emphasize the fact that He was human as well as divine.

Even though we do not have all the theological answers as to why Jesus prayed, we can learn from His example. Prayer was a way of life for Him. Every major decision He made was preceded by prayer and every action bathed in prayer. If the Son of God found it necessary to pray so frequently and so fervently, then we sinners ought to feel an even greater need. How many of our decisions would be made more wisely if we would pray more earnestly before we make them? How many mistakes might be avoided, how many successes attained? How greatly would our sorrows be reduced?

After spending the night in prayer, Jesus returned to His disciples. From among these disciples He chose twelve who would serve closely with Him for the remainder of His ministry. Because of this new relationship they were given a new designation—*apostle*. In the Greek, this term means "one who is sent." This was an especially appropriate designation for them, for before long they were sent out on a special teaching and preaching mission (Luke 9:1-6). Later they would be sent on an even greater mission, to carry the gospel to the whole world (Acts 1:8; Mark 16:15, 16).

Of the twelve whom Jesus chose, not one was really outstanding before coming to Jesus. They were, by human standards, rather ordinary. Whatever greatness they later showed came as a result of their association with the Master. With the exception of Judas, all of the men were from Galilee. Several were fishermen, a profession not usually accorded a very high social status. Matthew was a tax collector and probably a man of above modest means. At the same time, men of his profession were generally despised both because they extorted money from the people and because they collaborated with the despised Romans. At the opposite pole politically was Simon the Zealot, who belonged to a political party dedicated to the overthrow of the Romans.

The names of the twelve apostles are listed in the Synoptic Gospels (Matthew 10:2-4; Mark 3:16-19; and Luke 6:14-16) and in Acts 1:13. In each listing the names are presented in groups of four. Each list has the same men in each group, though the four are not always in the same order. While we should be hesitant about attaching too great a significance to their order, it is worth noting that Peter heads each list. Judas Iscariot is named last in each list, except in Acts, where his name is omitted because he is no longer living and a successor is soon to be named to take his place.

In the first quartet Luke names Simon, his brother Andrew, James, and John. These men were all fishermen and hailed from Bethsaida, a village on the Sea of Galilee near Capernaum. We are also told that Jesus gave Simon the name Peter (Cephas in the Aramaic, John 1:42), which means Stone. This name was to stick with him the rest of his life, a tribute to the steadfastness that he later developed. Mark notes that Jesus called James and John Boanerges, which means "sons of thunder." They may have received this title because of their tempestuous personalities.

Philip heads the second group of four. Like Andrew, he bore a Greek name. Other than that, we know little about him. The name Bartholomew means "son of Tolmai." His given name probably was Nathanael (John 1:45-51). Matthew also bears the name Levi (Mark 2:14; Luke 5:27). Thomas was called Didymus (John 20:24), which means Twin.

In each list the third group is headed by James the son of Alphaeus, so called to distinguish him from James the son of Zebedee, who is listed in the first group. Each list has also Simon the Zealot. In some versions he is called the Canaanite or Cananaean in Matthew and Mark. This is taken from the Hebrew word for zealot. There is another interesting difference in this group. Luke lists Judas the son of James, while Matthew and Mark have Thaddeus. Matthew in the *King James Version* has "Lebbeus, whose surname was Thaddeus" (Matthew 10:3). There is no conflict here; this apostle probably bore all three names: Judas Lebbeus Thaddeus.

The last apostle named in all of the lists is Judas Iscariot. Luke identifies him as the one who became a traitor. His name Iscariot may be interpreted as "man of Kerioth." It is generally believed that Judas came from Kerioth, a town in southern Judah. Probably the other eleven were all from Galilee.

The choice of Judas raises some questions. Was he an honest disciple when Jesus chose him? If so, when and how did he become so corrupted that he betrayed the Savior? The Scriptures give us no information that directly helps us answer these questions. Jesus by divine foreknowledge certainly must have known that Judas would become a traitor. Knowing this, why did He choose him? The safest course to follow is to admit that we are incapable of plumbing the depths of God's wisdom.

The choosing of the twelve apostles marks the beginning of another phase in Jesus' ministry. They would soon be given new responsibilities in preaching and teaching. More importantly, they would be prepared to continue that teaching when Jesus returned to His Heavenly home. Perhaps the most important lesson we can draw from all of this is that the advance of Christ's kingdom does not depend upon a few brilliant geniuses. Christ showed us that ordinary men with rather ordinary talents can accomplish great things if they make an extraordinary commitment.

71

The Sermon on the Plain

Luke 6:17-49

Every religion has a body of doctrine that must be believed. It has certain rituals and practices of worship that are observed. And it has certain standards of conduct that are expected of its adherents. Christianity is no exception. In this lesson we find the basic teachings about conduct set forth. Jesus did not proclaim these teachings as a legal code such as we find in the law of Moses. Rather, He laid down broad principles that, properly understood and applied, cover every situation one may encounter in life.

This body of teaching is sometimes referred to as the "Sermon on the Plain." Some hold that it is not to be identified with the Sermon on the Mount recorded in Matthew 5—7. However, several similarities make it appear that we have two reports of the same sermon. For one thing, both accounts begin and close in the same way. The substance in both is similar. And after the close of the sermon, both state that Jesus went to Capernaum where He healed a centurion's servant.

The differences are unimportant and are not contradictory. Luke tells us that Jesus with His disciples came down from the hills and "stood on a level place." Matthew states that He went up on a mountainside. It seems quite possible that Jesus prayed alone on a hilltop, then called His disciples there and selected the twelve apostles (Luke 6:12-16). As they came down from the mountain, a multi-

72

tude went up to meet them. Jesus chose a level spot on the mountainside where He stood and healed those who came to Him.

Luke states that He stood while He performed miracles of healing. Matthew does not contradict this when he says Jesus sat down to teach. It is quite reasonable to suppose that He stood to heal and then sat down to deliver this long discourse.

It seems quite likely that Matthew and Luke give us two condensed versions of the same sermon, which may very well have taken two or three hours to deliver. In that day listeners were not programmed for twenty-minute sermonettes. But after all, what difference does it make whether we have two condensed reports of the same sermon or condensed reports of two similar sermons? In either case we are enriched by Jesus' amazing teaching. Barclay calls this discourse "a series of bombshells." Deissmann says Jesus' sayings here are "flashes of lightning followed by a thunder of surprise and amazement."

A Time of Healing
Luke 6:17-19

A large crowd gathered with Jesus on the mountainside. Luke indicates that two different kinds of people were there. One group is designated "his disciples." The word here used means learners or pupils. These were persons who already knew something about Jesus, had committed themselves to Him, and were eager to learn more about Him.

The other group came from various backgrounds. Some came from Judea. Though Jerusalem is in Judea, it is specifically mentioned, perhaps because those from Jerusalem may have been critics, seeking some basis to attack Jesus. Others were from Tyre and Sidon, two cities on the coast of Phoenicia, north of Galilee. We are not told that they were Gentiles, but since they came from a Gentile area, that possibility does exist. Their presence indicates that Jesus' fame had spread beyond the boundaries of Palestine. The meeting was in Galilee, and of course throngs of Galileans were there, though Luke does not name Galilee. Perhaps Judea here means the whole land of the Jews, including Galilee.

These persons gathered for differing reasons. Some came to hear Jesus. They were certainly not going to be disappointed. Others came to be healed. Luke distinguishes between those with ordinary illnesses and those troubled by evil spirits. Persons with both types of afflictions were healed. The crowd pressed about Jesus, trying to touch Him. Some scholars say they had a superstitious belief that touching Him would bring healing; but superstitious or not, God accepted their faith in Jesus and rewarded it with healing. "Power was coming from him and healing them all."

Blessings and Woes
Luke 6:20-26

Once the sick had been healed and those troubled by evil spirits cleansed, Jesus turned to His disciples. This group was not limited to the twelve that had just been called as apostles, but included the larger group mentioned in verses 13 and 17. While the sermon was addressed specifically to the disciples, others present heard it and were moved by it. Many, no doubt, were led to become disciples as a result of this sermon.

Whether Matthew and Luke report the same sermon or different ones, both begin with Beatitudes, blessings pronounced upon people of certain conditions, attitude, and behavior. Matthew lists nine of these while Luke mentions only four. Our word *beatitude* is derived from the Latin word that means *blessed.* The Greek word that is rendered *blessed* is difficult to translate. Some modern translations have it *happy.* But happiness as many people think of it depends on external conditions. When these conditions change, the happiness disappears. Jesus was talking about an attitude that transcends circumstances.

Luke mentions first a blessing upon the poor. The parallel in Matthew is upon the "poor in spirit," and this seems to be the intent of Luke also. Jesus was not saying that any great virtue is to be attached to being physically poor. Probably most of those who heard this sermon would qualify as being poor, yet poverty alone would not insure their being blessed. But poverty can and often does lead one to a total dependence upon God. When people realize that only God can supply their needs, this attitude prepares them to become citizens of the kingdom of God.

Yet one need not be in the throes of dire poverty to feel dependence upon God. Peter, Andrew, James, and John were successful businessmen, not beggars. Matthew was affluent enough to give a substantial banquet (Luke 5:29). All of these were willing to give up their wealth and follow Jesus, indicating that they were "poor in spirit."

The poor in spirit possessed the kingdom of God. While the other three Beatitudes look to some future fulfillment, this one is realized in the present. The point Jesus was making is that persons who humbly surrender to God already know the joys and blessings that are reserved for citizens of His kingdom. They do not have to wait till they get to Heaven to enjoy these fruits. The words of the saints across the centuries bear ample testimony to this fact.

Luke's second Beatitude parallels Matthew's fourth Beatitude (Matthew 5:6). Realizing this can help us to understand that Jesus was not putting any great value on physical hunger. While fasting may have some value both physically and spiritually, that is not what Jesus was talking about. He was commending those "who hunger and thirst for righteousness." Such persons long for godliness and holiness as intently as a starving man longs for bread. Jesus assured His audience that such striving would be rewarded. But the irony is that when one is filled spiritually, his appetite for spiritual things is only sharpened. The holier a person is, the more intensely he feels the pangs of spiritual hunger.

Luke's third Beatitude is for those who weep. The parallel in Matthew addresses itself to those who mourn, but there is no contradiction here. Weeping is but one visible sign of mourning. In this context Jesus clearly had reference to the weeping that arises over spiritual matters. He certainly did not intend to include those who weep because they have been caught in their misdeeds or have failed in some evil enterprise. This is a worldly sorrow that leads to death (2 Corinthians 7:10). Rather, Jesus was commending godly sorrow that leads to repentance.

The last Beatitude embodies a dire prophecy, one that the disciples would begin to see fulfilled within a few months. Ordinarily we do not consider it a blessing when we are hated, yet Jesus insisted that this is a blessing. This hatred was not just a passive attitude on the part of enemies. Jesus' followers would be expelled from the synagogue, imprisoned, beaten (Matthew 10:17, 18). One incident occurred before long when a blind man healed by Jesus was thrown out of the synagogue (John 9:34). Persecution became furious in later years (Acts 5:40; 7:57—8:3).

Instead of grieving or sorrowing when persecution became their lot, Jesus' followers were to rejoice. This rejoicing would be open and unrestrained—they were to "leap for joy." They had good reason for such exultation. They would receive a great reward in Heaven.

Jesus was not teaching His followers that they should deliberately court persecution. In most periods in history this has not been necessary. Persecution has been frequent and severe enough even when it has not been sought. Jesus was simply preparing His people for the persecution that was certain to come if they followed His teachings.

Nor did Jesus teach that suffering or martyrdom would necessarily insure Heavenly blessings. Salvation comes to those who in faith surrender themselves to Jesus Christ. This kind of commitment to Christ may lead to suffering and even martyrdom, but it is the faith, not the martyrdom, that is the basis for salvation.

Jesus went on to remind His audience that God's saints have always suffered. We can immediately think of many of the prophets who were mistreated and abused by the Hebrew people. Elijah opposed the wicked Ahab and Jezebel. He saw many of his fellow prophets imprisoned and slain, and he himself had to flee the country for his life. Amos became exceedingly unpopular because he exposed the greed and hypocrisy of Israel. Jeremiah, known as the "weeping prophet" for good reason, suffered all kinds of mistreatment at the hands of his countrymen. Since the fathers had so mistreated God's holy prophets, Jesus' followers had best be prepared to suffer in a similar fashion.

After expressing four blessings, Jesus turned to the other side of the page to reveal four woes. These are mirror images of the blessings. Like bells that toll the message of doom, these woes ring out as pronouncements of judgment upon those who stubbornly resist the will of God. The first of these is aimed at the rich. In the context we are not to understand that Jesus was condemning wealth as such. Rather, He was condemning greed that gets wealth unjustly, and the arrogance and self-sufficiency that a reliance upon riches often brings. Most of the opposition to Jesus arose from the rich and arrogant. Men covet riches for the comforts that wealth can bring. Jesus pointed out to His hearers that such comforts are fleeting. Riches may bring comforts now, but in no way can wealth assure that these comforts will be transferred to the next world. Sad indeed will be any person who supposes that he can "take it with him."

This warning should be heeded by affluent Americans. In our privileged land even those who live below the so-called poverty level fare much better than most of those to whom Jesus spoke. God has allowed us to be blessed with physical possessions beyond the dreams of even our parents and grandparents. There is no reason to feel guilty about these possessions. Instead, we should look upon them as a sacred trust. If we commit these things to the glory of God's kingdom and refuse to allow them to become our masters, we can escape the woe that Jesus pronounced upon the selfish rich.

Jesus' next woe is pronounced against those "who are well fed." This does not suggest that there is inherently any virtue in malnutrition. Those condemned here are the same rich who are condemned in the previous verse. Their wealth allows them to have their appetites sated. They seek to find new taste thrills that will arouse their sated taste buds. Their sin is not in having wealth, but in using it so selfishly and so wastefully.

Jesus directed the third woe against those "who laugh now." We are not to suppose that He was condemning all laughter. In the context He was condemning the boastful, haughty laughter of those who were self-satisfied and showed no concern for others who were hungry or suffering.

The final woe was reserved for those who win all the popularity contests. One can gain universal popularity only by resorting to deception and flattery. Just as one can be known by the friends he makes, so he may also be known by his enemies. One who takes a stand for truth, no matter how lovingly he may do so, is certain to alienate those who have committed themselves to falsehood. Jesus reminded His hearers that only the false prophets gained wide popularity. The true prophets were met by hatred and rejection.

Love Your Enemies
Luke 6:27-36

These verses sum up what are probably Jesus' most discussed teachings. And no wonder! When He taught men to love their enemies, He was asking them to fly in the face of everything that they were naturally inclined to do. The so-called Golden Rule is not just a standard that requires us to avoid doing harm to others. Many thoughtful persons follow such a policy out of self-interest. It is a matter of living and letting live. By contrast, the Golden Rule obligates us to do positive good to everyone we can, even to those who are our avowed enemies.

Love stands at the heart of the Golden Rule. At this point the Greek language is more expressive than English. At least three or four words, each with a different shade of meaning, are used to express the idea of love. *Eros* means the physical love between a man and woman, sexual love. *Philia* is the warm affection of friendship. The word here used, *agape*, means intelligent good will toward another.

Eros is essentially a selfish love, one that seeks self-gratification through another. *Philia*, the love of friendship, is directed toward a person that is attractive or lovable. By contrast, *agape* may be directed deliberately toward one who is undeserving and even repulsive. It seeks intelligently to work for his good, even when those efforts are rejected.

Because *eros* and *philia* originate in the emotions, they cannot be commanded. But *agape* originates in the will, and so God can command us to love our enemies. It is precisely for this reason that God can command us to do what goes contrary to all of our selfish instincts. Hate your enemies, the world says. Or as one prominent politicial put it, "Don't get mad when your rival cheats you. Get even!"

Jesus' words must have sent a shock wave through His audience. Some, no doubt, refused to believe their ears. Others began to rationalize away the radical aspects of what He said. To make sure that no one would misunderstand or find a way to avoid the full impact of His words, He gave several specific examples to explain exactly what He meant. We are to bless those who curse us, pray for those who mistreat us, turn the other cheek to those who strike us, and give both our shirts and our coats to those who ask for our coats.

Jesus established an ethic that demanded that the Christian go beyond the conventional. After all, even sinners love those who love them. What special credit does one deserve for doing a good deed for those who are certain to return the good deed? Persons who practice such conventional morality are likely to feel good about their actions, but they are able to feel good only because they compare themselves with themselves. The situation changes dramatically when they compare themselves with the standard Christ set.

Jesus concluded this portion of His sermon by giving the basic reason for setting such high standards for His followers. These standards reflect the way God acts. Because God is "kind to the ungrateful and wicked," we ought to be also. We are to be merciful just as our Heavenly Father is merciful. This kind of conduct marks us as sons of the Most High.

A Warning Against Judging
Luke 6:37-42

If the Golden Rule meant anything, it meant acting mercifully, just as the Father has acted mercifully toward us. With this as the background, Jesus turned to an all-too-prevalent sin among the Jews of His day—judging others. The Pharisees, who came into being to purify the Jewish faith, fell readily into this fault. Their basic approach toward life prepared them to become censorious judges of others, lacking in compassion and often hypocritical.

Jesus was certainly not condemning moral discernment. Every day we are called upon to make judgments about whether an action is right or wrong. In fact, almost every decision we make has moral implications. There is no way we can avoid making these decisions, for in many cases to evade making a judgment is to judge.

Jesus gave a good reason to avoid critical faultfinding. We will be judged by the same standards that we apply to others. Jesus' statement also implied that behind whatever judgment we make stands the judgment of God. As we judge others, so He will judge us.

Just as we are to be generous in our judging, so we are to be generous in our business dealings. We are to give full measure "pressed down, shaken together, and running over." We probably wouldn't want to take this too literally if we happened to be selling strawberries or ripe tomatoes. But the point is obvious. The way we treat others will determine how we will be treated.

At this point in His sermon Jesus seemed to single out the Pharisees, who glaringly failed to live up to the principles He had just set forth. They were blind guides certain to fall into a pit, causing their followers to fall in after them. Since the Pharisees and scribes were guilty of making censorious judgments, their followers would do the same unless they found better guidance.

On occasion Jesus spiced His message with a few bits of humor. The audience must have chuckled when Jesus depicted a man with a plank sticking out of his eye trying to help another remove a tiny speck from his eye. Such obvious hypocrisy is laughable. The trouble is that in real life such hypocrisy is not always so obvious, and when it is obvious it is not so comical.

Judging
Luke 6:43-45

In verses 37-43 we see that Jesus cautioned men against making critical judgments; in verses 43-45 we see that He urged them to exercise moral discernment, to distinguish between honest men and hypocrites. Two trees may look alike until harvest time approaches. Then the quality of the fruit they bear reveals what kind of trees they are. We expect a good tree to bear good fruit and a bad tree to bear bad fruit. We do not expect to gather figs from thornbushes nor grapes from briers. In the same way, a good man brings forth good

79

things out of the good stored in his heart. Unfortunately, the converse is also true. An evil man produces evil from what he has stored in his heart. Science has never invented an X-ray powerful enough to penetrate a man's heart and discern what is there—evil or good. But we really don't need an X-ray. All we have to do is listen to a person talk awhile, especially in his unguarded moments. His speech will sooner or later betray what is really in his heart.

The Wise and Foolish Builders
Luke 6:46-49

In the concluding part of His sermon, Jesus set forth claims that are breathtaking in their scope. To proclaim Jesus as Lord is not enough. Words must be followed by appropriate actions. One who obeys Jesus' commands is like a person who wisely builds his house upon solid rock. It will stand the test of time and tide. In contrast, the foolish man takes the easy way out and refuses to heed His commands. He is like a person who builds on nothing but the earth. The first driving rain will wash away the foundation, causing the house to collapse. This portion of the sermon no doubt served to inspire the hymn writer: "On Christ the solid rock I stand; All other ground is sinking sand."

Jesus boldly stated that the way of salvation lay in following His teachings. Such a claim can properly be made only by the Son of God. Whether the audience understood the full implications of this we do not know. But as Jesus concluded His sermon, a silence must have fallen upon the audience. Even if they did not understand that He was claiming to be God's Son, they certainly sensed that He was different from the other rabbis they had heard. Matthew concludes the record in this fashion: "When Jesus had finished saying these things, the crowds were amazed at his teaching, because he taught as one who had authority, and not as their teachers of the law" (Matthew 7:28, 29).

A Time of Healing and Teaching

Luke 7:1-50

The Sermon on the Mount closed with the people amazed at Jesus' words. He spoke with authority and not as one of the scribes (Matthew 7:28, 29). If the sermon reported in Luke 6 was not the same one, it was so similar that it probably had the same effect. Some of Jesus' followers were perhaps beginning to realize that He was more than a mere man. The seventh chapter of Luke relates several events that continue His self-revelation as the Messiah. In some cases this was accomplished by His actions, in others by His words.

The Healing of the Centurion's Servant
Luke 7:1-10

The language of Luke would lead us to believe that Jesus, as soon as He had finished His sermon, made His way into Capernaum. This suggests that the place where the sermon was delivered was not far from Capernaum.

As at other times, Capernaum became the scene of a striking miracle. Luke sets the stage for this by providing the background. Strictly speaking, a centurion is the commander of a hundred men. This was a position of some authority. Several centurions are mentioned in the New Testament—the centurion at the cross (Matthew 27:54), Cornelius (Acts 10:1, 2, 22), and the centurion who accompanied Paul on his voyage to Rome (Acts 27:1, 43). These were all intelligent, sensitive men. That such capable men were in positions of leadership says something about the Roman army of that day.

In Capernaum a servant (literally, slave) of the centurion had fallen ill. The centurion's benevolent attitude toward the slave gives us an insight into his character. A Roman citizen had the power of life or death over his slaves, and it was common practice to consider them no more than tools that could be discarded when they became too old to work. Luke does not tell us the exact nature of the man's illness, but Matthew says he was "paralyzed and in terrible suffering." It was serious enough that he was about to die. The centurion's concern led him to take the only steps he knew to save the servant's life. He sought help from one whose power over disease had been proved many times.

We are not told how the centurion learned about Jesus, but it would be hard to be in Capernaum in those days without knowing about Him. Jesus had been in Galilee for several months, and often in Capernaum. His miracles were the talk of the town (Luke 4:36, 37). Crowds gathered wherever He was (Luke 4:40; 5:1, 19; 6:17). Probably one duty of the centurion and his men was to watch such crowds to be sure no riot or insurrection was developing. The centurion certainly was well informed about what Jesus was doing, and may have witnessed some of His miracles. He had reason to think Jesus could help him.

Matthew's report of this episode says the centurion came to Jesus (Matthew 8:5). However, Matthew gives an abbreviated account of this event and apparently ascribes to the centurion what the centurion accomplished through others. We often speak in the same way. Not long before this was written, for example, a news account reported that President Reagan had invaded Grenada. As a matter of fact, the President probably had not come within a thousand miles of the island. The reporter was simply ascribing to President Reagan what the President accomplished through the Marines. In like manner, Matthew ascribes to the centurion what that officer accomplished through others who acted on his behalf.

Rather than approach Jesus himself, the centurion sent a delegation of Jewish elders to plead his case. He must have believed they would have a better chance of getting a hearing than he, a Gentile, would. The elders could also tell that the man was a friend of the Jews and had built their synagogue for them. If that was the only synagogue in Capernaum, then Jesus had already taught there (Luke

4:31-37). The fact that the man had built the synagogue indicated that he was more than just a good neighbor who wanted to help his Jewish friends. It seems quite likely that he had left behind his paganism and was taking more than a passing interest in Judaism. It would have sounded like boasting had the man himself reported this to Jesus. The account seems to indicate that the men brought this information to Jesus of their own free will and without any coaching from the centurion.

When the centurion learned that Jesus was coming to his house, he became quite concerned. Sensing his own unworthiness, he sent friends to stop Jesus. He did not want to create a problem for Jesus by allowing Him to come into the house of a Gentile. This was considered a serious taboo by the Pharisees in Jesus' day. Had Jesus violated it, He would have offended many of the more scrupulous Jews. Perhaps Jesus would have done that without hesitation, but the thoughtful centurion wanted to spare Him any difficulty.

Through his friends, the centurion insisted that Jesus did not need to come to his house in order to heal his servant. From his own life he drew an illustration that showed his great faith. Jesus was very much impressed, so much so that He turned to the crowd following Him and commended the faith of this Roman. What a contrast between this man and the people of Jesus' hometown! There Jesus was amazed by their lack of faith, and as a result He did few miracles there (Mark 6:4-6). (And do we not also limit the things He can do among us by our lack of faith?) When the messengers returned to the centurion's house, they found that the servant was well. Without even being in the house or seeing the man or saying a word, Jesus' power had reached out and healed.

A Widow's Son Is Raised
Luke 7:11-17

Shortly after this miracle in Capernaum, Jesus and His companions traveled to the town of Nain. Nain was located on the slopes of Little Hermon at the edge of the Plain of Jezreel about a half dozen miles south and east of Nazareth. Having left Capernaum, Jesus was apparently on a teaching circuit around Galilee. His arrival at the gate of Nain was most timely. In fact, it is hard to believe that it was coincidental: It is not unreasonable to suppose that Jesus planned His arrival just as the funeral procession was leaving the village. Since the procession was coming out the gate, it is obvious that this was a walled town.

Luke tells us that the dead person was the only son of a widow. Accompanying the body was the mother and a "large crowd" from the town. Apparently the mother had many friends. For some funerals, professional mourners were hired to cry and wail, but it is not likely that the bereaved widow could afford many of them.

Seeing this sad procession, Jesus was moved with sympathy. "His heart went out to her." The word here used indicates very strong feeling. Jesus was not just an unconcerned, dispassionate passerby. He was physically and emotionally involved. His first words to the bereaved widow were words of sympathy: "Don't cry." The poor woman faced a most trying situation. Having already lost her husband, now she had lost her only son. This was reason enough for her sorrow, but on top of that she faced a world where the plight of widows without children was especially difficult. The poor woman's world had collapsed about her, and her future looked bleak indeed. Then as everyone watched, Jesus approached the coffin and touched it. This was not a wooden or metal box such as we are familiar with. It was probably a wicker stretcher for carrying the body to the tomb.

When Jesus touched the coffin, those carrying it stopped, surprised no doubt by the behavior of this stranger. But Jesus moved with such authority that no one challenged Him. Without saying a word to the coffin bearers, Jesus spoke directly to the young man in a voice loud enough that those about could hear Him: "Young man, I say to you, get up!" It is interesting to note that in the other two resurrections performed by Jesus, he spoke to the victims in a similar way (Luke 8:54; John 11:43).

In the other two resurrections, Jesus elicited faith and hope from the survivors before He performed the miracle. Here Jesus spoke to the widow only to console her. There is scarcely a hint of what was to follow. The crowd—both those who were in the funeral procession and those who were accompanying Jesus—were filled with fear. Some of them had undoubtedly witnessed miracles of healing, but they were still hardly prepared for a resurrection.

Their immediate response was that Jesus was a prophet. They may have had in mind the two Old Testament prophets, Elijah and Elisha, who had performed miracles of resurrection. In any event, the people recognized that Jesus was a special messenger from God and no ordinary rabbi. For more than four hundred years since the time of Malachi, the last of the Old Testament prophets, no prophet of God had arisen in the land. False prophets there had been, but none of these could offer the credentials that Jesus in just one miracle was able to present. The people called Jesus a prophet, and they were also quick to recognize that God through Jesus had come to help them.

Although the people were ready to recognize Jesus as a prophet, they were not ready to recognize Him as the Son of God. Nor should we expect them to come to this position after witnessing only one miracle. To accept Jesus as the divine Son of God was a radical conclusion that most people could not reach quickly. It meant laying aside their long-held views of the Messiah. It also meant making a life-changing personal commitment that people are seldom quick to make.

Without radio, television, or newspapers, the word of this miracle quickly spread through Judea and its surroundings. *Judea* here probably refers to the whole area of Palestine rather than to the small province surrounding Jerusalem.

Questions From John the Baptist
Luke 7:18-23

John had been imprisoned by Herod some time earlier. This was Herod Antipas, King of Galilee and Perea. He was angry because John rebuked him for "all the other evil things he had done," but especially "because of Herodias, his brother's wife" (Luke 3:19, 20). This woman had deserted her husband to live with Herod. The king was reluctant to take further action against John, "knowing him to be a righteous and holy man" (Mark 6:20). According to Josephus, a Jewish historian, Herod kept John imprisoned in his castle at Machaerus. This castle was located in a remote area east of the Dead Sea.

Word of Jesus' miracles had reached John in his isolated dungeon, stimulating his questions. Did John ask these questions because doubts had begun to creep into his own heart? Or did he raise them with the expectation that their answer by Jesus would reassure his disciples? Scholars have long debated this, and good arguments have been advanced on each side of the question.

We can never know with certainty John's motives, but we must always bear in mind that he was human. Confined as he was and facing almost certain death, it would be most unusual if he did not have some doubts. Even if he never wavered a moment in his belief that Jesus was the promised Messiah, he might very well have had some doubts about Jesus' methods. John had come preaching judgment; Jesus had come preaching love and bringing healing. The rough desert prophet may have had some trouble adjusting to that.

Jesus certainly knew what was in John's heart. Instead of trying to formulate a theological answer, He invited John's disciples to stay and watch. We don't know how long they remained with Jesus, but in that time they witnessed a variety of miracles. He cured many with diseases, cast out evil spirits, and restored sight to the blind. To these powerful evidences of divine approval upon His ministry, Jesus added a mild admonition in the form of a beatitude: "Blessed is the man who does not fall away on account of me." The answer was adequate, for never again do we hear a voice of doubt from John's cell.

Jesus' Tribute to John
Luke 7:24-35

As soon as John's messengers had left, Jesus sought to remove any erroneous conclusions that may have arisen about John. John was no frail reed swayed by every passing breeze. Such a fickle person would never have been able to attract the great crowds that sought him out even in the remote desert. Nor was John a fawning syco-phant who assured himself of his master's favors by bowing and scraping. John was in a palace, true enough, but he was in its dungeon, not enjoying its luxuries. John had earned a reputation as a man of resolute courage. Jesus reminded the people of this so that none would criticize John for his question.

Jesus went further. John was a prophet, but he was more than a prophet. He was also the fulfillment of a prophecy. Malachi had predicted that God would send Elijah before that great and dreadful day of the Lord (Malachi 4:5). Matthew reports that Jesus indicated that John was Elijah (Matthew 11:14).

Then Jesus added a paradox. On the one hand, no one greater than John had ever been born of woman. (Can one think of a higher tribute from a higher source than this?) Yet on the other hand, "the one who is least in the kingdom of God is greater than he" (Luke 7:28). Jesus was in no way casting doubt upon John's greatness. But John lived under the Old Covenant. Its blessings could not compare to the blessings of the New Covenant. Even the least under the New Covenant would have the advantage of knowing of the resurrection and the greater blessings it brought. May God give to us who live under the New Covenant the wisdom and grace to appreciate and enjoy these blessings as we should!

The *New International Version* takes verses 29 and 30 to be paren-
thetical, added by Luke. But it seems better to follow the *King James*
and several modern translations that make these verses a continuation of Jesus' words in which He was continuing to talk about John's
ministry. When the publicans heard John's message, they accepted it
and were baptized. Most of the Pharisees and lawyers, on the other
hand, rejected John's teaching and refused to be baptized by him.

Jesus then turned specifically to His critics with an extended sim-
ile. They were like children who, while sitting in the marketplace,
decided to play some children's games. Their first choice was to
play a happy game—a wedding, perhaps. And so they piped a
happy tune, but some refused to dance. Then they decided to play a
sad game—a funeral, maybe. The disgruntled ones still refused to
participate.

Then Jesus made His point. John came with a somber message
and an ascetic, austere life-style. The religious leaders rejected him
as some kind of a religious nut. "He has a demon," they said.

Since they rejected John for his austerity, they logically should
have been pleased with Jesus' conduct. His life-style was quite normal. He lived among the people and did not withdraw from them.
But they were just as critical of Him. "Glutton, drunkard, friend of
tax collectors and sinners," they charged. But Jesus insisted that
eventually wisdom would be vindicated. And how right He was!
Enemies denounced Him as a friend of sinners, but now that is
recognized as one of the great strengths of the Christian faith.

The problem that Jesus dealt with was not unlike many that we
face today. Certain people, even some within the church, are difficult, if not impossible, to please. No matter what course of action
one takes, they will not be satisfied. We must learn to find the
correct course of action and then, like Jesus, pursue it without wav-
ering. Jesus was not turned aside by the questions from John, nor
was He intimidated by the hostility of the Pharisees and scribes. If
we persist in the truth with wisdom and courage, we can be sure
that wisdom will eventually be recognized by her children.

Jesus in the House of Simon the Pharisee
Luke 7:36-50

Jesus' fame as a teacher and healer had by this time become
widespread, and it is likely that He had many invitations for dinner.
We can only guess at Simon's motives in inviting Him. Not all
Pharisees were critics of Jesus, and so it is possible that Simon had a

sincere desire to learn more from this young rabbi. But Simon's failure to offer the ordinary courtesies to his guest makes this motive unlikely. Simon, on the other hand, may have planned to use the occasion to trap Jesus and criticize Him.

There is yet another possibility. Simon may have been one of those persons who liked to associate with celebrities. Jesus at this time was enjoying great popularity, and it may have been that Simon wished to bask a bit in Jesus' limelight.

Some say that this incident is the same one reported in Matthew 26:6, 7; Mark 14:3; and John 12:1-3. There are some parallels, but the two events come at different times in Jesus' ministry and other differences rule out this possibility. Some have identified this woman as Mary Magdalene, but there is no basis for this either.

As was the common practice, the guests at the banquet reclined about the table, each resting on his left arm and eating with his right. Their feet would be away from the table, making them accessible to anyone beside the table. At feasts such as this, it was not uncommon for uninvited persons to come and stand about the walls of the room watching the guests. This was one way that the rich could flaunt their affluence.

One of these uninvited guests was a woman of the town, a well-known sinner. While she is not specifically called a prostitute, that is a common inference. This woman had evidently heard Jesus teach, and learning that He was at the house of Simon, came bringing an alabaster jar of perfume. Once there, she was so overcome by emotion that she wept freely, the tears falling upon Jesus' feet. Then she let down her hair, an act considered quite improper in public, and wiped His feet with her tresses, pouring the perfume on them as she did.

Simon watched all of this without saying a word, but he was thinking in typical Pharisee fashion. "If Jesus were a prophet," he said to himself, "He would not permit a woman like this to touch him." The conclusion Simon came to in his own mind was that Jesus was not a prophet.

Jesus knew exactly what was on Simon's mind, and without revealing His intentions, He began to tell a parable. According to the parable, two men fell into debt—one for five hundred denarii and the other for fifty. (A denarius was a coin worth a typical day's wage for a worker.) When neither could pay, their creditor forgave them both. Now came Jesus' question: "Which of them will love him more?"

Simon obviously missed the import of the question and answered rather nonchalantly, "I suppose the one that had the bigger debt cancelled."

"You passed the first part of the test," replied Jesus. But poor Simon failed the second part. The woman, who came in humility and seeking forgiveness, had done all the things that Simon as a proper host should have done. Simon had not offered to wash Jesus' feet when He entered his house, but this woman had bathed His feet with her tears. Simon had not offered Jesus a kiss, but the woman had continued to kiss His feet. Simon had not anointed Jesus' head with oil, but the woman had poured perfume on His feet.

This sinful woman knew overwhelming gratitude because her great sins had been forgiven. The self-righteous Simon, however, had felt no need to seek forgiveness because he felt he was not a sinner.

Not satisfied with this rebuke, Jesus shocked his host even more. Turning to the woman, He said, "Your sins are forgiven." To a pious Pharisee such a statement seemed little short of blasphemy, for they believed, and rightly so, that only God could forgive sin. But they kept their objections to themselves, fearing that another challenge to Jesus would only increase their humiliation.

This scene was brought to a close when Jesus commended the woman for her faith and sent her forth with His blessing: "Go in peace."

10

The Bearer of Glad Tidings
Luke 8:1-56

Following Jesus' anointing by the sinful woman, His popularity continued to grow. This gave Him an opportunity to extend His ministry to many towns and villages in Galilee that had not previously been visited by Him. The twelve accompanied Him, as did several women who had been cured of evil spirits and diseases. These women, apparently of some means, helped support Jesus in His ministry. This statement, along with a few other hints of support from friends, indicates that Jesus did not resort to His miraculous powers to care for His own physical needs.

It is worth noting that some of these women were among Jesus' most faithful followers. They stood by Him at the time of the crucifixion when even the apostles fled. Of all the women mentioned in the Gospel accounts, no one of them is said to be hostile to Jesus. Most of them served Him faithfully—a commendable example for women today.

The Parable of the Sower
Luke 8:4-15

As Jesus traveled from town to town, a large crowd followed Him, intent on hearing the good news He brought. Though He had used parables earlier, He began to use them more extensively in this period of His ministry.

A parable has been defined as "an earthly story with a heavenly truth." Each parable served at least one of three purposes. First, it might be used to illuminate a spiritual truth that otherwise would elude the understanding of Jesus' listeners. Second, it might help a hearer remember the truth longer or more accurately. The third reason that Jesus used parables, paradoxically, was to conceal the truth. Jesus knew that people needed an intellectual challenge in order to grow spiritually. We understand better and appreciate more those things we have to labor to acquire. Used in this way, parables served as a tool to divide the sincere seekers after truth from those too lazy or too hostile to seek truth beyond the surface level.

The parable of the sower is one of those that separated the sincere from the casual. At this period in His ministry Jesus had a great popular following, but many of the followers had little serious interest in Jesus' real mission. They were mere curiosity seekers whose interest would quickly pass away. This parable not only separated the serious from the shallow; it also illustrated their different responses to Jesus' teachings.

Luke does not make it clear where Jesus spoke this parable, but the parallel passages in Matthew and Mark indicate that it was on the shore of the Sea of Galilee. There the crowd so pressed upon Him that He got into a boat and rowed out a few feet from the shore. This boat became His pulpit. Sitting in it He was able to teach the crowd most effectively (Matthew 13:1, 2; Mark 4:1).

Jesus' listeners were quite familiar with the scene He described. Perhaps many of them were farmers, and all of them had seen farmers in their fields sowing their grain by hand. The fields in Palestine were not large. Paths crisscrossed them, dividing them into individual plots. There were not many fences or hedges. Most of a field was broken up by plowing, but some of the seed broadcast by the sower would fall upon the paths that were packed hard by constant use. There it was not hidden in crevices as it was on the plowed ground. The birds promptly found it and feasted upon it. The farmer had no harvest from that seed.

Some seed fell on the rock; that is, a thin layer of soil on top of the underlying rock. Much of the soil in Palestine was like this, thin and unproductive. Seed sown in this shallow soil would quickly sprout, and it would even grow during the winter rainy season; but as soon as the rain stopped and the warm sun came out, the immature plants withered and died. "They had no moisture" because the shallow soil became dry right down to the rock.

Every farmer knows the bane of thorns and weeds, which seem always to spring up more quickly than do the good seeds. The thorns may have been perennials whose tops died back in the winter but which quickly sprang to life from the roots once spring came. Growing rapidly, the thorns quickly choked out the grain.

But all was not lost. Some of the seed fell on good soil, where it germinated and in due season brought forth a bountiful crop. Matthew and Mark say the yield was thirty, sixty, or a hundred times as much as was sown. Luke, giving an abbreviated account, mentions only the hundredfold yield.

Jesus closed this parable with an admonition for His audience to heed it carefully. He used this exhortation many times in His preaching, and when He did, it usually indicated that what He had just said was quite important. Here He was suggesting that this parable had a deeper meaning that would yield itself to those who paid attention with an open mind.

Even the disciples did not get the point of the parable. Mark tells us that when Jesus was alone, the twelve and others of His disciples asked Him about it. Their question gave Jesus a chance to explain why He used parables. The time had come in His ministry to separate the serious disciples from the casual curiosity seekers. This was His way of challenging His followers to seek the deeper meaning of His teaching. Then He quoted from Isaiah who, even as God commissioned him to preach, was warned that most of the people would not heed him.

In Isaiah's day, most of the people had hardened their hearts against his message from God. His further proclamation of that message served only to further harden their hearts. By quoting this passage from the prophet, Jesus seemed to be saying that many of the people who had heard Him had hardened their hearts in the same way.

But it was not Jesus' intent to hide His message from His disciples who sincerely sought the truth. Quickly and plainly He explained the parable when they asked about it. Others could have heard the explanation if they had cared enough to ask. Jesus himself was the sower. The seed was the word of God. The hardened pathway represented those who heard the word but resisted it until the devil came along and snatched it away.

Why do men reject the word of God without ever really giving it a chance to take root in their lives? Some reject it because they reject the messenger himself. Others have become so calloused by the world that nothing spiritual seems able to penetrate their defenses. But even though the devil comes quickly to snatch the word away, Jesus did not excuse these people for their rejection of it. No person can escape his responsibility to respond to God's message.

The second group of hearers, represented by the shallow soil, were persons who readily received the word and responded to it. For a time they showed great promise, but when responsibilities were placed upon them or they faced opposition, their enthusiasm waned and they soon fell away. All of us have known persons like this. They are enthusiastic at first and seem eager to serve, but then one day we look around and they are missing. They think the Christian life is a hundred-yard dash, when really it is a marathon run.

The third group, represented by the thorny soil, also heard and responded to the word. Their intentions were good; but the burden of the world, whether worldly cares or temptations of wealth and pleasure, kept them from producing a crop. The membership rolls of every church carry the names of persons who fit in this category.

Finally, some of the seed fell on good soil. The people who are represented by this soil respond when they hear the word, and they have the depth to keep growing and the strength to overcome the distractions represented by the thorns.

Matthew's and Mark's reports of this parable mention a thirtyfold and sixtyfold as well as a hundredfold yield. This may carry another important suggestion. Persons who respond positively to the gospel do not all yield the same fruit. Differing levels of talent lead to differing levels of fruitfulness. But Jesus did not praise the hundred-fold yield any more than He did the thirty or sixtyfold yield. The important thing is that many hearers were faithful; and being faithful, they were fruitful.

We usually take this parable as a warning against hardening our hearts to the word of God or accepting it in such a casual way that it will not be fruitful. However, this is also a parable of hope. The enemies of Jesus were beginning to take steps to silence Him. Soon there would be persecution against both Jesus and His disciples. Some were almost certain to fall away. Every farmer who plants grain knows that some of it does not sprout or does not grow to maturity. But he plants nevertheless, knowing that some of the grain will bear a crop. Jesus' message was a word of encouragement to His followers to sustain them when the persecution came and many fell away. They could find hope in the knowledge that at least some would bear a harvest.

The Parable of the Lamp
Luke 8:16-18

The discussion of the meaning of the parable of the sower was carried on with the disciples, not the larger crowd. The parable of the lamp seems to be a continuation of that discussion. It is perfectly obvious that no one lights a lamp and then hides it in a jar or under a bed. (The *King James Version* says "candle" rather than "lamp," but this is an anachronism. Candles were not invented until several centuries later.) The lamp Jesus had in mind was a small clay vessel with a spout for the wick. The fuel was usually olive oil. When we realize that the bed in Jesus' day was a pallet unrolled on the floor, we know that it would be not only foolish but downright dangerous to hide a burning lamp under it.

The meaning of this parable seems quite obvious. The message that Jesus was giving to His disciples should not be hidden but should be shouted from the housetops. Everything that was hidden in parables was eventually to be made known. As apostles, they would be sent for that very purpose.

Then Jesus added a warning. Because they would soon be responsible for spreading the light of the gospel, they were to listen carefully and take it all in. Since they had had the opportunity to be with Jesus and hear His teaching more than others had, they had the greater responsibility to share that teaching. Any person who refused to share what he had received would lose even that which he had.

Jesus' True Relatives
Luke 8:19-21

At some point during Jesus' teaching, His mother and brothers came to speak to Him. There is no reason to doubt that these brothers were younger sons of Mary and half-brothers of Jesus. Mark 3:21 indicates that they came to take Jesus home because He was "out of his mind." He was arousing the opposition of leaders in a way that seemed reckless to them.

The appearance of His family created a rather delicate situation for Jesus. He had always been obedient to His mother, but to obey her now would mean abandoning a very helpful ministry. Though their intentions were good, His brothers were not at this time believers. His mother certainly knew the truth about Him, but somehow she was persuaded to join them in this effort. Gently but firmly Jesus made it clear that they could not control His ministry.

He turned this ill-advised effort into an opportunity to teach a great truth. The real brothers and sisters of Jesus are those who hear and obey God's will. Spiritual relations are more important than physical relationships. The spiritual family is far more important and far more lasting than any physical family can be.

Jesus Calms the Sea
Luke 8:22-25

Luke doesn't tell us what day it was when Jesus stilled the sea, but Mark 4:35 says it was the same day in which Jesus taught in parables. It must have been late in the day, when Jesus was tired from His busy activities. The soft sounds of the rowing and the gentle sway of the boat lulled Him to sleep, and He slept so soundly that He was not awakened by roaring wind, dashing spray, and the violent motion of the storm-tossed boat. Jesus was the divine Son of God, but He was also human, which means that He could suffer fatigue just as we do.

He had not slept long before a sudden squall swept down upon the boat and threatened to swamp it. Nestled as it is among surrounding high hills, the Sea of Galilee is subject to sudden, violent storms. Although several of the disciples were fishermen and experienced at handling a boat in a storm, they were frightened. They quickly realized that they could not cope with this tempest alone. They did the only thing they knew to do—they woke up Jesus, pleading for His help.

Once Jesus awoke, He immediately addressed the storm: "Quiet! Be still!" (Mark 4:39). At once the storm subsided and the water was calm. Then turning to the disciples, Jesus chided them for their lack of faith. We may very well sympathize with the disciples in this situation. Few things are more terrifying than a violent storm at sea.

Once the waves had been stilled, the disciples began to talk among themselves. Their fear had given way to awe and wonder. Because of their experience on the Sea of Galilee, they realized that the sudden and complete calming of the waters was a miracle. It was evident that Jesus was no ordinary man. The wind and the waves do not obey mortal men.

They had seen Jesus perform many other miracles, but this one seemed different, even overwhelming. Some people today have a similar problem. They can accept the healing miracles, perhaps because they think these can be explained as psychosomatic. But there is no way this miracle can be explained away. The response of the disciples and modern skeptics is notably different. The disciples were overwhelmed by awe; the skeptics still cling to their doubts. Perhaps the disciples still had no more than a vague idea of Jesus' deity, but their minds were open and they were growing.

The Gerasene Demoniac
Luke 8:26-39

Once the storm was stilled, Jesus and the disciples proceeded across to the eastern side of the lake. Since they started late in the day and were delayed by the storm, perhaps all of them slept in the boat and moved to the shore in the morning. There they were met by a strange welcoming party—a naked man possessed by demons. (Matthew mentions two demon-possessed men, but Luke concentrates on the more prominent of the two.) This pitiful creature made his home among the tombs that had been carved out of the limestone cliffs. Driven by demons within, he was constantly injuring his own body (Mark 5:5).

As soon as the man saw Jesus and the disciples, he ran down to meet them. Then when he, or rather the demons that controlled him, saw who it was, he fell prostrate before our Lord. They recognized who Jesus was and also realized that He would challenge their domination of the man. We are certainly aware of the power of Satan and his hosts, but we need also to recognize that their power is not absolute. Confronted by the Son of God, their power quickly faded away.

The demons knew the fate that awaited them—the abyss. The *King James Version* calls it the deep, but it is not the deep Sea of Galilee that is meant. It is the bottomless pit of Revelation 20:1-3, the prison of Satan. The Scriptures tells us very little about what this may involve, but these demons obviously wanted to avoid that fate. They pleaded with Jesus to allow them to enter a herd of swine that was nearby. One would not expect to find swine in a Jewish community, but many Gentiles lived in the area. The hogs probably were owned by Gentiles and destined to be eaten by Gentiles.

Once the demons entered them, the pigs immediately went berserk. They ran pellmell down a steep slope and plunged into the lake, where they drowned. The swineherds watching over the pigs apparently were close enough to see and hear the whole thing. They immediately rushed into town to report what had happened. They were terrified by what they had witnessed, but they also wanted to make sure they were not held responsible for the loss of the swine.

96

The townspeople soon arrived at the scene. Imagine their surprise when they saw the former demoniac, now clothed and in his right mind, sitting at the feet of Jesus. Did they rejoice because their neighbor was restored to health and sanity? If they did, their joy was almost lost in a stronger emotion: "They were overcome with fear." Added to fear of supernatural power over demons was dismay at the loss of hogs—two thousand of them (Mark 5:13). "All the people of the region" asked Jesus to leave their territory. A herd of swine was worth more to them than was the sanity of a man.

While we piously reject the crassly materialistic values of these Gerasenes, we need to look a bit more closely at our own values. We license the profitable sale of alcoholic beverages that every year kill and maim thousands on the highways, destroy countless marriages, and reduce thousands of people to a pitiful chemical slavery. We countenance the destruction of a million or more fetuses every year simply to satisfy selfish desires. We are forced to confess that the Gerasenes had no monopoly on materialistic attitudes.

Even as the Gerasenes rejected Jesus, the reclaimed man wanted to cling to Him. Perhaps he dreaded having to return to a society from which he had been an outcast. It is more likely, however, that the man wanted to go with Jesus as an act of love and devotion. But Jesus had other plans for him. He was to remain among his own people as a missionary. Once he realized that this was Jesus' will for him, he obeyed without further question. Indeed, the man went beyond the circle of his family and friends. He "told all over town how much Jesus had done for him." Mark 5:20 indicates that he spread the news even more widely "in the Decapolis," an area of ten important cities.

Jairus' Daughter Raised
Luke 8:40-56

Since Jesus no longer was welcome among the Gerasenes, He and His disciples crossed the Sea of Galilee to the west side, probably to Capernaum. Almost as soon as they landed, Jairus, the ruler of a synagogue, came to Jesus, begging Him to come to his house and heal his twelve-year-old daughter.

On the way to Jairus' house, a woman who had a bleeding problem was healed simply by touching Jesus. Jesus indicated that her faith had made her whole. But even as Jesus was speaking, a messenger from the house of Jairus brought the tragic news that the girl was dead. Since she was dead, they felt that there was nothing Jesus could do for her and so they might as well leave Him alone. But Jesus rejected this conclusion and reassured the father.

Arriving at the house, Jesus kept everyone out but the girl's parents and Peter, James, and John. He also silenced the mourners, who by this time must have been setting up a horrible din. The mourners were quite skeptical of Jesus' power. When He insisted that the girl was only asleep, they laughed at Him.

But Jesus, as He always does, confounded the skeptics. He took the dead girl by the hand, and immediately her spirit returned and she stood up. The cure was instantaneous. There was no weakness, no period of slow recovery. Since she had been without food during her illness, Jesus thoughtfully asked that she be given something to eat.

Death had been cheated of his prey. This resurrection stands as a symbol of a greater resurrection, a greater victory over death, that Jesus would later accomplish through His own death and resurrection.

Jesus Concludes
His Galilean Ministry
Luke 9:1-50

In chapter 9 of Luke we see Jesus' Galilean ministry come to a climax. Somewhat earlier His ministry had taken a new direction when He had begun to teach in parables more extensively, thus separating followers who were really interested from those who were merely curious. Now He added another element. He began to speak openly of His coming death in order to prepare His followers for that event. In the earlier part of the Galilean ministry, the twelve had followed Jesus about, observing His miracles and absorbing His teaching. In the concluding phase of this ministry, they were increasingly involved. They had been trained to the point where they could begin to carry the good news, and they had matured to the point where they should be able to understand something about His suffering and death.

Jesus Sends Out the Twelve
Luke 9:1-6

Jesus' ministry had carried Him back to the vicinity of Capernaum. Since several of the twelve made their homes there, Capernaum made a convenient starting place for their preaching mission. The first thing Jesus did was to give them the power and authority necessary to carry out their work. *Power* refers to their ability to fulfill their mission; *authority* refers to their right to do so. Their power and authority allowed them not only to heal diseases but also to cast out demons. Thus they could work very much as Jesus had been working.

Once they were equipped, they were given their commission. Jesus had spent weeks traveling through Galilee, preaching, teaching, and healing. Now as His Galilean ministry was coming to a close, it was necessary for Him to reach out once more in the time that remained and consolidate His work. Several preaching teams going out separately could cover more area than could be covered if the twelve remained with Jesus. Their task was to preach (the word actually means "herald") the good news that the kingdom of God was at hand.

Anyone who goes out as a herald must be equipped both intellectually and spiritually. But more than that, he must also be equipped physically. Jesus did not neglect their physical equipment, although in this case it was meager. They were not to take a staff, bag, bread, money, or an extra tunic. If this seems an unusual way to send messengers out, we must keep in mind two things. First, they were going out into familiar territory. They would be passing through areas they had previously visited, and they had many friends there. The second thing we need to keep in mind was the traditional Jewish hospitality. Even a stranger traveling in the area could expect to be provided with the necessities of life. And so those who came as friends and benefactors need have no concern about being taken care of. Obviously, when we today send missionaries out into hostile territory, we have to make more adequate provisions for their welfare.

Although Luke does not mention it, Mark 6:7 tells us that they went out two by two. Anyone who has done evangelistic calling can readily understand the wisdom of this. They were given specific instructions for their conduct on the road. If they entered a village and were invited to stay in a home, they were not to move later to another home. This would prevent their being tempted to move to a more comfortable abode should an invitation arise.

Suppose they came to a village that didn't welcome them, then what? Under such conditions they were to move on, pausing only long enough to shake the dust off their sandals. This action symbolically declared God's displeasure with those people. This may seem a bit harsh to us, but we need to realize that they were on a hurried mission to reach as many people as possible in a short time. If they paused to argue and debate, others would miss the opportunity to hear. Every modern evangelist faces the same dilemma. How much time should we spend on an unresponsive person when there are many others who also need the good news?

Luke concludes this section by briefly summarizing the activities of the twelve. They went from village to village, not only preaching but also healing. Those villages that turned them away missed not only the good news but also the healing that accompanied it.

A King With a Troubled Conscience
Luke 9:7-9

While the apostles are carrying out their mission, Luke inserts an aside involving Herod the tetrarch. This is Herod Antipas, a son of the infamous Herod the Great. The title *tetrarch* means ruler of one-fourth. Herod was so called because he inherited one of the four parts of his father's kingdom. The four parts are listed in Luke 3:1.

Antipas was responsible for the death of John the Baptist (Mark 6:17-28). As more and more news about Jesus reached him, he became increasingly perplexed. Several suggestions were offered about Jesus' identity. Some felt He was John the Baptist come back from the dead. The messages of the two were similar, but their ministries were in many ways quite different. John preached in the wilderness, while Jesus kept to the populated areas. Further, so far as we know, John did not perform any miracles. These differences should have made it clear that Jesus was not John restored to life, but a conscience-stricken man like Herod was not limited to logical conclusions.

To satisfy his curiosity, Herod sought to see Jesus. Apparently this was not a wholehearted wish, however. Certainly the ruler could have arranged a meeting with Jesus had he desired it strongly enough. Herod was eventually to see Jesus, but under quite different circumstances at Jerusalem (Luke 23:6-12).

Jesus Feeds the Five Thousand
Luke 9:10-17

When the apostles returned from their mission, they were both excited and exhausted. Jesus knew exactly the treatment they needed—a time of relaxation to unwind. And so they boarded a boat and sailed across to the east side of the Sea of Galilee. The hills there might provide a quiet, deserted place where they could rest and discuss the mission just completed. As it turned out, however, their time in the boat was the only time they had in private. A large crowd followed them afoot around the northern end of the lake to a spot near Bethsaida. It may seem surprising that so many people made such an effort to hear Jesus once more. But we must realize that Jesus was then at the peak of His popularity, and this popularity had been enhanced by the mission of the twelve.

Although Jesus had sought some time alone with the disciples, He showed no irritation when the enthusiasm of the people thwarted His efforts. Instead, He welcomed them, taught them, and healed many who needed it. But as the day wore on, a problem arose. Jesus had preached well past the lunch hour. Unlike modern audiences, the people had not complained. Now it was late in the afternoon and they were still without food. Realizing the problem, the twelve suggested that Jesus pronounce the benediction and send the people home. Since there was no MacDonald's or Holiday Inn nearby, they would have to be on their way soon if they were to get home before dark. Jesus' reply seemed to make no sense at all. "Feed them," He said.

"But how can we?" they complained. "We have only five crackers and a couple of sardines. Why, it would take half a year's salary to feed this crowd. And besides, where would we buy food in this deserted place even if we had the money?"

Jesus didn't waste any more time with their excuses. Without giving any hint of His intentions, He told the apostles to have the crowd sit down in groups of about fifty. The twelve must have been mystified by this action, but at least they obeyed Jesus without any hesitation. Since there were five thousand men present, not counting women and children, they must have occupied quite a large area.

Once the people had been arranged in groups, Jesus took the five loaves and two fish and blessed them. Then He broke them—presumably both the bread and the fish—and gave the pieces to the disciples to distribute to the people. The verb that Luke uses for *give* suggests continuing action—"He kept on giving." This would indicate that the miracle occurred in Jesus' hands. If this was the case, it must have taken some time for Jesus to produce enough food for the whole crowd. Further, handling that much food would have been physically exhausting.

How simply this miracle is related! In fact, we're not even told that it was a miracle. But the results leave no doubt that a miracle was performed. Some modern writers have raised questions about this, attempting to explain it away by saying that actually many had brought their lunches but refused to share with others and kept them hidden. Then because of Jesus' teaching, their selfish hearts were melted and they began to pull their food out and share it. As a result everyone had enough to eat. But of course there is nothing in the account to suggest that anything like that happened, and so we must reject such an explanation as pure imagination.

After this meal was over, the broken pieces that remained were gathered up—twelve baskets full in all. Two lessons may be drawn from this. First of all, God provides bountifully for His children, more than they need. But even though He makes generous provision for us, He expects us to use His gifts carefully and without waste.

Luke gives us an abbreviated account of this incident, and he does not tell of the people's response to the miracle. From John 6:14, 15 we learn that the people wanted to take Jesus and make Him king. And why not? With Jesus as king they would have cradle to the grave security—all the food they needed plus free medical insurance on top of that. When it became obvious that the people wanted to take Him by force and make Him king, Jesus sent the disciples by boat back to Capernaum, while He went up into the hills to find solitude to pray (Mark 6:45, 46).

John supplies a sequel to this story. The disciples in the boat encountered a strong head wind and were having trouble in making their way across the lake to Capernaum. But in the night Jesus came to them, walking on the water, and then they finished the trip with no more difficulty.

The people who have enjoyed the feast of loaves and fish were eagerly looking for Jesus the next morning. When they finally found Him in Capernaum, they were disappointed. Instead of another free meal, He gave them a profound sermon on spiritual food, the bread of life. At that, some of the people lost interest in Jesus, but the apostles did not. As Simon Peter put it, "You have the words of eternal life" (John 6:16-69).

Peter's Good Confession
Luke 9:18-27

Luke in his Gospel omits several events that are mentioned in Matthew and Mark. The feeding of the five thousand raised the people's expectations to such a pitch that they threatened the whole course of His ministry. To escape the crowds whose thoughts were mainly on a physical kingdom, Jesus left the area of Capernaum and carried on work in Phoenicia, the Decapolis east of the Sea of Galilee, and then in the area around Caesarea Philippi. It is here that Luke again takes up the narrative.

Caesarea Philippi was located in the northern part of Palestine near the foot of lofty Mount Hermon. One of the important sources of the Jordan River arises here. It was an ancient city, the site of a Canaanitish sanctuary dedicated to the worship of Baal. The town had been enlarged by Herod Philip, who named it to honor Caesar and then added his own name to it to distinguish it from the city of Caesarea on the Mediterranean coast.

Jesus was alone with the twelve on this occasion and took the opportunity to do some private teaching. Like many good teachers, He began by quizzing the class. "Who do the crowds say I am?" He asked.

There were several answers, each having some element of plausibility. Herod, for example, was afraid that Jesus was John the Baptist come back to life. Others suggested Elijah, Jeremiah, or another of the prophets (Matthew 16:14).

Jesus then gave them the final question: "What about you? Who do you say I am?"

Peter, who so often spoke up first, again took the lead. "The Christ of God," came his answer. Since none of the others objected, it is safe to assume that Peter expressed the sentiments of all of them. As he so often does, Luke abbreviates the incident. Matthew's Gospel gives us a more complete report of the reply and the discussion that followed (Matthew 16:16-20). Peter's complete answer was "You are the Christ, the Son of the living God." Theologians may debate just how completely Peter understood the full implications of his confession. But it is clear that in using the title "Christ" he accepted Jesus as God's long-awaited Savior, "the anointed one of God."

Jesus then pointed out that this confession would be the solid rock upon which the church would be built. He also warned them to keep this information a secret. When we understand the excitement then running through the crowd, we can understand the reasons for this restriction. Galilee was a hotbed of Jewish nationalism ready to explode in flames. This information about Jesus could very well have led to an upheaval against Rome that would have resulted in great bloodshed.

To make sure that the disciples were not swept away by this popular misunderstanding about the nature of His kingdom, Jesus began to warn them about what the future held for Him. He must suffer many things from the religious leaders, who would finally kill Him. But His death would not end His mission. Instead, He would be raised on the third day. Earlier in His ministry Jesus had hinted about these future events, but now He came out with a plain statement that they were not likely to misunderstand (Matthew 16:21).

Matthew informs us that Peter did very well understand Jesus' prediction and objected strenuously to it. But Jesus rebuked him, calling him a tool of Satan (Matthew 16:22, 23). This exchange gave Jesus an opportunity to present further teaching about the nature of His kingdom. Self-denial is at the very heart of service to Him. One must be willing to lose his life for Christ if he really wants to save it. He concluded this challenge with the assurance that His kingdom was not far in the future. Indeed, some of those present would live to see its coming (Matthew 16:24-28).

A Mountaintop Experience
Luke 9:28-36

There is something about a mountain that seems to capture and hold our attention. For one thing, a mountain is big and obvious. Also, from its heights we are offered views that we would not otherwise have. Mountaintops also provide us solitude that we sometimes need. These things may help us understand a little better the unusual mountaintop experience that Jesus shared with three of the apostles.

About a week or so after Peter's good confession at Caesarea Philippi, Jesus took Peter, James, and John up on a mountain. Traditionally, the mount of transfiguration has been identified with Mount Tabor, a small mountain about six miles east and south of Nazareth. A more likely spot for this dramatic event is Mount Hermon, which towers more than nine thousand feet above sea level. Its peak is usually covered with snow during much of the year, and it can readily be seen from all over Galilee. Matthew 17:1 says "a high mountain," and Hermon fits that description.

Jesus sought privacy for a time of prayer. As He prayed, His appearance changed. His face shone "like the sun" (Matthew 17:2), and His clothes were as bright as a flash of lightning. Then Moses and Elijah appeared and began to speak with Him about His impending death in Jerusalem. Just why Moses and Elijah appeared with Him we do not know. However, we can speculate that these two men represented the two ways by which God sought to guide His people in the Old Testament period, Moses representing the law and Elijah representing the prophets. All of God's revelation pointed to the mission of Jesus; and of all things in Heaven and earth, these three were most concerned about Jesus' death for the sins of the world.

The three apostles, perhaps exhausted by the climb up the mountain, had fallen asleep. They awoke to see Jesus in His glory standing with the two men. They must have been dumbfounded at first. Peter, who seemed always to have to say something, came up with a suggestion. "Why not build three shelters—one for Jesus, one for Moses, and one for Elijah?" The shelters he had in mind were booths or tents, temporary dwellings. Just why Peter suggested this is not certain. Indeed, the Scriptures tell us that he didn't know what he was saying, that he hadn't thought through the idea before he spoke.

Jesus did not need to give a reply to Peter's idea, for even as the apostle spoke, a cloud enveloped them. In the Old Testament, God's presence was sometimes indicated by a cloud. Then, as at Jesus' baptism, the voice of God came: "This is my Son, whom I have chosen; listen to him."

Matthew informs us that the apostles were so terrified at the sound of God's voice that they fell on their faces (17:6). Then when Jesus touched them, they arose to find that Jesus was all alone. No doubt these men were greatly moved by this experience. Jesus told them not to tell others about it until after the resurrection (Matthew 17:9).

The transfiguration served two important purposes. It helped encourage Jesus and prepare Him for the ordeal He would face in Jerusalem in a few months. It confirmed the three apostles' faith in Jesus, coming as it did only a few days after the good confession. It would also help them understand His suffering and death. This experience made a profound impression on Peter, who many years later recalled that it gave support and assurance to his faith (2 Peter 1:16-18).

The Conclusion of Jesus' Galilean Ministry
Luke 9:37-50

When Jesus came down from the mountain the next day, He was immediately faced with a problem. During His absence a man had brought his demon-controlled son to the disciples for healing, but they were not able to drive the demon out. It seems strange that the nine could not exorcise this demon, since they had wielded this power in their tour through Galilee. Jesus' sharp criticism in verse

106

41—"O unbelieving and perverse generation"—may give us a hint. They were lacking in faith. Jesus later confirmed this plainly (Matthew 17:19, 20).

Jesus asked that the boy be brought to Him. The demon made one last effort to keep control, hurling the boy to the ground in a convulsion. But the demon's efforts were unavailing, and the boy was set free.

Then while the crowd was marveling at the miracle, Jesus took the opportunity to tell His disciples once again about His coming suffering. These verses provide an appropriate transition to the next phase of Jesus' ministry. Even as they were enjoying a moment of triumph, He took the occasion to warn them of the somber future that lay only a few months ahead. Very plainly He told them that He was going to be betrayed into the hands of men. Yet they did not understand. We marvel at how dense they were, but we need not be too smug about it. Jesus' intent is obvious to us only because we have the advantage of hindsight.

From Galilee to Jerusalem
Luke 9:51—12:12

An important phase of Jesus' ministry closed with Luke 9:50. His Galilean ministry, which had generated much enthusiasm, had now come to an end. The popularity He had known in Galilee was waning because He refused to be a military leader and establish an independent kingdom of Israel. Replacing that popularity would be the growing hostility of the religious leaders. Jesus set out on a way that would eventually take Him to Jerusalem, where loomed the cross. This section of Luke does not follow a strictly chronological pattern, but the direction of its movement is clear.

Jesus Sets Out for Jerusalem
Luke 9:51-62

The time of Jesus' death was rapidly approaching. Knowing this full well, Jesus "resolutely set out for Jerusalem." In the words of a song we sometimes sing, there was "no turning back." As Jesus and His disciples passed through Samaria, the people in one village refused to extend them common hospitality because they were obviously Jews on their way to Jerusalem. James and John, living up to their name, "Sons of Thunder," wanted to zap the whole town—call down fire from heaven upon them. The pair still misunderstood the nature of Christ's kingdom, and so He rebuked them for their harsh thoughts and moved on to the next village, which was more hospitable. Jesus' patient response to the Samaritan snub taught a lesson that John later learned, for eventually he became known as "the apostle of love."

Sometimes others were with them as they walked along. One indicated his willingness to follow Jesus anywhere. Rather than welcoming him with open arms, Jesus seemed to rebuff his offer by a strange saying: "Foxes have holes and birds of the air have nests, but the Son of Man has no place to lay his head." Apparently the man had not carefully thought through what he was saying. Jesus' response was designed to jar him back to stark reality.

Jesus challenged another man, "Follow me." The man seemed willing to obey after his father's funeral, but Jesus turned him away with a harsh answer. Before we are critical of Jesus, we must bear in mind that He knew the man's heart better than we do. Jesus' reply seems to indicate that the man's wish to bury his father was a shallow excuse. It may very well be that the father was still living and the man meant that he could not leave until his father died, which might be years in the future.

A third man wanted to bid farewell to his family—a normal enough request, we would think. But again Jesus saw through it. It was really an excuse to avoid making that final and complete commitment to Christ. Though love of family is commendable, yet it must not take priority over loyalty to Jesus. A man who tries to maintain dual loyalties is like a man who keeps looking back over his shoulder as he tries to plow. He certainly can't plow a straight furrow, and he is very likely to ruin his plow on some unseen boulder.

Mission of the Seventy
Luke 10:1-24

Only Luke tells of the sending of the seventy (or seventy-two, according to the *New International Version,* for there is a difference in the ancient manuscripts at this point). Scholars differ about whether the number is symbolic or whether this just happened to be the number of trained workers who were available at the time. Just as the twelve were sent out two by two, so the seventy went out in pairs. Anyone who has done calling recognizes the wisdom of this. Not only is the testimony of two stronger than the testimony of one, but companions can also assist and encourage one another.

Jesus often used examples from agriculture to illustrate His point. Since most people in Palestine were farmers or lived close to the soil, they would readily understand these figures. The field had been prepared and the seed planted by Jesus' earlier ministry. As a result of this previous work, many were now ready to accept the message these disciples would bring. Though the field was ready for harvest, there were not enough workers to complete the harvest during the time allotted. The agricultural illustration is most appropriate in this situation. Every farmer knows that if the grain is not harvested when it is ripe, the birds will get it, the heads will shatter and fall to the ground, or the stalk will fall over and the grain will rot.

Jesus made it very clear that He was not sending these men on a picnic. They should expect opposition and persecution. Indeed, Jesus described the situation in such a way that the mission seemed almost suicidal. They were being sent as lambs among wolves! They had only one defense: Jesus had sent them, and that was assurance enough.

They were to travel light, just as the twelve had done in the earlier mission. They were not to take money, provisions, or extra clothing. They were to stay where they were invited but not to linger where they were not welcomed. They were not to consider themselves beggars who relied upon others to support them. They were workers who were bringing a spiritual benefit to those who provided them food and shelter. They were laborers worthy of their hire.

They were not to remain where they were unwanted guests. When they were rejected by a town, they were to shake the dust from their feet as a symbolic testimony against that place. God's judgment would then be upon it. That judgment was no light thing. The unbelievers' fate would be worse than that of Sodom, the ancient symbol of evil that justified God's wrath. Their fate would be worse, not because they were more evil than Sodom, but because they had rejected God's grace when it had been offered through Jesus' messengers.

Jesus then singled out three cities that especially had earned God's wrath—Korazin, Bethsaida, and Capernaum. He compared them to three notorious cities of the past—Sodom, Tyre, and Sidon. Jesus set forth a most profound truth here. By any kind of moral standards Sodom, Tyre, and Sidon were far more wicked than the cities Jesus was condemning. But the point that He was making was that God's final judgment will be based upon the opportunities one had. The cities of Galilee had heard Jesus many times and they had rejected Him. They would have accepted Him as a bloody king to defeat Rome, but not as a king of peace and righteousness to rule their hearts. Sodom, Tyre, and Sidon, grossly wicked as they were, would have repented had they but had the opportunity that was available to Galilee.

The application of this truth to our situation is frightening. We may look at ourselves and thank God that we are not as wicked as Sodom, Tyre, and Sidon. We may even try to argue that we are actually pious. But Bethsaida, Korazin, and Capernaum would have felt the same way, and these were the very towns that called down Jesus' condemnation. Jesus set forth the principle that to whom much is given, from him much will be required.

Jesus concluded His charge to the seventy-two by setting forth the authority under which they would proclaim the good news. The message they would carry would be Jesus' message. But more than that, it would be the message that God sent His Son to deliver. The realization of the importance of this message must certainly have placed a heavy responsibility upon the shoulders of the messengers.

Luke does not tell us how long it took the seventy-two to complete their mission. It may have been completed in a few days, or it may have extended for several weeks. Apparently Jesus had set an established time and place for them to reassemble. Their spirits were high when they returned. Jesus had prepared them for possible rejection, but instead they had achieved many victories. The thing that seemed to excite them most was that even the demons were subject to them.

In the midst of their victory celebration, Jesus made a strange statement: "I saw Satan fall like lightning from heaven." In this context Jesus seems to be saying that in casting out demons the disciples had gained a notable victory over Satan. It also prefigures future victories over the evil one, victories so dramatic that Satan could be described as lightning falling from heaven. This victory over Satan also brought protection from the evil forces of nature that he might use to thwart their mission. As important as this victory was, however, it could not begin to bring the joy that having their names written in Heaven would bring.

Who Is My Neighbor?
Luke 10:25-37

This parable, which is found only in Luke, has been a favorite down through the centuries. Its theme has been portrayed in the art of the early church and the tapestries of the Middle Ages. Because it deals with a universal problem, it has sounded a note that will continue to reverberate so long as the Gospel of Luke is read.

We don't know where or when this incident occurred, but it must have happened shortly after the return of the seventy-two. A lawyer, that is, one of a special group of men who gave themselves to the study of the Old Testament law, arose to challenge Jesus. These scholars had been growing increasingly suspicious of Jesus because He did not always follow their interpretations of the law. The question that he asked was a crucial one: "What must I do to inherit eternal life?" But the thrust of his question betrayed his belief that one could earn salvation by good deeds.

As He often did, Jesus answered a question with a question: "What is written in the Law?" The man's reply was right on target. One must love God with all his heart, soul, strength, and mind, a summary of the law from Deuteronomy 6:5. The second part of his reply set forth the necessity of loving one's neighbor as himself (Leviticus 19:18). Jesus gave the man an A for these answers.

But the lawyer was unwilling to leave it that way. Still determined to find some way to beat Jesus, he resorted to a lawyer's trick—demand a definition of terms. "Just who is my neighbor?" he asked. Jesus, refusing to play the lawyer's game, gave an example rather than a definition.

The route from Jerusalem to Jericho, passing through rugged terrain that was sparsely populated, was a high crime area. No doubt some of Jesus' listeners had taken that route and knew very well its potential dangers. In this case the traveler became a victim. There he lay stripped and half-dead when a priest came upon him. Seeing the man, he quickly moved to the other side of the road and passed him by. After all, if the priest stopped to care for the man, he would be late to an important religious convocation. Besides, if the man died, and the priest touched him, he would be considered ceremonially unclean. Or if the priest was only going home after his term of service in the temple, his wife and children were eager to see him. It wouldn't be right to keep them waiting, would it?

A Levite came along next, and he too passed by on the opposite side of the road. After all, the brass candlesticks in the temple probably needed polishing, and as a laborer in the temple, he dared not neglect his duties in the house of the Lord—even if it meant leaving a man to die.

Then the Samaritan arrived. In terms of Jewish prejudice, he should have been the villain in the situation. But Jesus' story didn't follow the usual plot, and so the Samaritan turned out to be the hero. As soon as the Samaritan saw the wounded man, "he took pity on him." Without hesitation he stopped and administered first aid. In stopping he might have been endangering himself, since bandits sometimes pretended to be hurt in order to decoy unwary travelers into a trap. But if this danger ever crossed the Samaritan's mind, he gave no indication of it. Once he had treated the man's wounds, he mounted him on his own donkey and took him to an inn. There he gave the innkeeper two denarii (equivalent to two day's wages) and promised to pay more if further expenses should be incurred. So actual out-of-pocket expense was added to His risk, loss of time, and the inconvenience of walking.

Once Jesus had completed the story, He was ready for the next question. "Which of these three do you think was a neighbor to the man?" He asked.

The answer was so obvious to everyone that the lawyer could not avoid it. But even though he had to give the answer Jesus wanted, his prejudice would not allow him to say a good word about the Samaritan, and so in lawyer fashion he answered, "The one who had mercy on him."

Jesus was not interested in winning debating points, and so He wasted no time gloating over the vanquished lawyer. Instead, He urged him to good works. "Go and do likewise," was our Lord's admonition, and after all these centuries that admonition still rings in our ears.

It is unfortunate that some are so committed to legalistic orthodoxy that they neglect the deeds of mercy that cry out on every hand. Every age has produced its lawyers who would rather quibble about the definition of the word *neighbor* than go out and serve the neighbor who is in need. Jesus made the word so broad that anyone in need is a neighbor, regardless of the color of his skin or the shape of his creed. No one compromises his Biblical faith when he helps someone who is hurting. Indeed, he compromises it seriously when he passes by on the other side of the road.

Two Sisters Disagree
Luke 10:38-42

Luke gives us little data by which we may date or locate this incident that occurred in the house of Mary and Martha. Luke doesn't even tell us that Mary and Martha lived in Bethany. (We find that information in John 11:1 and 12:1-3). At some point the people of this household had become dedicated disciples of Jesus, and their home was open to Him whenever He was in the area.

113

On this occasion Jesus had not been there long before a dispute erupted. Martha was an activist who had to be doing things. And with thirteen guests (we assume that the twelve accompanied Jesus) coming for dinner, there were many things to be done. Mary, on the other hand, was the quiet thinker who did not become upset when every detail was not attended to.

As Martha busied herself with preparing the meal, her resentment toward Mary began to build up. Finally she exploded, "Tell her to help me!" In her anger she didn't stop to think how inappropriate it was to make such a request of an honored guest. Gently but plainly, Jesus set her straight. Martha's problem was that she was concerned about things, relatively little things that really didn't matter all that much. Mary, on the other hand, chose to sit and listen to Jesus, a far more important thing. Or to put it in our language today, Mary had her priorities straight.

The Marthas are still with us, always scurrying about making sure that every detail is just right. It is a Martha who stays home from church to fix a meal on the Sunday the preacher is coming for dinner. It is a Martha who frets about the petty things and misses the important matters, and irritates everyone around her in the process. The mundane things of this life will pass and no one will remember much about them either way. But the spiritual values, if faithfully pursued, cannot be taken away.

Teach Us to Pray
Luke 11:1-13

Nothing teaches better than a good example. We don't have the words that Jesus used as He prayed (verse 1), but the prayer made such an impression on the disciples that they wanted special instruction on how to pray. Since John had taught his disciples to pray, Jesus' disciples also wanted some guidance. And don't we all feel the need of some help in our praying?

The result was what we often refer to as the Lord's Prayer. It would be more appropriate to call it the Model Prayer, since it was not a prayer that He prayed but one designed for their use. Luke's version of this prayer is shorter than Matthew's as stated in the Sermon on the Mount (Matthew 6:9-13). It seems reasonable to suppose that this prayer was given on two separate occasions. Some time had elapsed since it was given in the Sermon on the Mount; and if the disciples were like most people we know, their memories were not infallible. Every teacher knows the value of repetition. Besides, some in the group may not have been present when Jesus gave this prayer the first time.

Jesus began by addressing God as Father. This plainly teaches that the God we serve is no remote, impersonal force, but is a Father who loves and is concerned about His children. Though He is our Father, God is high and holy, to be approached with reverence and awe. There is no place in our service to Him for an attitude of casualness and flippancy. It is after we have rendered the reverence due Him that we have a right to raise our petitions to Him.

The prayer next concerns itself with the coming of God's kingdom. Pious Jews of Jesus' day might understand this to refer to their regaining autonomy as a nation and once again becoming a world power. But this clearly was not Jesus' intention. Some feel it refers to Christ's return to claim His own at the end of time. The best explanation is found in Matthew's version of the prayer, where the petition for the coming of the kingdom is followed by these words of explanation: "Your will be done on earth as it is in heaven." In other words, the kingdom comes to our world to the extent that God's will is done in our lives. As we obey Him and lead others to obey Him, we are helping the kingdom to come.

As a model, this prayer covers our needs for the present, the past, and the future. First of all, it asks for daily sustenance—for bread, not for cake, mind you. When we ask for bread, the necessities of life, our Father out of His bounty often supplies us with cake, even cake with icing.

The prayer is for things of the past in the sense that our sins of the past need to be forgiven. Every day we need to make this kind of prayer both for the sins of omission and the sins of commission. This is a dangerous prayer to pray, for in praying it we ask God to forgive us as we are willing to forgive others. Of course, in the absolute sense, God's forgiveness is based upon His grace as expressed through the death of His Son, not upon our forgiveness of others. But the attitude we express towards others really reflects the attitude we have toward God's wonderful grace. If we come before Him in humble contrition, we will certainly extend that attitude toward others.

Finally, this prayer contains a request for the future. Just as we are concerned that sins of the past be forgiven, so we must be concerned that we avoid sins of the future. Of course, God does not lead us into temptation, but He does allow us to be tempted. Paul assures us God will not allow us to be tempted beyond what we can bear (1 Corinthians 10:13). At the same time we must bear some of the responsibility for avoiding temptation. God expects us to use our intelligence and knowledge of His Word to avoid those situations and those persons that are likely to cause us to fall into sin. And if we do come into temptation, we are to fight it with intelligence and determination. "Resist the devil, and he will flee from you" (James 4:7).

After giving the model prayer, Jesus went on to give some examples that illustrate just what kind of a Father our God is. The first point He made is that persistence in prayer is a virtue. A person in an emergency need of food in the middle of the night went to a neighbor's house for help. Understandably, the neighbor was irritated because he was awakened in the middle of the night, and his first response was to send the man away. Yet because he persisted in his knocking, the neighbor finally supplied the man's need. The point that Jesus was making was that if an irritated and unhappy neighbor would supply a request, how much more can we expect from our loving Heavenly Father.

Jesus sums up the teaching of this parable with three words: ask, seek, knock. The idea of asking suggests humility. When we seek, we become more active. Knocking is more persistent yet. All three verbs are in the present tense, indicating continuing action, not something that is done once and then forgotten.

Jesus concluded the discussion on prayer by emphasizing God's loving concern for us. No father would honor his son's request for a fish by giving him a snake. Nor would he hand him a scorpion ready to sting if he asked for an egg. Surely, then, if our earthly fathers know how to give good gifts, how much more can we expect from our loving Heavenly Father. He will give us the Holy Spirit, who is the source of all good gifts.

Growing Conflict
Luke 11:14—12:12

In the latter part of chapter 11 and the first part of chapter 12, we see Jesus' conflict rising to new heights. Unable to deny that Jesus had power over demons, his enemies declared that He got that power from the ruler of demons, Beelzebub or Satan. Calmly Jesus showed how absurd that declaration was (11:14-26). He said the people who rejected Him would fare worse in the final judgment than would the queen of Sheba or the people of Nineveh (11:29-32). His enemies were living in darkness because they were looking for evil, rather than for good. They needed to open their eyes to the light of Jesus so that their lives might be flooded with light (11:33-36).

Though the enmity was growing, one of the Pharisees invited Jesus to dinner. On that occasion Jesus plainly pointed out some of the faults of Pharisees and legal experts, and they opposed Him with greater fury (11:37-54). In the first twelve verses of chapter 12, we read Jesus' warning to His disciples. Those who were furious with Jesus would be furious with His disciples too. The disciples must prepare to face their fury without flinching, depending on the Holy Spirit to guide them in answering the charges that would be brought against them. They must not tremble before rulers or mobs that could no do more than kill the body, but they must take care to be loyal to the Lord in order to escape the Hell that awaited His enemies.

13

Lessons From Parables
Luke 12:13—15:32

Jesus used many different teaching methods, employing the method that would best meet the needs of the lesson and the people being taught. One favorite method seems to have been the parable. In writing his Gospel, Luke did not always follow a chronological approach, but often organized his material topically instead. This seems to have been the case in chapters 12—18. Here we see a collection of parables, but we need not suppose Jesus gave all of them in one day or one week. Included in this section are some of the best-known and most-loved parables.

Teaching About Possessions
Luke 12:13-21

On one occasion when Jesus was teaching, someone from the crowd asked Him to settle a property dispute between himself and his brother. Perhaps an elder brother had not properly divided the inheritance that belonged to both, and the younger brother sought justice through Jesus' intervention. This request was not unusual, for the Jews did not distinguish between religious and civil matters. Thus a rabbi might be called upon to interpret the law in such a case. Jesus refused to become involved in the case because He knew that the man was motivated by greed, and Jesus would do nothing to encourage such a motive.

Instead, Jesus used this as an occasion to present a powerful lesson on the proper attitude toward wealth. According to the parable, a rich farmer had a bountiful crop, so bountiful that he had no place to store it. And of course there was no government agency to buy the surplus. So he did the prudent thing and tore down his barns and built bigger ones. He had it made, no question about it. He had everything all figured out. He forgot just one thing—his own mortality. For that crucial omission, God labeled him a fool.

It is hard to imagine a lesson that modern Americans need more than this one. This rich man did everything that was correct by our modern standards. He had worked hard to buy a farm, and he had cared for it so well that it was quite productive. The account gives no indication that he had broken any laws to gain his wealth, nor had he taken advantage of any of his workers. Today such a man would be considered a pillar of the community, and he would probably be a leader in the local church. What then was his sin?

First of all, the man was completely self-centered. See how many times he used the first-person pronoun, I or my. Every thought seems to have been upon his own interests, activities, and possessions. In the second place, he completely neglected the needs of others. When he found that his barns would not hold the grain, he might very readily have helped some poor people who could use it. But there is not a hint that such a thought ever crossed his mind.

It is good to work and earn a living (2 Thessalonians 3:12), but it is bad to do nothing else. A Christian is alert to every opportunity to do good for others (Galatians 6:10). Such opportunities may seem more obvious when one has more wealth than he knows what to do with, but they come also to those who think themselves poor. If we really want to help others, we can find a way.

The rich man's worst mistake was leaving God out of his life. He conveniently forgot that God had created the land and given the rain and sunshine to make the crops grow. There is nothing in the parable to show that the man ever thanked God for the wealth he acquired. It is no sin to acquire wealth, but sooner or later every person must give an accounting of how he has used his wealth. In this rich farmer's case it came sooner: his "many years" became God's "this very night." When a person dies, people sometimes ask how much he left. Whether the deceased was as rich as Howard Hughes or as poor as a beggar, we can be sure of one thing—he left it all! Or as one sage remarked, "You never see a Brink's truck following the hearse to the cemetery."

Teaching About Anxiety
Luke 12:22-34

Another besetting sin of our times is anxiety. Though it is often associated with greed, its roots may often be found elsewhere. Jesus pointed to the birds of the air and the flowers of the field. Even though they do not labor or store the fruits of labor, God cares for them. If God cares for these lower forms of life, how much more will He care for man, who is made in His image!

A thin line separates a proper concern for the necessities of life from the anxiety about them that Jesus condemned. Most of us do not have to worry about the necessities of life. The vast wealth that God has poured out upon America insures that all of our necessities will be provided for. But how quickly the things we once considered luxuries become "necessities"! Then we become anxious when we can't have all the things we see advertised on every hand. When the neighbors have better houses and furniture, better cars and lawn mowers, better boats and vacations, who among us can be really content with what we have?

We become anxious about things other than material possessions too. We become unduly concerned about our appearance, our social prestige, our health. Will worrying about our health add an hour to its length? Quite the contrary. Worry is almost certain to shorten it. If we become too anxious to gain social prestige, we induce snickers behind our backs and lose what little prestige we already have.

Men have devised many different ways to measure and accumulate wealth. We measure it in money, gold, cattle, real estate, jewels, stocks, or bonds. Yet all of these are subject to erosion by time, the elements, political tides, and economic variations. The only treasure that will survive is that which we lay up in Heaven—spiritual treasure. This is not so easy to count as money is. But the approval of God and good men, the fellowship of people we have helped— these we can enjoy forever.

Then Jesus concluded with a truth that at first thought seems backward. He said that where our treasure is, there our hearts will be. We would probably have stated it the other way around: where our heart is, there our treasure will be. But Jesus understood better than we that things have a powerful pull on the hearts of men. A few people may be able to resist this pull, but most of us succumb sooner or later to the subtle magnetism of things. If we generously invest our material wealth in spiritual things, we will find our heart goes with it.

Teaching About the Future
Luke 12:35—13:17

Once Jesus had helped establish the proper attitudes toward material possessions, He turned His attention to attitudes about the future. The spiritual kingdom that Jesus was establishing was designed to move toward a definite goal. That goal was the final return of our Lord in triumph. Some of Jesus' disciples had come to expect that triumphant return in the very near future. However, this was not to be the case. Jesus knew that a long delay in His return would cause some people to become lazy and indifferent. Thus the teachings in this section are designed to prepare people for that delay.

Jesus told about some servants who were ordered to be ready and waiting for the return of their master from a wedding feast. Jewish wedding feasts customarily were extended affairs, with guests lingering far into the night. And so the servants had no idea when to expect their master. Under such circumstances, they would be tempted to become careless and fall asleep. But if they were watching as the master had ordered, he would reward them by serving them a meal. This rather surprising conclusion suggests that the master in the parable is Christ himself, who is servant of all.

The next parable again stresses preparations and watchfulness. A thief comes when one least expects him. We who live in rather constant fear of burglaries can identify with this parable. If thieves would only be considerate enough to let us know ahead of time when they were coming, we would be ready for them. But of course thieves don't operate that way.

Jesus used this parable to emphasize two points. First of all, the exact time of His return will be unannounced. The second point is that regardless of when He comes, we should be prepared. This parable, along with other teachings of Jesus, should caution us against those who are quite sure they know when He is returning.

These two parables caused Peter to raise a question. "Are these teachings just for us, the leaders, or for everyone?" he asked. Jesus did not answer directly but gave another parable to help Peter understand. The thrust of this parable is that, indeed, leaders have a greater responsibility to be watchful, but certainly the task is not exclusively theirs.

In this case the master put one of the servants in charge of the other servants. His task was to see that they were cared for and that they did their work. But unfortunately the trust in this steward was misplaced, and he soon began to take advantage of his position to indulge himself and abuse the other servants. Then came the day of reckoning when the master returned unexpectedly. The punishment by the master was swift and severe: "He will cut him to pieces and assign him a place with the unbelievers." This punishment seems shockingly severe to us. Jesus often used hyperbole, intentionally exaggerated language, for emphasis, but we need to realize that here He is dealing with eternal judgment. The conclusion is not exaggerated. The problem is that Christians today are unwilling to face up to the fact that God's judgment will not be a mere slap on the wrist.

The verses that follow (47, 48) are often quoted to show that there will be degrees of punishment in Hell. It seems only fair that those who knowingly and deliberately sin should receive more severe punishment than those who fall unwittingly into sin. This is a sobering teaching for ministers and other leaders in the church. If we understand the parable correctly, unworthy leaders are represented by the stewards who mistreat the other servants and indulge themselves. Their punishment will be appropriately severe. Yet no one will escape with a suspended sentence. This fact ought to intensify our concern for the plight of those who have never known our Lord.

Jesus then added another element to His teaching about the future (Luke 12:49-53). We often refer to Jesus as the "Prince of Peace," and rightly so. Yet He is also the Lord of Justice, and the execution of justice almost invariably brings division and suffering. As Jesus looked to the coming of the church, He knew that the gospel would not always be enthusiastically received. Some, perhaps most, would reject it. Although it was not His intent to bring division among people, their response to the gospel was destined to bring division. All of us have seen examples where His prophecy became true quite literally. Families have been divided and friends have been separated.

After this Jesus criticized the people because of their lack of perception. They knew how to look at the sky and predict the weather, but they were unable to realize the nature of the drama that was unfolding before them. Centuries before, the prophets had foretold the coming of the Messiah. During the intervening centuries men had increasingly looked forward to this great event. Then when that great age finally dawned, few were able to recognize it. Many factors contributed to their blindness. First of all, they were blinded by their Jewish nationalism. They were looking forward to a militant Messiah, one who would lead them against the Romans. Instead, He came as a suffering servant. They expected Him to come with regal splendor. Instead, He was born in a stable to a peasant girl.

Those who ignored such warnings received yet another warning when news came that Pilate the governor had ordered the slaughter of some Galileans, perhaps terrorists or guerillas. Those men were now dead, but all those who rejected Jesus would also be dead unless they would change their way of thinking. This was illustrated by a little parable of a fruitless fig tree. The owner waited patiently, but not forever. Finally the tree was destroyed. So the Lord patiently waits for His enemies to repent—but He will not wait forever (Luke 13:1-9).

Jesus' enemies themselves provided a parable. Even on the Sabbath they freed their domestic animals so they could drink. Then why did they think it was bad for Jesus to release a woman whom Satan had bound for eighteen years? Is one of God's own people worth less than an ox or a donkey? (Luke 13:10-17).

Teachings About the Nature of the Kingdom
Luke 13:18—14:24

As the weeks passed, Jesus spoke more frequently about the nature of the kingdom of God. Often this teaching came in the form of parables. Some of these, such as the parables of mustard seed and yeast, were quite brief. The mustard seed was quite small. Yet when the farmer planted it, it began to grow rapidly. It might reach ten or twelve feet in height in one year, high enough for birds to come and perch in it. The point that Jesus was making here is that the church, like the mustard plant, had small beginnings; yet, like the mustard plant, it would grow to a substantial size. This parable may have come in response to the opposition that came when Jesus healed a woman on the Sabbath (Luke 13:10-17). Jesus was saying that opposition could not destroy God's plans for the church. Even with meager beginnings, it would grow and prosper.

The growth of the kingdom would also resemble the growth of yeast or leaven in dough. Leaven sometimes carried a bad connotation (Matthew 16:6; Luke 12:1; 1 Corinthians 5:7), but here it is used in a good sense. In the previous parable the emphasis was on great growth from a small beginning. In this one, the emphasis is on the process of growth that goes on quietly and unseen. Yet in the end it permeates the whole batch of dough.

The next teaching about the kingdom that Luke records came some time after this as Jesus was traveling to Jerusalem (13:22-30).

123

Someone in the crowd that was following Jesus had been perceptive enough to catch the idea that citizenship in the kingdom was not easy or simple. "Lord, are only a few people going to be saved?" he asked.

Jesus in answering refused to get into the business of telling how many would be saved. Instead, He directed His reply personally to the questioner. In effect, Jesus said, "Don't worry about how many will be saved. Just make sure that you are among that number." The entrance of salvation is through a narrow door. Not everyone who tries to enter will be able to squeeze through. Further, once the owner closes the door, no one else can enter. After the door is closed, some will beg to enter because they followed Jesus and heard His teachings. But this casual relationship is not enough. They will be turned away as evildoers.

Jesus then injected another sobering thought. They would see Abraham, Isaac, Jacob, and the prophets in the kingdom, but they themselves, because they had sinned away their day of grace, would be cast out. But Jesus' next statement must have been even more infuriating. People from the four corners of the compass—Gentiles, that is—will come and take their places at the Father's great feast. The Jews, who as God's chosen had all along thought themselves to be first, suddenly found themselves to be last. The very idea that Gentiles might be permitted in the kingdom was anathema to many Jews, but to suggest that the Gentiles would go in ahead of them must have been considered almost blasphemous. Obviously Jesus was no politician trying to curry the people's favor when He made this statement! He mourned over the fate of Jerusalem, but there was no way to avoid it unless Jerusalem would repent.

Another parable of the kingdom that sounds a similar note is reported in Luke 14:15-23. The parable tells of a banquet, suggested by the fact that Jesus was a guest at a banquet when He told it. A certain man prepared a great feast and sent out invitations, the parable began. The "certain man" is God himself. Once the feast was ready, his servant (Jesus) was sent to summon the guests. But they began to make excuses. If anyone doubts that Jesus had a sense of humor, he needs only to read this parable. The audience must have roared with laughter as each ridiculous excuse was given.

The first guest said that he had bought a field and needed to go out and look at it. What a flimsy excuse! What man in his right mind would ever buy a field without looking at it first? The second said that he had just bought five yoke of oxen and needed to try them out. Can you imagine anyone buying five used cars he had never seen? The last excuse must have brought an uproarious response: "I just got married, so I can't come." What Jewish man would ever admit to anyone that he was henpecked?

Angered by these petty excuses, the master sent the servant out into the street to bring in the poor, the crippled, the blind, and the lame. When this did not fill the banquet room, the servant was sent again, this time to the roads and country lanes, to invite guests urgently. Like the previous parable, this meant that the Jews had rejected God's gracious invitation, and that God would throw open the doors of His banquet hall that the whole world might come in. Undoubtedly this parable antagonized the Pharisees and other religious leaders. They must have seen that they were represented by those who rejected the initial invitation. But to suggest that their place would be taken by common sinners and even Gentiles must have infuriated them.

As the fury of enemies was growing, Jesus warned would-be followers that it was costly to follow Him. They had better be prepared! (Luke 14:25-35).

Teaching About the Lost
Luke 15:1-32

Even as Jesus' teachings were alienating many of the religious leaders, they were at the same time attracting many of the outcasts in society—the tax collectors and "sinners." This further scandalized the Pharisees and teachers of the law. Their attitude provided the occasion for the parable of the lost sheep.

The content of this parable would be familiar to all of Jesus' listeners. It was built upon an experience that many shepherds had had. Sheep have a knack for getting lost. They wander away, get caught in the bushes, or fall into a pit. Since these Palestinian shepherds knew their sheep by name, they were soon aware of any that were missing. As soon as the shepherd realized that one of his flock was gone, he left behind the ninety-nine and went to hunt the missing one. In this case his efforts were rewarded and he found the lost sheep. Immediately the shepherd was filled with joy, a joy that he shared with his friends and neighbors.

In the same way, Jesus added, there is more rejoicing in Heaven over the one lost person who is found than over ninety-nine who were never lost. This was a subtle but barbed attack upon the religious leaders. They would rejoice over the recovery of a lost sheep, but they did no rejoicing over lost sinners who were saved. Indeed, they even strongly resented Jesus' association with them. There must also have been a touch of sarcasm in Jesus' concluding statement about the "righteous persons who do not need to repent." The religious leaders deemed themselves righteous persons who did not need to repent, but at every turn Jesus showed that such was not the case. More than anyone else, they needed repentance.

Jesus then added a second parable that stressed the same theme. A woman possessed ten drachmas, each coin worth about a day's wage. One day she lost one of these coins in her house. Though peasant houses were quite small, they were also quite dark. The one small door and one tiny window admitted the only light. The floor was usually covered with rushes, making it quite easy to lose a coin.

It is likely that the woman was very poor, making the loss of even one small coin a major disaster. Some have suggested that these coins were linked together and worn as a headdress or jewelry almost as we would wear a wedding ring. If so, she had sentimental as well as monetary reasons for searching for the coin. Under these circumstances, her great joy at finding the coin is readily understandable. The application is the same as in the previous parable. There is rejoicing in the presence of God when a sinner repents.

The third parable in Luke 15, one of the best known and beloved of all the parables, adds another element. We sometimes call this the parable of the prodigal son, but we might appropriately call it the parable of the two lost boys, for the elder son who stayed at home was surely just as lost as the younger son.

The details of this parable are quite familiar. A younger son, chafing under what he considered to be a restrictive father and a super-upright older brother, wanted out. It may surprise us a bit that the father gave the younger son his inheritance when it is obvious that the boy was too immature to handle it. Yet this is the kind of a decision every parent has to make sooner or later. If a young person is never given a chance to try his wings, then he may never become mature.

The young man blew it. The inheritance accumulated by his father over many long years was quickly dissipated, and soon he was reduced to dire poverty. His degradation was intensified when he was reduced to a lowly swineherd, groveling with the pigs in their pen for a few scraps of food. But this miserable experience shocked him back to his senses. Thoroughly humbled, he returned to his father.

All this while, the father back home had never given up. Every day his eyes watched far down the road for the sight of a familiar figure. The young man was quite unprepared for the gracious reception the father gave him. (We have the same problem understanding the generous love of our Heavenly Father.) Completely ignoring the young man's speech of humble repentance, the father embraced him and welcomed him home to a sumptuous feast.

All this time, the elder son had been in the background. But when he had his chance, he blew it too. He resented his younger brother who had wasted his inheritance, and he resented his father who was apparently condoning such waste. Whatever the elder brother possessed in moral rectitude, he lacked in a forgiving spirit.

Jesus had made His two points. His first was that God is a loving, forgiving Heavenly Father. The younger brother represented the publicans and sinners, who by repenting from their sins found their way back to the Father. The elder brother represented the religious leaders. They carefully observed all the conventional moralities, but somehow missed the fact that love and forgiveness are at the very heart of our commitment to God.

Preparing Men
for the Kingdom
Luke 16:1—18:30

In the previous lesson we examined several of Jesus' parables that dealt with various aspects of the kingdom of God. In this lesson we will take the opportunity to look at several parables that deal especially with preparing men for the kingdom of God.

The Clever Manager
Luke 16:1-18

This is a most difficult parable to interpret. In it Jesus seems to be praising a group of scoundrels who were out to take advantage of a rich man, who apparently was a big businessman. The first crook was the manager or steward who was placed in charge of some of the master's business. Although he was not accused of deliberately defrauding his master, he had seriously mismanaged his affairs. Word of this eventually reached the rich man—as it usually does, sooner or later. Called for an accounting, the manager realized he had to do something and do it quickly. He considered himself too weak to do manual labor, and he was too proud to beg.

His scheme was to reduce the bills that various debtors owed the master. Some of these debts were substantial. Eight hundred gallons of oil was reduced to four hundred gallons, and a thousand bushels of wheat to eight hundred. These two are given as examples; probably many others were involved in the scheme. The size of the debts shows that these men were commodity dealers, not just small farmers. By reducing these debts, the manager hoped to ingratiate himself with the debtors so that they would take care of him when he was fired. The manager obviously knew the debtors very well. They all fell for the scheme. Once they agreed to go along with the plan, they were hooked. They could now be subjected to blackmail if they did not take care of the manager. Theirs was a familiar pattern. Their greed led to larceny, which in turn led to their entrapment.

It did not take the owner long to discover what had happened. There is nothing in the account to indicate that he could recover the money he had been cheated out of, and so he had good reason to be furious. But even though he did not approve of his manager's crookedness, he did admire his shrewdness. The man had made clever, even though illegal, use of his master's money.

The man's cleverness is the point that Jesus was making in this parable. He did not have to take time to condemn the man's wickedness. That was clearly wrong. What Jesus was saying is that men of the world in dealing with their own kind use money and skills shrewdly to gain an advantage for themselves. "People of the light"—Christians—ought not to do anything crooked, but they ought to use their possessions and talents to gain the great advantage of being welcomed in the world to come.

We must avoid the conclusion that our clever use of possessions for the purpose of serving God will insure our entrance into Heaven. It was not Jesus' purpose to teach that we earn salvation by our good works. Rather, our good works indicate the kind of faith in God that places us in a position to receive His eternal blessings.

Jesus continued this teaching on management by showing that faithful stewardship begins with one's character, not with one's possessions. One who is trustworthy in small matters will be able to handle large matters in the same faithful manner. Conversely, if one cannot be trusted in small matters, he certainly cannot be trusted in larger matters. The Christian recognizes that the possessions he often calls his own do not really belong to him but are granted to him as a trust. How he manages these will determine whether or not he will be entrusted with "true riches"—Heaven, in other words.

Jesus concluded this teaching by pointing out the danger of the divided heart. In some situations, of course, it is possible for one to work for two different employers without any conflict of interest. But Jesus was not talking about this kind of a situation. He was talking about household slavery, a situation in which the master had control over the slave twenty-four hours a day. Under such conditions it was impossible for a person to serve two masters except as his real master ordered him to serve the other. In a very real sense we are slaves either of God or of money, which represents worldly possessions. To be equally loyal to both is an impossibility. Satan has a way of blinding us to this fact by suggesting all kinds of little compromises that will seemingly allow us to serve both God and money. But this is a delusion, a delusion that can have spiritually fatal consequences.

The Pharisees, "who loved money," caught the brunt of this lesson. Their sneering response was predictable. But their sneers were not an adequate answer to Jesus' indictment. Not only were the Pharisees lovers of money, but worse, they were hypocrites. They cleverly concealed their greed and managed to make themselves look good in the eyes of men. But in so doing they fooled themselves most of all, for what men approve may be detestable in the sight of God.

In Luke 16:16-18, two short paragraphs illustrate how one serves God rather than money or self. First, he has a high regard for God's Word. Second, he is faithful to his wife according to God's plan. Certainly both of these reminders are much needed in our time of hasty marriages and easy divorce without regard for God's plan that is made plain in the Scriptures.

The Rich Show-off and the Beggar
Luke 16:19-31

Luke 15 contains three parables that hold up the right attitude toward persons. The opening verses of chapter 16 deal with the proper attitude toward possessions. Now in another parable, the two emphases are combined to provide a lesson on the proper use of possessions in regard to persons.

This parable tells of a rich man who is sometimes called *Dives*. This is not actually his name, but is derived from a Latin adjective meaning "rich" that is found in a Latin version of the Bible.

The rich man had it made, and he wanted to make sure everyone knew he had it made. So he dressed in the latest and most expensive fashions. ("Purple and fine linen" were usually worn only by royalty or the very rich.) He lived in luxury every day. One translation has it "living in dazzling splendor day in, day out." Being rich is not of itself a sin. Abraham was rich, and Joseph must have been exceedingly rich, and yet neither was condemned for his riches. God judges one not on what he has but on how he uses what he has. In this parable there is nothing to indicate that the man had gained his wealth illegally, but he certainly was using it improperly.

Contrasted to the conspicuous affluence of the rich man is the dire poverty of the beggar, Lazarus. His name is a shortened form of the Hebrew name *Eleazar,* which means "God has helped." This is the only parable in which Jesus used a personal name. As a result, some feel that the persons in the parable were not fictional, but real persons known by many in the audience. It seems more likely, however, that Jesus assigned the name to the beggar because of its meaning.

Lazarus' condition was pitiful. Apparently he was crippled, which caused his terrible poverty. More than that, he was covered with ulcerating sores, a condition often caused by inadequate diet. It would seem that he had no family to care for him, and those who brought him to the gate of the rich man's mansion had little concern for him. This is evidenced in the word translated *was laid,* which more often means *thrown.* We are left with the impression that Lazarus was unceremoniously dumped at the gate. What a terrible condition he was in! He was poor, hungry, crippled, covered with sores, too weak to fend off the scavenger dogs that roamed the streets, and without family or friends. His greatest wish was just for the scraps that fell from the rich man's table.

We do not know how long he may have lain at the rich man's gate. But he had been there so long or so often that the rich man certainly knew about him, and yet the rich man was so totally lacking in compassion that he had made no effort to help him.

Only death brought relief to Lazarus. But with relief came a dramatic change in his status. No longer was he a miserable beggar seeking a few scraps of food; at his death he became a privileged person. He was borne by angels to the side of Abraham. At last his name, *God has helped,* was fulfilled.

Death stalks the back alleys and the hovels, but it also haunts the boulevards and the mansions. The rich man must have enjoyed seeing people bowing and scraping before him, but he eventually learned that death bows before no man. Death was no relief to the rich man. It cast him into the bowels of hell. The word here for hell is *hades,* a Greek word that meant the place of the dead, good and bad. But this man was in torment, and so the translators have chosen to translate it *hell.*

131

In his desperate situation, the man looked up and saw Lazarus in the company of Abraham. He asked only one tiny favor (which was more than he had ever given Lazarus in this life). "Send Lazarus to dip the tip of his finger in water and cool my tongue," he pleaded.

Abraham stated two reasons why he could not permit this. First of all, the rich man didn't deserve it. He had enjoyed the good life in this world and had done nothing to ease the burden of Lazarus. Now the tables were turned, and justly so. But an even more important reason why Abraham could not grant his request was that between him and the rich man was a great chasm over which none could cross. Death settles some things with awful finality. After that, man's eternal destiny is fixed and no one can change it. This parable gives no support to the doctrine of purgatory, which teaches that one can move from the area of punishment into Heaven.

Realizing that his own fate was fixed, the rich man's thoughts turned from himself to his brothers. Yet even now his concern was narrow. His thought was just for his brothers, not for the whole world that needed such a message. His request was that Abraham send Lazarus to warn his brothers. He still thought of Lazarus as a subordinate who might be used as a servant or errand boy.

Abraham rejected his plea because the brothers already had Moses and the prophets: that is, the writing of these men. The rich man protested that the testimony of the Old Testament was inadequate to bring conviction. At least, in his own life it had not brought him to faith. If one should come back from the dead, he thought, the testimony of a resurrected man would bring conviction. Once more Abraham rejected his argument. Men who will not believe the Scriptures are not inclined to believe the testimony of one returned from the grave, especially if that testimony condemns the sinful life of luxury they want to live.

The attitudes of the rich man and Lazarus after death present some interesting contrasts. The rich man, even in torment, did not display the slightest evidence of repentance. In fact, in his refusal to accept the responsibility for being where he was, he subtly hinted that God had not really given him a fair chance. If only God had sent someone from the dead to warn him, he would have repented. Lazarus, on the other hand, did not complain about his lot in this life, nor did he gloat over the plight of the rich man. And when the rich man suggested that he be sent back to this world, he offered no objection, although it might have placed him again in a painful, humiliating situation.

In pointing out that the rich man's brothers would not believe even if one came from the dead to warn them, Abraham stated a truth that we need to be aware of today. Whether one accepts the gospel or rejects it depends much less on the quality of the evidence presented than upon the condition of the heart of the hearer. We sometimes feel guilty, feel that we have failed, when we present the gospel only to have people reject it. If we have presented the gospel faithfully and lovingly, we have met our responsibility and need not apologize for our apparent failure. We must be willing, then, to allow the word to work on the hearts of our hearers.

In mentioning the fact that men will not believe even if one rise from the dead, Jesus was undoubtedly looking forward to His own resurrection only a few short months away. When He arose from the grave, Jesus did not appear to the religious leaders and try to convince them. He knew that their hearts were too hard. He showed himself, instead, to His followers.

A Lesson in Gratitude
Luke 17:1-37

Chapter 17 begins with some brief teaching on sin and forgiveness, faith and duty. Then verse 11 begins a poignant lesson in gratitude.

Some time earlier Jesus had set out for Jerusalem (Luke 9:51). That does not mean He then went directly and swiftly to that city. He spent much time in what seemed to be leisurely teaching, yet Jesus was not ignoring the timetable God had set for Him. Luke reminds us of this again when he tells us that Jesus was "on his way to Jerusalem" when He encountered ten lepers on the border between Samaria and Galilee.

These men met Him and His disciples as they approached a village. Their loathsome disease forced them to live outside the town. Probably they had built some kind of shelter and were living together, almost completely removed from their neighbors. Interestingly, one of these lepers was a Samaritan. Misery and disaster know no boundaries; indeed, sometimes they break down the barriers that men erect between themselves.

Standing at a distance, the men cried out for Jesus to have pity on them. Jesus did not touch the men as He had done in the healing mentioned in Luke 5:13. He did not even say, "Be healed." Instead He sent them to show themselves to the priests. One duty of priests was to act as health officers. When one recovered from leprosy they must examine him and pronounce him well before he could end his isolation. Sending the men to the priests was Jesus' way of requiring them to show their faith. They all passed the test, starting off obediently while still afflicted. As they went, they were healed.

One of the men, when he discovered that he had been healed, rushed back and threw himself at the feet of Jesus, giving thanks and praising God. Luke, himself a Gentile, must have taken some pleasure in reporting that this man who showed gratitude was a Samaritan. Jesus was obviously grieved that only one man returned. "Where are the other nine?" He asked. We may try to excuse the nine by arguing that they were so excited that they forgot to show their gratitude. Better still, we may note that they were doing what Jesus told them to do. Yet it would have taken so little time for them to return and say a simple thank you! Ingratitude is an extremely common sin, and in our own times, it seems especially prevalent. Let us not be guilty of bringing pain to our Lord or our fellowmen by failing to say thank you.

The last part of chapter 17 brings another warning. Some people are more interested in God's timetable than in doing God's will. Jesus wants us to reverse that. If we are doing right all the time, we have no need to worry about when Jesus will come and make His kingdom complete.

Two Parables About Prayer
Luke 18:1-17

Luke 18 begins with two parables about prayer. The first parable teaches perseverance in prayer. The two characters in the parable were a judge, "who neither feared God nor cared about men," and a persistent widow. We are not given the details of the case, but apparently the widow had been defrauded. She presented her case before the judge, but he turned down her plea. It is clear that he was motivated by neither mercy nor a sense of justice.

But the widow was unwilling to take no for an answer. Again and again she returned until the very sight of her approaching must have made the judge cringe. Finally he ran out of excuses and patience and granted her the justice she deserved. The *New International Version* says, "So that she won't eventually wear me out with her coming!" A more literal translation would put it more strongly: "So that she won't give me a black eye." Whether the judge really had fears of a physical attack or was just exhausted by the whole affair, he finally granted the woman her petition.

The point Jesus was making was this: If a wicked judge can be moved to grant justice because the petitioner is persistent, is it not reasonable to believe that a loving Father will grant our persistent prayer? God sometimes does seem to delay answering our prayers, at least in the way we hope He will answer. Jesus gave this parable to encourage us to continue to pray when the answer is not immediately forthcoming. Jesus' ended with a rhetorical question: "When the Son of Man comes, will he find faith on the earth?" That is something each of us must answer for himself. Will He find faith in you?

The second parable deals with one's attitude in prayer. Jesus directed this parable to "some who were confident of their own righteousness and looked down on everybody else." Among these were the Pharisees. One of the characters in the parable, a Pharisee, went up to the temple to pray. He prayed about himself, reminding God of how good he was and how many good deeds he had done. His remarkable record of piety would have qualified him for leadership in almost any congregation. He seemed to be saying, "God, aren't You lucky that I'm on Your side!"

The other man, a despised tax collector, was so contrite that he would not even lift his eyes to look up to Heaven. Instead, he beat his breast in spiritual anguish and prayed the prayer that every one of us must make if we are to come before God with the right attitude: "God, have mercy on me, a sinner." It is quite obvious to us who the good guy was and who the bad guy was. But just to make sure that no one in the audience, especially the Pharisees, missed the point, Jesus spelled it out for them: "He who humbles himself will be exalted." The painful point of this parable is that there is a bit of Pharisee in every one of us.

The teaching of humility was reinforced by an event that happened about that time. God's people must accept God's rule humbly, like little children (Luke 18:15-17). The kingdom is not for those who cherish their pride.

Money Again—the Rich Young Ruler
Luke 18:18-30

A critic might say Jesus was always preaching about money. At least He spoke frequently about possessions and how we are to use them. One occasion for such a lesson was the coming of a young ruler—probably a leader in the synagogue—who wanted to know what good thing he needed to do to inherit eternal life. This young man may have been somewhat shallow in his theology, but his sincerity and humility are a refreshing relief from the spiritual arrogance of the Pharisees.

Jesus then gave the examination. "You know the commandments. Have you kept them?" The young man had kept all of them from his youth. He passed with an A plus. Well, not quite. Somehow, the young man had really overlooked the full implications of a couple of the Commandments. Take the tenth Commandment, for instance. It is quite likely that he had not coveted his neighbor's house or wife, and yet covetousness was at the heart of his problem. Or how about the first Commandment? The simple truth was that he had placed another god—money—before Jehovah.

Jesus moved swiftly to the heart of the young man's problem. He demanded radical surgery as the only cure: "Sell everything you have and give to the poor." Tragically, the young man was unwilling to pay the price. With a heavy heart he turned away. Jesus' heart must have been equally burdened. Mark's record tells us that "Jesus looked at him and loved him" (Mark 10:21). We can't escape wondering what happened to this young man. Did he go back to his gold and silver to find consolation there? Or did he eventually find the courage to do what Jesus required? But an even more important question is this: How do we respond to this same challenge? If we are not asked to sell all we have, we certainly are asked to put God's will above all we have. Have we succeeded in doing this?

15

The Road to Jerusalem

Luke 18:31—19:27

In many sections of his Gospel, Luke does not attempt to present his material in a strictly chronological pattern. Often he follows a topical pattern instead. We have seen this in the past two chapters of this book, in which much of the material has been arranged in a logical pattern in order to bring together certain teachings of Jesus that were not presented at the same time.

Now Luke seems to be returning to a chronological pattern of presenting his data. It seems that the rich young ruler came to Jesus in Perea, the region east of Jordan. Some weeks earlier Jesus had been in Jerusalem at the feast of Dedication, but the bitter opposition of the religious leaders made it necessary for Him to leave and find security in Perea (John 10:22-42). The severe illness of Lazarus in Bethany caused Jesus to be called there. The raising of Lazarus intensified the opposition. Plots against Jesus' life made it expedient for Him once more to retire to Perea. But now the time was approaching when Jesus must come to Jerusalem for the last time.

Jesus Predicts His Death
Luke 18:31-34

As Jesus turned His course toward Jerusalem, He tried to prepare His disciples for the tragic sequence of events that would culminate in His crucifixion. Mark 10:32-34 indicates that the disciples noticed something unusual in the attitude or behavior of Jesus at this point: "The disciples were astonished, while those who followed were afraid."

Many things had happened in the past few weeks. Jesus' teaching had grown more solemn and pointed. Lazarus' resurrection had aroused bitter antagonism among the religious leaders. The disciples knew that if Jesus appeared in Jerusalem, a confrontation leading to violence was almost certain to follow. Although they had confidence in Jesus, they could not face the prospect without some fear. They were not organized or trained or armed for battle.

On other occasions Jesus had warned them that He must go to Jerusalem and die. The first clear warning had come just after Peter's good confession at Caesarea Philippi (Luke 9:22). Moses and Elijah had talked with Jesus on the mount of transfiguration about His coming death (Luke 9:31). Following this experience, Jesus had once again given a clear warning of His impending death (Luke 9:44, 45). Yet in spite of these warnings "they did not understand what this meant. It was hidden from them. ... " They were convinced that Jesus was the Messiah, and they thought the Messiah must live and rule forever (Isaiah 9:7). Apparently they thought His talk about dying and rising was figurative language that they did not understand (Mark 9:10).

Now in Luke 18:31 we read that Jesus took the twelve aside and told them they were going up to Jerusalem. There everything that had been written about Him by the prophets would be fulfilled. Interestingly, Jesus designated himself as the "Son of Man." This term suggests His special relationship to the whole human race and not just to the Jewish people alone. He would suffer and die for the sins of the whole world (John 3:16; 1 John 2:2).

In this prediction of His coming suffering and death, Jesus included more details than in the earlier predictions. Matthew and Mark report that He said He would be "betrayed to the chief priests and teachers of the law," and that those leaders would "condemn him to death." Jesus said further that He would be turned over to the Gentiles, who would mock Him, flog Him, and kill Him. Mark and Luke include the prophecy that they would spit upon Him. Matthew, Mark, and Luke all record the triumphant good news that He was to arise on the third day.

Thus Jesus laid out the course of coming events in greater detail than He had done before. For the first time He included the information that His death would be at the hands of Gentiles, the Romans.

Further, He indicated that He would die by crucifixion, a horrible form of execution designed for the worst of criminals. See Matthew 20:17-19 and Mark 10:32-34 along with our text in Luke.

The really amazing thing is that the disciples did not understand this. Their minds were still wedded to the idea of an earthly Messianic kingdom, and they could not believe that what Jesus was saying was literally true. Later, when all these prophecies had been fulfilled, they would remember these words in vivid detail.

A Blind Beggar Receives His Sight
Luke 18:35-43

Moving from Perea across the Jordan River, Jesus and the disciples approached Jericho. When we compare the records of Matthew, Mark, and Luke, some problems emerge. Matthew and Mark say the blind man called when Jesus was leaving the city, while Luke says that it happened as Jesus approached the city. One suggested solution to this problem is that there were two Jerichos: the old Jewish city and the newer one built by Herod the Great. Perhaps Jesus was leaving one of these cities and approaching the other.

Another problem is seen because Matthew mentions two blind men while Mark and Luke speak only of one. But there is no necessary contradiction here. Mark and Luke do not say that Jesus healed *only* one man. Apparently they mention only the spokesman for the pair. Mark gives us the man's name–Bartimaeus, which means son of Timaeus. See Matthew 20:29-34 and Mark 10:46-52.

As the crowd accompanying Jesus passed by, the blind man became aware that something unusual was happening and asked about it. When someone told him that Jesus of Nazareth was passing by, he immediately became excited. In a loud voice, he began to cry out to Jesus for mercy. He addressed Jesus as "Son of David." This indicated that he thought Jesus was the Messiah. David was looked upon as the most glorious king in the whole history of Israel, and it was well known that the Messiah would be a descendant of David.

The man's appeal to Jesus raises another question. Just how did he know that Jesus could help him? Very little of Jesus' ministry had been spent in the area around Jericho, and so it is not likely that the man had heard Him before. It seems that Jesus' reputation as a healer had spread all over the country. A few months earlier, when Jesus was in Jerusalem for the feast of Tabernacles, he had healed a blind beggar (John 9:1-7). That healing had created so much controversy that it probably had been reported in Jericho as pilgrims were returning from Jerusalem. Bartimaeus could hear as well as his neighbors could, and news of sight given to a blind man surely would be impressive to him. Probably he had been wishing he could get in touch with the famous healer.

The man's cries upset many in the crowd, and they tried to quiet him. Perhaps they were intent on listening to Jesus' teaching and did not want to be interrupted. Or perhaps they thought Jesus should not be bothered by anyone so unimportant. But the man refused to be silenced. The crowd was concerned about being inconvenienced, but for the blind man, getting Jesus' attention was a matter of desperate concern.

Jesus refused to allow the crowd to determine what He should do. He knew the man's need, and He waited till the man was brought to Him. Then Jesus tenderly asked him what he wanted. Of course Jesus already knew, but he wanted the man to express his need for the crowd to hear.

The man's request was simple and to the point: "Lord, I want to see." He knew what he wanted, and he had the faith to believe that Jesus could supply it.

Jesus met his request just as simply as he had made it. "Receive your sight," He said. "Your faith has healed you." The man's faith had led him to take the action necessary to gain the healing he wanted.

Matthew's account tells us that Jesus touched the man's eyes. In one earlier healing of a blind man, the healing process took place in two steps. First the man saw only dimly, reporting that people looked "like trees walking around." At the next step of the healing the man saw clearly (Mark 8:22-26). In another case, Jesus gave the man a task to complete before the healing was accomplished. Jesus mixed saliva with the soil to form mud, which He placed on the man's eyes. His sight was restored only after he went to the pool of Siloam and washed away the mud (John 9:1-7). We don't know why Jesus treated each case differently. We can only conclude that He knew what was best in each case.

When the man of Jericho was healed, he responded immediately and enthusiastically by giving praise to God. His friends and neighbors who witnessed the miracle joined in the celebration. We are told also that the man "followed Jesus." Does this mean only that he joined the crowd that was accompanying Jesus to Jerusalem, or does it mean that he actually became a disciple of Jesus? We can only speculate. But it would not be at all surprising if the man did become a loyal follower of Jesus after such a tremendous healing.

Zacchaeus, the Tax Collector
Luke 19:1-10

Jesus and the crowd that followed Him, now increased by others from Jericho who had joined them, made their way through Jericho. Their progress must have been slow because of the crowds and the narrow streets. At this point Luke introduces us to Zacchaeus. We immediately learn two things about him. He was the chief tax collector for the whole area. For a price, Rome farmed out the right to collect taxes in an area. A person who had purchased the taxing rights for a large area would then subdivide that area and sell taxing rights to others. These tax collectors, or "publicans" as they were called by the Romans, made handsome profits in the process. The whole system was also open to oppression and corruption. It is little wonder that the tax collectors were thoroughly detested among the Jews. The other thing we learn about Zacchaeus is that he was rich. Probably that made his neighbors dislike him even more.

Like the blind man, Zacchaeus had heard much about Jesus. He wanted to see Him with his own eyes. Because of his small size, he could not see over the crowd; and because the people were so closely packed together, he could not push his way through. Indeed, because he was so thoroughly disliked, people probably went out of their way to keep him from getting close to Jesus.

But Zacchaeus was a determined man. In spite of his riches and his position, he was not happy. He probably had few close acquaintances and even fewer friends. Men pay a steep price for acquiring ill-gotten gain. And so there was an emptiness that gnawed at his heart and drove him to take unusual means to find relief. He still had enough moral sensitivity to see in Jesus a hope for his problem. Without regard to what others might say or think, Zacchaeus ran ahead of the crowd and, casting aside his dignity, he proceeded to climb up into a tree that was on the route Jesus was taking. The tree, called a "sycamore" in the *King James Version* and a "sycamore-fig" in the *New International Version,* was a variety often planted along roadsides. It grew to a considerable size and was easily strong enough to support a person.

When Jesus reached the tree, He stopped and, looking up, spoke to Zacchaeus. It was hard to believe that Jesus' stopping at this tree was an accident. With divine insight Jesus knew Zacchaeus' name and his need, and so He ministered directly to that need without the benefit of any formal introduction. Jesus did not ask if He might come and visit Zacchaeus, nor did He need to, for He knew the man's heart. Zacchaeus must have scrambled down the tree in record time and joyfully made Jesus welcome.

But Zacchaeus' response was not matched by that of the people of Jericho. Their deep-seated antagonism against tax collectors would not allow them to understand Jesus' actions in this matter. Tax collectors were "sinners" of a very special category. Prejudice against them was based on two mistaken ideas: first, that all tax collectors were alike, and second, that no tax collector could change. How often are our prejudices based on similar misconceptions?

We gather that Luke gives us an abbreviated account of what followed. It seems reasonable to suppose that Jesus spent some time teaching Zacchaeus about the standards for citizens of the kingdom. Perhaps this teaching, as did much of Jesus' teaching, occurred during a meal. Zacchaeus' heart was ready for the truth when Jesus presented it. His generous response indicates that he caught the spirit of what Jesus was saying. Unlike the Pharisees, he did not quibble about legalistic details. First of all, he was willing to give half of his possessions to the poor. But he went beyond this. He was willing to repay fourfold anyone he had cheated, an offer that was more generous than the Old Testament law required. In an ordinary case of cheating, the law required the offender to give back what he had gotten unjustly and to add a fifth of its value (Leviticus 6:1-5). In case of outright theft, a thief must restore twice as much as he had stolen (Exodus 22:4, 7, 9). Only when stolen livestock was butchered or sold must the thief restore fourfold or fivefold (Exodus 22:1).

Jesus' response indicated that He understood the sincerity of the man's offer. Salvation, that is, forgiveness of his sins, was his. Even though he had been disowned by his own people, now he was a "son of Abraham" in a higher sense. He was now more than just a physical descendant of Abraham; he was a spiritual descendant. This pronouncement gave Jesus an opportunity once more to set forth His mission to this world: to seek and to save the lost. Both the seeking and the saving are a part of this mission.

The Parable of the Ten Minas
Luke 19:11-27

This setting also provided Jesus an opportunity to present a parable with two purposes. One purpose was to correct the notion that "the kingdom of God was going to appear at once." Jesus was going to Jerusalem, where the rulers were hostile to Him. Many people thought He was going to take over the government. This parable made the point that there would be an extensive delay before the Lord came to claim His kingdom. The second purpose of this parable was to teach that every citizen should exercise careful stewardship of the things entrusted to him.

Some attempt to equate this parable with the parable of the talents (Matthew 25:14-30), but the differences between the two indicate that they are not the same. The two parables were told at different times, the amounts of money are different, the number of servants is different, and so are some other details.

When Jesus spoke of a certain nobleman in this parable, He may very well have had in mind a specific historic event. At the death of Herod the Great, three of his sons sought his throne. One of these sons, Archelaus, made a trip to Rome to plead his case before Caesar. Archelaus displayed many of the cruel traits of his father, and so some of his subjects also went to Rome to thwart his efforts. As a result Archelaus received only a portion of Herod's kingdom, and before long he was deposed by Rome because of his excessive cruelty. Jesus' purpose, however, was not to recount history but to draw lessons from historical events.

According to the parable, the nobleman called in ten of his servants and entrusted each of them with a mina. A mina was worth one hundred drachmas, with each drachma worth a day's pay for a laborer. Thus the amount entrusted to each of the ten servants was equivalent to more than three month's pay. After the nobleman gained the kingship, he returned home and demanded an accounting of his servants. The first servant had done quite well; he had earned ten more minas. The second had done well also; he had earned five more minas. These faithful and resourceful servants were rewarded for their efforts. The first was given charge over ten cities; the second, over five cities.

It was a different story with the third servant. Knowing that his master was a hard man, he was afraid to invest the money but carefully hoarded it. The nobleman judged the man by his own standards, condemning him because he did not at least put his money out to interest. The one mina he had so fearfully preserved was taken from him and given to the man who had ten.

This prompted some to question why the nobleman did this. His action and his reply seem at first glance to be contrary to the generosity we would expect from our Lord, who in this parable is represented by the nobleman. He seemed to be commanding that money be taken from the poor to give to the rich to make them richer. We need to keep in mind, however, that the parable is not really concerned with physical riches. It deals with more important things that are committed to us: the abilities we are given and the gospel entrusted to us. One who diligently makes use of these can both increase his abilities and build up the Lord's church. His reward will be great when the Lord returns. On the other hand, one who neglects to develop these riches will justly lose everything.

Jesus closed this parable by describing the frightful vengeance the nobleman brought upon those who had opposed him. This may seem harsh to us and out of keeping with a loving, forgiving Savior. But we must keep in mind that the return of the nobleman corresponds to the return of our Lord for final judgment. Those who hate and reject the Lord will face fearful retribution (Matthew 25:41). We deem God's judgment harsh only because we underestimate the heinousness of man's rejection of His loving offer of salvation.

16

Jesus Enters Jerusalem

Luke 19:28—21:38

Above the main entrance to the National Archives building in Washington, D.C. are these words: "The past is prologue." We have reached a point in this study from which we can look back over three years of Jesus' ministry and make the same pronouncement: "The past is prologue." Everything that occurred prior to this time was but preparation for the climax of His ministry. Everything pointed to the last few days when He would be seized, tried, crucified, and raised from the dead.

Early in Jesus' ministry there were scattered hints of what lay in store. But His popularity was high and the opposition was only beginning to develop, and few if any understood these hints. Then as the months passed, Jesus stated ever more plainly that He would be put to death. Still the disciples refused to believe it.

They saw the growing opposition and realized the danger, however. A few weeks before Jesus went up to Jerusalem for the last time, He and the disciples were in Perea when word came of the illness of Lazarus. When Jesus indicated that He was going to Judea, the disciples tried to dissuade Him. "A short while ago the Jews tried to stone you," they said, "and yet you are going back there?" (John 11:8). Thomas probably expressed the sentiments of the other disciples when he grimly commented, "Let us also go, that we may die with him" (John 11:16).

No one died on that trip, however. Instead, Lazarus was restored to life. Jesus avoided a confrontation with the hostile rulers by leading His disciples quickly back to Perea. But only a few weeks later He turned His steps toward Jerusalem again, in spite of the apprehension of His followers (Mark 10:32).

Jesus Enters Jerusalem
Luke 19:28-44

After giving sight to a blind man and reclaiming lost Zacchaeus in Jericho, Jesus went on toward Jerusalem. Whatever fears the disciples may have had at this stage, they went unrecorded by Luke. The quiet determination that Jesus displayed may have silenced this concern. Some commentators believe that Jesus left Jericho early Friday and arrived at Bethany, the home of Mary and Martha, Friday evening, just before the beginning of the Sabbath. If so, this was no easy trip, for it was no less than sixteen miles and it was all uphill. Jesus rested there on the Sabbath and was entertained at a meal, perhaps on Saturday evening after the Sabbath ended at sunset (John 12:1, 2).

On Sunday Jesus resumed His trip to Jerusalem. On the way, He and His disciples approached the village of Bethphage. The exact location of this village is unknown, but it must have been near Bethany and not far east of the crest of the Mount of Olives. Here Jesus sent two of His disciples into the village to bring back the colt upon which He was to ride into Jerusalem. Jesus may have had made arrangements earlier with its owner. They found the colt and soon returned with it. It is Matthew who points out that the Messiah's coming on a colt, the foal of a donkey, is a fulfillment of a prophecy found in Zechariah (Matthew 21:4, 5; Zechariah 9:9).

By this time a sizeable crowd had gathered. In addition to the residents, many visitors had come to Jerusalem early in preparation for the Passover. Others had accompanied Jesus when He came from Jericho. Word quickly passed among these people that Jesus was boldly going to enter Jerusalem, an open challenge to His enemies. Jesus' friends naturally wanted to be there to support Him, and the curiosity seekers wanted to be there to witness the confrontation.

This was no ordinary occasion for Jesus' friends. As He approached the brow of the hill, they spread their garments on the road before Him and began to shout and praise God. They especially praised Him for the miracles they had seen. Persons from

Jericho had seen the healing of the blind man recently; residents of Bethany rejoiced over the raising of Lazarus; pilgrims from Galilee could report many other miracles.

All four of the Gospel accounts report the triumphal entry, but each reports some different details, especially the shouts of the crowd. One of the shouts of acclaim reported by Luke—"Blessed is the king who comes in the name of the Lord"—is a quotation from Psalm 118:26, which was often sung during the Passover. It was certainly a most appropriate quotation to use for this occasion. They also shouted, "Peace in heaven and glory in the highest!" This reminds us of the angels' song at Jesus' birth (Luke 2:14).

But the shouting and rejoicing were not shared by everyone. Some of the Pharisees were quite upset. They understood that people were hailing Jesus as the King, the Messiah. Since they rejected Jesus' claims, they considered the crowd's acclamations as blasphemous. They may also have feared that such a tumultuous crowd would attract the attention of the Roman officials and lead to greater oppression on their part.

The Pharisees realized that Jesus was so popular with the crowd that they dared not try to silence the happy people. Instead they worked their way up through the crowd and appealed directly to Jesus. Jesus responded to their request, but not in the way they had expected. "There is no way they can be silenced," He replied, "for if the people are silent, even the very lifeless stones will take up the cry."

At this point Jesus paused in His approach to Jerusalem. Looking down over the city, He could see the massive walls and the beautiful temple that had been built by Herod. But He could see more, much more. With the prophetic eye, he could see the temple a smoldering ruin, the city walls leveled, and the citizens dead or carried into slavery. Little wonder that He wept over it! Earlier Jesus had raised a similar lament (Luke 13:34, 35) in an attempt to warn the people. But their hearts had only become hardened, and now the terrible drama was moving swiftly to its close.

Jerusalem—that is, the Jerusalem controlled by the political and religious leaders—had had its chance. The city had stubbornly and arrogantly refused to recognize Jesus as the Messiah, the way of escape that God had provided. When men harden their hearts, God's gracious offer only hardens their hearts the more. Jesus' way of peace was hidden from their eyes because they were blinded by their prejudice. With their hearts hardened and their eyes darkened, they went on with their furious plots to kill Jesus, and after that there was little they could do except wait for the coming of God's righteous judgment. And come it did forty years later in A.D. 70 when the Roman legions finally overwhelmed the city with horrible destruction and death.

Jesus in the Temple
Luke 19:45-48

The Gospels record that Jesus twice cleansed the temple. The first time, mentioned only in John 2:13-17, was near the beginning of His ministry. At that time the moneychangers and the sellers of animals were driven out. But the huge profits they had been realizing soon led the merchants to forget Christ's wrath, and they quickly returned to their old haunts. This suggests that reform efforts are not likely to have permanent results unless they strike at the root causes of evil.

It was three years later when Jesus' triumphal entry brought Him into the big outer court of the temple and He found the market was there again. Mark records more details. It was late in the day when Jesus came to the temple. He merely looked around at everything that was going on, then went back to Bethany with the twelve. On Monday He came again to the temple, this time ready to take action. (Mark 11:11-15).

Luke tells us that He drove out those who were selling. Matthew and Mark tell us that there were moneychangers and sellers of doves. Cattle and sheep also had been on sale three years before. They are not mentioned here, but possibly they had been brought back along with the doves.

The Passover season was the busy time of the year for the temple merchants, rather like our Christmas shopping rush. People by the thousands were coming in from the provinces for the occasion. Since it was difficult for them to bring their own animals for sacrifices, they found it convenient to buy animals after they arrived. This was an acceptable practice, but Jesus objected to giving it a place within the temple area, making those sacred precincts look, sound, and smell more like a stockyard than a house of prayer.

Jesus also objected because they were making the place a "den of robbers" by charging exorbitant prices. Animals for sacrifice had to be perfect, without any blemish. If a person brought an animal from his own farm, he might find it rejected by the official inspectors. He then would have to buy from the temple merchants. Their animals, of course, always had the priestly "seal of approval." Thus the approved merchants had a monopoly on the sacrificial animal business and could set the prices very high. The moneychangers operated a similar racket. Jews were required to pay a tax to maintain the temple services, and the fee could be paid only with Jewish coins. Since Jews from outside of Palestine would not have Jewish coins, the moneychangers made unfair profits by changing the money for these visitors.

Jesus' charges were certainly quite justified, and apparently the people supported Him. Of course the religious leaders were furious. In cleansing the temple Jesus had not only cut into their sinful profits; He had also humiliated them before the people right in their own stronghold. They had two choices. They could repent and clean up their act, or they could destroy Him. If there were any voices for reform within the Jewish leadership, they were quickly silenced. Their thoughts turned exclusively to one solution to their problem—get rid of Jesus as quickly as possible. The only thing that kept them from carrying out their intention was their fear of the people who "hung on his words." To arrest Jesus might precipitate a riot (Mark 14:2).

Jesus' Authority Challenged
Luke 20:1-8

Luke's "one day" (Luke 20:1) does not tell us what day it was, but from Matthew's account we gather that it was Tuesday when Jesus faced the religious leaders in what has been called "the great day of controversy." Entering Jerusalem triumphantly late on Sunday, Jesus observed what was going on in the temple and then went to Bethany for the night. Returning on Monday, He cleansed the temple and then stayed there to heal the blind and lame who came to him. In the evening He went again to Bethany (Matthew 21:12-17). On Tuesday He returned to the temple to teach and preach, but He was soon interrupted by the "chief priests and the teachers of the law, together with the elders." In their controversy with Jesus the main event was now at hand, and so the first team was called out. The situation was too close to home, too desperate, to trust to the second stringers.

Undoubtedly Jesus' enemies had planned their strategy carefully. Their first attack was upon His authority. If they could just raise doubts about this in the minds of the people, they knew they could readily dispose of Him as a threat. "Tell us by what authority you are doing these things?" they asked. "Who gave you this authority?" Their questions were not for the sake of information, for a few months earlier they had heard Jesus make it clear that His authority came from the Father (John 7:16, 17; 8:42). Further, He had given overwhelming proof of that authority by countless miracles (John 10:25). They raised the question to cast doubt upon His authority in the thinking of the people.

Knowing their purpose, Jesus did not answer directly but with a counter-question. "John's baptism," He asked, "was it from heaven, or from men?" His opponents realized at once that they were trapped in a dilemma. If they admitted that it came from Heaven, they knew that Jesus would ask them why they had not accepted it. On the other hand, if they said it was from men, they would anger the people, who might even stone them. Faced with these options, they chose to play it safe and offer no comment. Thus Jesus was free to refuse to answer their question. Clearly, Jesus won the first round.

The Parable of the Wicked Tenants
Luke 20:9-19

This gave Jesus an opportunity to use a parable aimed directly at the religious leaders. A wealthy landowner planted a vineyard and then rented it out to farmers when he left the country for an extended period of time. This practice of absentee land ownership was a well-known and accepted arrangement in Palestine. According to the terms of the contract, the owner was to receive a stipulated portion of the crop at harvest time. At the proper time, the owner sent a servant to receive his share of the harvest; but the tenants beat him and sent him away empty-handed. Another servant was sent and he was treated even worse. We have to marvel at the owner's patience, for he sent still another servant. This one was seriously wounded and thrown out.

The owner made one last effort by sending his son. "Surely," he said, "they will respect him." Quite the contrary. These depraved rascals saw in this a chance to seize the vineyard for themselves by killing the son. Their violent action aroused the owner to seek swift justice. The wicked farmers were killed and their places taken by others.

By this time the people were totally involved in Jesus' presentation of the parable. They understood its point and cried out that it not be fulfilled. They understood that God was the landowner and the Jewish nation was the farmers. The servants were the prophets

God had sent to garner spiritual fruit. Some of them perhaps even grasped the idea that Jesus was God's Son.

Jesus' words were not particularly reassuring. He quoted from Psalm 118:22, which tells of a rejected stone that becomes the cornerstone. That cornerstone then becomes the standard by which men are measured. Some trip over it and fall; others are crushed by it. The people were concerned about how they might avoid the terrible fate predicted in the parable. The leaders, on the other hand, were enraged by it because they knew full well that it was aimed at them. Though they had not yet killed God's Son, they were already plotting His death.

Taxes to Caesar
Luke 20:20-26

The leaders were so embarrassed before the people that they dared not face Jesus again. They laid a trap for Him by sending spies who pretended they were sincere seekers after truth. These tried to be more clever than their superiors. Instead of being trapped in a dilemma they would trap Jesus in one.

First of all, they approached Him with flattery. He was brave, they said. He would not be afraid to tell the truth, no matter who might be offended. Then they sprang their trap. "Is it right," they asked, "to pay taxes to Caesar?" If Jesus said no, they could charge Him with sedition before the Romans. If He said yes, He would alienate the people. They had to pay the taxes, but they thought it was cruel and unjust. They would turn against Jesus if He said it was right for God's people to be taxed by heathen. Without the people's support, Jesus could readily be seized by the religious leaders.

Jesus saw through their hypocrisy and had no difficulty in avoiding their trap. He asked for a denarius, which was a widely-circulated coin equivalent to a day's wages. It was a Roman coin commonly used in paying Roman taxes. One of the questioners produced a coin, apparently without realizing the implications of his action. Jesus asked, "Whose portrait and inscription are on it?"

This question seemed innocent enough, and so they gave the obvious answer: "Caesar's."

"Exactly!" said Jesus, "and so you ought to give to Caesar what rightfully belongs to him." This was more than a matter of giving Caesar's picture to Caesar, of course. The fact that these Jews were carrying Roman coins showed that they were really under Roman government. The government that provided the coins also provided

151

good roads, police protection, order and stability. As citizens enjoying these benefits they ought to pay for them. Jesus' words are just as binding on us today. Nobody enjoys paying taxes, but responsible citizens recognize that taxes are necessary if we are to enjoy the many benefits that our government provides.

But Jesus' answer did not stop there. "Give to God what is God's," He added. While there is a realm that rightly belongs to civil authority, Jesus was saying, there is a higher realm—God's kingdom—that takes precedence over all civil rulers. Our dual citizenship may at times raise issues for which we have no easy answers, but we must never forget that God's authority is supreme.

The spies who had come to trap Jesus were surprised and overwhelmed by His answer. In the face of such an embarrassing defeat, they kept a discreet silence.

Marriage and the Resurrection
Luke 20:27-40

Jesus' enemies did not give up easily. Still another group, the Sadducees, decided to challenge Him. The Sadducees were the skeptics of that day. They did not believe in life after death, nor did they believe in angels. They curried favor with the rich and the powerful; and since they were comfortably fixed, they sought to maintain the status quo. Thus they were probably more concerned about the political aspects of Jesus' teaching than the religious. If too many people became followers of Jesus, the Sadducees' comfortable positions might be jeopardized.

They came to Jesus with what they were sure was a real stumper. Undoubtedly they had used it effectively already against the Pharisees. The Old Testament law provided for a practice that is now called levirate marriage. That name comes from the Latin word *levir,* a husband's brother. According to this law, if a married man died without any children, the man's brother was to marry his wife to raise up a child to his name. The first child of this union was considered the child of the brother who died (Deuteronomy 25:5, 6). In the Sadducee's story this happened six times so that the same woman was married to seven brothers one after another. Now came the question that was supposed to stump Jesus. If all of the parties enjoy life in the next world, whose wife will she then be?

This seemed to be another perfect dilemma. It was totally unacceptable to any Jew that a woman could be married to seven men at the same time. The alternative was that there was no resurrection.

Of course, what the Sadducees didn't realize was that there was a third possibility. Jesus' reply jarred them out of their smug complacency. Matthew 22:29 reports that Jesus said, "You are in error because you do not know the Scriptures or the power of God." In other words, their neat little trap had been conjured up out of their own ignorance.

Jesus then went on to point out that the resurrected life will be lived in an entirely different dimension. Marriage will not be a part of that life, for men will be as angels. Then Jesus concluded His reply with a strong argument for life after death. He based it upon facts recorded in the Old Testament. When God spoke to Moses from the burning bush, He spoke as the God of Abraham, Isaac, and Jacob (Exodus 3:6). These men died long before God spoke to Moses; but God is the God of the living, not of the dead, and so it is evident that Abraham, Isaac, and Jacob are living long after their death. Jesus' reply brought amens from some of the teachers of the law. There was some more discussion that day (Matthew 22:34-46), but finally Jesus silenced His critics. They were afraid to ask Him any further questions.

A Question for the Questioners
Luke 20:41-47

To add to the critics' discomfort, Jesus had a stumper for them (Luke 20:41-44). Everyone knew the Christ was to be a son of David. Then how could David call him Lord, as he did in Psalm 110? By immemorial custom, the father is lord of the son. The answer, of course, is that the son of David is also the Son of God, and therefore the Lord of David and everyone else—the King of kings and Lord of lords. But Jesus' critics did not answer. Perhaps they had never thought of that question, though they were well acquainted with the psalm. Perhaps they wanted to think it over. Perhaps they were afraid Jesus was laying a trap for them, as they had been doing for Him. Whatever the reason, they let the question go unanswered.

Jesus concluded this period of open controversy with a stinging denunciation of the religious leaders (Luke 20:45-47). He denounced them because they publicly paraded their religion to gain the applause of men. They sought the chief seats in the synagogues and at banquets. They made long showy prayers, yet at the same time they devoured widows' houses. In due time, Jesus concluded, they would get their just punishment.

153

Prophecy of Things to Come
Luke 21:1-38

As Jesus was leaving the temple, His disciples were admiring the beauty and magnificence of it. Sadly Jesus told them it was to be utterly destroyed. Naturally the disciples wanted to know when that would happen, and chapter 21 of Luke records what Jesus told them.

First, He said the end of Jerusalem would not be the next week or the next year. The world would be troubled by wars, earthquakes, famines, and epidemics. The disciples would be persecuted. They should prepare themselves to endure all these things and still be faithful.

But the time would come when Jerusalem would be surrounded by armies. Then the disciples should get out, and fast! Then the city was going to be destroyed, and the suffering of its people would be terrible.

It was forty years later when this happened. Rome grew tired of little rebellions and guerrilla warfare among the Jews. Roman troops crushed Jerusalem and scattered its people.

Jesus said the city would be trampled "until the times of the Gentiles are fulfilled." He did not say how long that would be, but He went on to tell what would happen later. We are still looking forward to this. Not only the earth, but the whole universe will be shaken as Jesus comes "in a cloud with power and great glory."

Before the end of Jerusalem, the disciples could see the coming armies and know it was time to leave (Luke 21:29-33). But there will be no such warning before Jesus comes. No one can escape. The thing to do is to live every day as His people ought to live, so that you may be able to stand before the Son of Man (Luke 21:34-36).

The Trial and Crucifixion
Luke 22:1—23:56

The Tuesday of Jesus' last week was filled with furious controversy as the religious leaders sought to discredit Him in the eyes of the people. When they failed in this, they concentrated on their efforts to plot His death. Jesus and His disciples spent Tuesday night outside Jerusalem on the Mount of Olives. Perhaps they went to Bethany as they had done before (Matthew 21:17); or possibly they camped in Gethsemane, a favorite spot (John 18:2). Jesus came back in the morning to continue His teaching in the temple. His schedule was the same for Wednesday and Thursday (Luke 21:37). Apparently He was able to teach the people without interruption from His enemies, who had already set in motion their plan for His destruction. Let us now consider how that plan was developed with the help of one of Jesus' disciples.

The Plot With Judas
Luke 22:1-6

The religious leaders were in a quandary. They dared not arrest Jesus in the midst of an admiring crowd—the people might overwhelm and destroy the police. On the other hand, the leaders realized that they had to act swiftly if they were going to dispose of Jesus. If they waited until the end of the week-long feast, Jesus might leave with a throng of pilgrims and thus slip through their clutches.

But Satan was already at work to make sure their scheme did not fail. The tool he used was Judas. All kinds of attempts have been made to understand this man's motives. Some have even attempted to portray him as a kind of hero who betrayed Jesus in order to force Him to reveal himself as the Messiah. They suppose Judas thought Christ would not allow himself to be killed, but would destroy His enemies and take over the government—and Judas was impatient for that to happen.

But the efforts to depict Judas as anything except a villain must fall in the light of what the Scriptures say about him. He was basically a selfish person who could not appreciate Mary's lavish expression of love for Jesus. He was hypocritical in saying the money ought to be used to help the poor. On top of that, he was a thief who had been dipping into the disciples' funds (John 12:4-6).

We may find it difficult to understand how one could spend three years with Jesus, watching Him heal the sick and hearing His wonderful teaching, and yet in the end betray Him. Many people turned away from Jesus because they did not understand Him or because they were unwilling to sacrifice to follow Him or because He would not accept earthly kingship. Yet even when they turned away from Him, they did not plot against Him or betray Him to His enemies. What is it then that makes a traitor? Money, disappointed ambition, resentment of Jesus, wounded pride, fear of being ostracized from the synagogue? Perhaps all of these figured in his decision. All of us know persons who might become traitors in such circumstances. For that matter, all of us need to take heed lest Satan find a way to enter our hearts and tempt us in similar fashion.

Judas took the initiative in the matter and went to the chief priests and officers of the temple. They were delighted with the opportunity he presented. He quickly agreed to their terms and then began to seek for an opportunity to turn Jesus over to them when the crowd was not around to give Him protection.

The Last Supper
Luke 22:7-38

On Thursday, the fourteenth of Nisan according to the Jewish calendar, Jesus sent Peter and John to prepare the Passover supper. Their first question was about where the meal would be held. Crowded as the city was by all the pilgrims who came for the feast, it would not be easy to find a room large enough to accommodate Jesus and the twelve. But from the instructions Jesus gave, it is obvious that He had already made arrangements for the room. It seems likely that the owner of it was a disciple of Jesus.

At the appropriate hour, Jesus and His disciples arrived at the upper room. Some translations say they sat about the table, but a more accurate translation of the verb indicates that they reclined, which was the practice of that day. Da Vinci's *Last Supper*, which has influenced our thinking about the scene, reflects Renaissance Italian customs rather than those of first-century Palestine. Luke gives us only a brief outline of the activities of the evening, but from this and the other Gospel accounts we see the trend of what occurred.

As the meal began, Jesus expressed the intense desire He had to eat this Passover with His chosen twelve. There was a reason for this great desire. This would be the last such meal He would eat with them "until it finds fulfillment in the kingdom of God." These words must have had an ominous sound in the ears of the disciples. Yet if they asked about their meaning, Luke does not record it.

At the close of the Passover meal, Jesus instituted what we commonly call the Lord's Supper or Communion. He took bread, gave thanks for it, and then gave it to the disciples. The bread He broke was the thin loaf of unleavened bread, the only kind available during this feast when all leavening agents were forbidden. "This is my body," He said as He handed them the pieces of the broken bread. Complicated theological conclusions have been drawn from this statement, and men across the centuries have divided and fought over it. It is obvious that Jesus here, as He did so often, was using highly figurative language to make His point in a decisive manner. The bread represented His body, which in a few hours He would give upon the cross for their sins. Across the centuries this simple memorial has kept us from forgetting the great sacrifice He made for us.

In a similar fashion He took the cup and shared it with them. This cup represented the blood of the New Covenant, shed on the cross for the sins of mankind. The Old Covenant that God had made with Abraham and his descendants was passing away. Replacing it was a New Covenant with better promises and a better sacrifice.

In the midst of this solemn occasion, Jesus injected a statement that surely must have shocked everyone. "I am going to be betrayed," He said, "and by one who is with me about this table." Jesus went on to point out that His death was necessary as a part of God's eternal plan. Yet that in no way relieved the traitor of his moral responsibility for his action. Step by step he had made the decisions that led to his terrible deed. Even in that very moment, Jesus' statement could have led him to repent. Yet he rejected this last opportunity, and only the woe of final judgment awaited him. Don't we all need to be alert to the warnings of God's Word and turn quickly when we see our way is wrong?

As terrible as the sins of Judas were, the rest of the disciples were not free of the sin of jealousy. At this point Luke reports a dispute that arose about who was the greatest. Luke does not always record events in the order in which they occurred, and this dispute may have erupted when they first came into the room and were vying for the best places at the table. We may find it hard to believe that they had not really understood Jesus' teachings about humility and were still quibbling about such petty things as seating arrangements. But we don't have to look far to see the same failings among ourselves. This dispute may have prompted Jesus to wash the disciples' feet as an object lesson in humility (John 13:2-11).

Following the meal, Jesus warned Simon Peter that Satan had sought to sift him as wheat, indicating that Peter was not immune from Satan's temptation. Peter vehemently insisted that he was ready to stand by Jesus even if it meant prison and death. He must have been chagrined when Jesus informed him that he would deny Him not once but three times. After these and other words designed to prepare them for the dark hours just ahead, they left the upper room and started toward the Garden of Gethsemane.

In the Garden of Gethsemane
Luke 22:39-46

When Jesus arrived at the Garden of Gethsemane, located on the slope of the Mount of Olives, He left the disciples and went on farther into the garden. Here He knelt and offered a simple but agonizing prayer. He prayed that this cup, that is, the terrible sufferings of the trial and crucifixion, might be taken away. This was not possible according to God's plan, and Jesus humbly submitted to God's will. Our limited human viewpoint does not equip us to comprehend fully our Lord's agony in the garden. Not only did He have to contemplate the physical suffering of His trial and crucifixion; He also had to bear the anguish of the sins of the world.

As Jesus prayed, an angel appeared to strengthen Him. The depth of His need and agony is shown by the fact that He sweat great drops of blood. It is interesting that Luke, the physician, is the only one who mentions this.

Jesus Arrested
Luke 22:47-53

When Jesus finished His prayer and returned to the disciples, He found them sleeping. The physical and mental pressures of the past few days had taken their toll. But it made little difference now, for the betrayer, along with a huge detachment of armed men, was approaching. As Judas came near to identify Him with a kiss, Jesus challenged him: "Judas, are you betraying the Son of Man with a kiss?" Such a comment should have stopped Judas in his tracks, but Judas had so completely surrendered himself to iniquity that even this did not touch him.

While Luke does not relate all the details in this scene, he does tell of the disciples' efforts to defend Jesus with physical violence. John 18:10 tells us it was Simon Peter who drew a sword and attacked the arresting officers, severing the ear of one of them. Peter's willingness to defend the Lord even in the face of great odds was commendable, but his action showed that he still misunderstood what Jesus' ministry was all about. Jesus reminded the officials that He had been available every day in the temple. They chose rather the night hours for their deeds because, as Jesus commented, "This is your hour—when darkness reigns."

Peter's Denials
Luke 22:54-62

All the disciples fled when Jesus was arrested. Peter, however, followed at a distance. In the courtyard of the high priest's house a servant girl recognized Peter and challenged him. Peter denied that he had ever been with Jesus. Fear does strange things to people. Only a short time before, Peter had been willing to fight the whole arresting force. Yet the tongue of a young woman drove him into a cowardly denial. But have we not on occasion all been guilty of Peter's sin, either by words of denial or by frightened silence?

Twice more Peter was guilty of the same kind of denial. Some have argued that Peter had no business being in the courtyard of the high priest, that if he had been where he belonged, he would not have fallen into sin. But were the actions of the other disciples who fled and hid any more commendable? After all, Peter did have a real concern about what was happening to Jesus, and the best way to know was to follow Him as closely as possible.

Almost as soon as Peter uttered the third denial, he heard a rooster crow. At the same moment Jesus turned and looked at Peter. It must have been a look of extreme sorrow, for Peter immediately remembered Jesus' words and realized how empty were his boasts about his courage. Brokenhearted and humbled, he went out and wept bitterly.

Jesus' Trials Before the Jews
Luke 22:63-71

None of the Gospels give all of the details of Jesus' trials, and so we must consult all of them to get a clearer picture of what happened. Apparently Jesus was taken to the house of the high priest for a preliminary hearing. John tells that He was taken first to Annas, the father-in-law of the high priest that year (John 18:12-14). Then He was sent to Caiaphas, the official high priest (John 18:24). In these hearings He was questioned, mocked, and beaten.

While these hearings were taking place, the Sanhedrin, the ruling council of religious leaders, was being assembled. According to Jewish legal procedure, no trial of one accused of a capital offense could be held at night. But by daybreak the group had come together and proceeded to question Jesus. From the record it is obvious that they were not seeking the truth but only a basis upon which they might condemn Him. Finally they asked Him point-blank, "Are you then the Son of God?"

This was the key question, and Jesus answered it without any hesitation: "You are right in saying I am." Other charges were brought against Jesus by false witnesses (Matthew 26:59-61), but His claim to be the Son of God was what sent Him to the cross. As soon as the Sanhedrin heard His affirmation, they were ready to condemn Him. According to their thinking, He was guilty of blasphemy.

There was just one problem. They could not carry out the death sentence against Him. The Romans reserved this right for themselves, and so the Jewish rulers were forced to take Jesus before Pilate, the Roman governor.

Jesus Before Pilate and Herod
Luke 23:1-25

When the assembly brought Him to Pilate, they did not charge Him with blasphemy. The Roman governor would not be concerned about disrespect to the God of the Jews. So the Jews accused Jesus of subverting the nation by opposing the payment of taxes to Rome. That charge was completely false. Only a few days earlier He had publicly insisted that men ought to render to Caesar the things that belonged to Caesar (Luke 20:25). They also charged that He claimed to be Christ, a king. This charge would carry more weight with Pilate because such a claim could be considered an act of rebellion against Rome's authority.

Pilate was no fool, however, and he quickly saw through their scheme. He was prepared to release Jesus. But the Jews insisted that He had given subversive teaching all over the country, beginning in Galilee. Seeing a chance to get off the hook, Pilate then sent Jesus to Herod, king of Galilee, who was in Jerusalem at that time along with many of his subjects.

Herod had long wanted to see Jesus. He had heard of Jesus' activities as a miracle-worker, and he probably thought of Him as some kind of magician. But it would not be dignified for the king to mingle with the throng of common people around Jesus, and there was no ground for having Jesus arrested and brought to court. Now at last Jesus was before him, and it seems that Herod wanted Him to entertain by putting on a magic show. Naturally he was quite disappointed when Jesus refused to cooperate, remaining silent when questioned. All the while this was going on, the chief priests and teachers stood about vehemently hurling their accusations. But Herod quickly tired of the show. Since it was said that Jesus claimed to be a king, Herod and his men laughed derisively as they dressed Him in an elegant robe, perhaps one of Herod's own royal robes, and sent Him back to Pilate.

Pilate then called the Jewish leaders together once again, and this time he also called the people. Then the procurator gave his decision. There was no basis in the charges they had brought. For good measure, he added that Herod had not found any reason to charge Him either. Certainly Jesus had done nothing to deserve death, and so Pilate indicated that he would punish Jesus, probably by scourging Him, and then release Him. Throughout the affair it is obvious that Pilate did not want to execute Jesus. He knew the prisoner was innocent, and he wanted to release Him. But the religious leaders would have none of that. They were determined to eliminate Jesus by one method or another.

Luke 23:18 gives us a hint of one more effort Pilate made to set Jesus free. Matthew 27:15-23 tells more about it. As a gesture of good will, the Romans made it a custom to release a prisoner at Passover time—any prisoner the people asked for. Usually this would be a political prisoner, one jailed for opposing Rome, and therefore a hero in the eyes of the Jews. Now Pilate gave the people a choice: did they want him to release Jesus or Barabbas, a notorious and murderous robber who had been caught?

Pilate knew the people had honored Jesus with a tumultuous welcome into Jerusalem just a few days before (Luke 19:28-38). He must have felt certain that the same people would prefer Jesus to a murderer. But it was still early in the day, and most of those people did not know what was going on. The crowd outside Pilate's house was composed largely of employees and other partisans of the priests and Pharisees. Directed by those leaders, this crowd yelled for Barabbas to be released and Jesus to be crucified.

Pilate then sent Jesus to be flogged and tormented by the soldiers. Perhaps he hoped the sight of the helpless, bleeding man would arouse sympathy among the crowd. But still the cry went up, "Release Barabbas!" For a time it seemed that Pilate would stand his ground and not give in. The Jewish leaders, however, knew his weak spot, and that was where they attacked. "If you let this man go," they said, "you are no friend of Caesar." Pilate knew they would report him to Rome if they did not get their way. They would say he was tolerating a rebel who claimed to be king. The higher authorities probably would agree that Jesus was innocent, but some other phases of Pilate's administration were not so blameless. He could not afford to be investigated. So he decided to sacrifice Jesus (John 19:1-16).

Even then Pilate went through one last desperate charade to shift the blame upon the Jewish leaders. Calling for a basin of water, he washed his hands before the crowd, declaring that he was not responsible for the unjust death of an innocent man. The crowd did not hesitate an instant in accepting this terrible responsibility: "Let his blood be on us and on our children" (Matthew 27:24, 25). So at last Pilate told the soldiers to crucify Jesus.

The Crucifixion
Luke 23:26-43

As the soldiers led Jesus toward the place of execution, He carried His own cross at first (John 19:17). But He was exhausted by His strenuous ministry, a sleepless night, and a terrible beating. Perhaps he could not go fast enough to suit the soldiers; perhaps He actually collapsed, as tradition says. Then a Cyrenian was pressed into service to carry the cross. Many of the crowd followed Him, and by this time many of His friends had joined the crowd. Some of these mourned and wailed for Him. Jesus took the occasion to pronounce a dire prophecy upon Jerusalem. The suffering of Jerusalem would be so great that men would cry out for the mountains to fall upon them and the hills to cover them (Luke 23:30).

The place of crucifixion was called The Skull—*Golgotha* in the language of the Jews (John 19:17). The Latin version calls it *Calvaria,* from which we have the name *Calvary.* Today we are not sure exactly where this place was. Tradition places it at the spot now occupied by the Church of the Holy Sepulchre. Many, however, feel that it was on a little mound, called Gordon's Calvary, just north of the present city wall. Crumbling caves on the face of this hill resemble the eye sockets of a skull.

At this place called The Skull, Jesus was nailed to the cross. As He hung there dying, the soldiers cast lots for His clothes; and the rulers sneered, "He saved others; let him save himself if he is the Christ of God, the Chosen One."

Even in the midst of His agony, Jesus had thoughts for His enemies. He generously prayed for them: "Father, forgive them, for they do not know what they are doing." Even in His dying hours He set for us an example of forgiving love.

Above His head was an inscription in three languages—Aramaic, Greek, and Latin—ordered by Pilate: "This is the king of the Jews." The chief priests protested that Jesus was not their king. They wanted Pilate to change the inscription. But Pilate, who had been bullied into crucifying Jesus, now stood his ground. "What I have written, I have written," he said (John 19:19-22).

Two criminals also were crucified, one on either side of Jesus. One of them hurled insults at Him, but the other defended Him. Then he asked Jesus to remember him when He came into His kingdom. What a wonderful response he got when Jesus told him that on that very day he would be in paradise!

Jesus' Death
Luke 23:44-49

At the sixth hour, which would be noon by our time, a great darkness came upon the land and lasted until the ninth hour, three o'clock in the afternoon. No natural phenomenon can adequately account for this. It certainly could not have been an eclipse, since the moon was full at the time of the Passover. We can only conclude that it was a miracle that symbolized both the terribleness of sin and God's judgment upon the sinful world. At this point Jesus uttered His final words: "Father, into your hands I commit my spirit."

Even as He breathed His last, in the temple the great curtain that separated the Holy Place from the Holy of Holies was miraculously rent from top to bottom (Matthew 27:51). The writer of the Hebrew letter gives us the symbolic meaning of this (Hebrews 10:19-23). According to the Old Testament law, once a year the high priest entered the Holy of Holies to make petition for the sins of the people. He alone was allowed to go beyond the curtain that separated the Holy Place from the Holy of Holies. But at the death of Jesus, this curtain was split. This symbolizes the fact that now all men through the blood of Christ may approach God and offer prayer for their sins.

Jesus' death was accompanied also by a great rock-splitting earthquake (Matthew 27:51). All this had a tremendous impact on those who observed it. The hearts of Jesus' enemies were made harder than ever. His disciples were overwhelmed with sorrow. The centurion in charge of the execution was so impressed that he said, "Surely this was a righteous man." Matthew and Mark report an additional statement that was even stronger: "Surely he was the Son of God." It is interesting indeed that a man with a pagan background could see and understand what the trained Jewish theologians rejected. None are more blind than those who refuse to see!

Jesus' Burial
Luke 23:50-56

Joseph of Arimathea was an admirer of Jesus. Although he was a member of the Sanhedrin, he had not consented to the council's action in condemning Jesus. It was he who went to Pilate and requested Jesus' body. Nicodemus, another member of the Sanhedrin, was there to help. He brought a generous amount of myrrh and aloes to be wrapped with the body. Tenderly they took the body from the cross and placed it in Joseph's new tomb, which was near to Golgotha (John 19:38-42; Matthew 27:57-60).

At sunset the day ended and the Sabbath began. Shattered by their experiences of the day, Jesus' followers could only return to their lodging places to grieve.

The Resurrection

Luke 24:1-53

The Gospel of Luke reaches a climax in chapter 24. The whole book leads up to this chapter, and if this chapter were omitted, the Gospel of Luke would not be gospel—good news—at all. Chapter 23 ends with Jesus dead and laid to rest in a tomb. There is no basis for hope in a story that ends like that. Yet, thanks be to God, there is chapter 24, and the story ends with a living Jesus and message of hope for the whole world.

The Empty Tomb
Luke 24:1-12

Each of the Gospel accounts, written at a different time and for different readers, reports different aspects of the resurrection. While there are no contradictions among these accounts, we cannot be sure as to the precise order of the events they report. Scholars for generations have sought to arrange these events in what seems to be the correct chronological order, but no such arrangement has been universally accepted.

Jesus' body was placed in the tomb of Joseph of Arimathea on Friday just before the beginning of the Sabbath at sundown. Nicodemus supplied about seventy-five pounds of myrrh and aloes to be wrapped with the body (John 19:39), but some devoted women wanted to add their own contribution of spices and ointments.

Among these women who had come with Jesus from Galilee were Mary Magdalene, Joanna, Mary the mother of James and Joses, and Salome. Some of them watched the burial of Jesus, but they did not bring their spices till the Sabbath was past. It was early on Sunday morning when they made their way to the tomb. John 20:1 tells that they began their trip while it was still dark, and Mark 16:2 says the sun came up as they were on their way. We certainly must commend these women for their dedication to this sad task. Yet at the same time, we can't avoid wondering about their faith. It seems strange that neither they nor the male disciples recalled Jesus' repeated promise that He would rise from the dead (Luke 9:22; 18:33). Even His enemies thought of that promise, and they took steps to be sure a resurrection would not be faked (Matthew 27:62-66).

As the women made their way to the tomb, their greatest concern was about who would roll the stone away (Mark 16:3). They did not know a guard had been posted at the tomb. The soldiers could have provided manpower to move the heavy stone, but they would not have dared to break the seal without orders from their superiors. However, the matter was taken out of their hands.

As the women were on their way to the tomb, an angel of the Lord came down and rolled back the stone (Matthew 28:2-4). His appearance was as brilliant as lightning and his clothes as white as snow. The guards were so overwhelmed by his appearance that they fell over "like dead men." By the time the women arrived, all they found was an empty tomb. Apparently the soldiers had recovered and fled in terror to report what had happened.

Naturally the women were quite perplexed at finding the tomb open and empty. It seems that Mary Magdalene left the group and hurried to tell Peter and John (John 20:1, 2). The other women lingered at the tomb, wondering. Had Jesus' enemies taken the body away? Had some of Jesus' friends moved it to another place? As they pondered these things, two men in brilliant apparel (obviously angels) stood beside them.

The women were as frightened as the soldiers had been earlier, and they fell on their faces before the angels. But the words of the angels were reassuring. "Why do you look for the living among the dead?" they asked. "He is not here; he has risen!" What a range of emotions must have flooded their hearts! They wanted to believe, but the news seemed too good to be true. Yet the news came from angelic messengers. How could they disbelieve? To strengthen their belief the angels reminded them that Jesus had said this would happen. He had told them He would be delivered into the hands of sinful men, crucified, and raised again on the third day. Now, with the angels' reminder, Jesus' predictions came back to them. "Why didn't we see that before?" they must have asked themselves. "How much sorrow we might have avoided if we had just understood!"

Luke gives us an abbreviated account of what happened after that. The women were told to go find the disciples and tell them what had happened (Matthew 28:7). We can be sure that they lost no time hurrying to find the disciples. What a contrast there must have been between their conversation as they came to the tomb and as they left it! But their story brought only disbelief from the disciples. "Emotional, overwrought women!" they must have exclaimed. "How can we believe what they have to say? This is utter nonsense."

Peter and John got the report first from Mary Magdalene, who had left the tomb without seeing the angels. Hurrying to the tomb, they found the linen that had wrapped the body; but Jesus was not there. John reports that he "saw and believed," but it does not seem that he yet believed Jesus had risen. He believed what Mary had said: the body was gone.

Weeping at the tomb after Peter and John were gone, Mary Magdalene was the first one to see Jesus after He rose from the dead (John 20:10-18; Mark 16:9). What exciting news she carried then as she ran again to find Peter and John and the other disciples!

Meanwhile the other women were finding the other disciples and reporting both the empty tomb and the message of the angels. The disciples must have been staying at different places in and around Jerusalem. Before all of them were reached, the women met Jesus himself! (Matthew 28:9). They went on then to spread a more joyous message.

On the Road to Emmaus
Luke 24:13-35

Luke condenses all this into a few words, not even mentioning that the women saw Jesus himself. Then he gives a more detailed account of an incident on the road to Emmaus, a village about seven miles west and north of Jerusalem. In this account he for the first time describes an appearance of Jesus after His resurrection.

Two people, Cleopas and an unnamed companion, were making their way from Jerusalem to Emmaus. It is probably safe to assume that one or both of them lived here. As they walked, they talked of events that had occurred in the past few days. While they were

167

engrossed in their conversation, Jesus began to walk along with them, but miraculously they were kept from recognizing Him. Jesus entered their conversation by asking what they were talking about. This caused the two to stop as if such a question was totally unexpected. Their sorrowful expressions gave away their feelings. They found it difficult to believe that anyone could have been around Jerusalem the past few days without knowing what had been happening. "You must be the only one living in Jerusalem who doesn't know about these things," exclaimed Cleopas.

"What things are you talking about?" Jesus asked. He was not asking for information, of course, but was raising the question to cause the two to think more carefully and logically about what they had been discussing. We often speak in an illogical or disorganized way about a subject until we have to explain it to someone else. Then we begin to organize our thoughts. That's what Jesus' question forced them to do.

Since they assumed that Jesus was completely ignorant of these events, they began with the simplest facts. Jesus, who was the center of all of these activities, was from Nazareth. "He was a prophet, powerful in word and deed": that is, He had made an impression on them both through His teaching and through His miracles. They went on to explain how their chief priests and rulers had delivered Him up to be crucified. They clearly placed the blame on the Jewish leaders rather than on the Romans.

Then came the source of their sorrow and disappointment: "We had hoped that he was the one who was going to redeem Israel." But now, as far as they were concerned, that hope was gone. Yet now on the third day there was just a tiny glimmer of hope again. Some women had gone to the tomb and found it empty. They had told of seeing a vision of angels who said Jesus was alive. Others had gone to the tomb also, and they had found it empty. Cleopas and his companion were suspended in that agonizing position between faith and unbelief. They would like to think Jesus was alive again, but how could they? They knew He had died. If they accepted the word of a few excited women, would they just be disappointed again? Other followers of Jesus must have been going through this same kind of struggle.

Jesus broke into their recounting of recent events. He chided them for being foolish and slow of heart, for failing to believe everything the prophets had spoken. Like most of the Jews of their day, they accepted the prophecies that told of the glory and triumph of the promised Messiah. But like most, they missed those passages that referred to the Messiah as a suffering servant. Had they not been so slow of heart, they would have recognized that it was necessary for the Messiah to suffer all those things before He entered into His glory. Then beginning with Moses—that is, the first five books of the Old Testament—Jesus showed them all the things the Scriptures taught about himself.

When the travelers reached Emmaus, Jesus seemed to be going farther. But the two insisted that He stay with them for the night, since the day was nearly over. At their insistence, He agreed to stay with them.

This unknown traveler was a remarkable conversationalist along the way, and He proved to be a remarkable guest. At the table He took the bread, gave thanks, and broke it as if He were the host. At this point their eyes were opened and they recognized Him. They had been miraculously kept from knowing Him before, but now suddenly they saw the familiar face of their Master. But was there something else they recognized? As followers of Jesus they had shared meals with Him in the past. Did He break the bread in a characteristic way? Was there something familiar in the tone of His voice or the words He used in blessing? Did they notice the nailprints in His hands? Whatever details were involved, suddenly they knew their guest was Jesus.

As soon as they recognized Him, He disappeared, leaving them to be swept along by a flood of emotions—joy that He was alive, chagrin that they had not recognized Him, hearts set aflame by the Scripture that He had expounded for them. Filled as they were by joy and excitement, there was no way they could stay in Emmaus until morning. The darkened road back to Jerusalem may have held dangers, but in their exhilaration they were oblivious to these.

Once back in Jerusalem they found the eleven and others assembled together. The term *eleven* seems to be used to designate the apostles as a group rather than to count them. Thomas was not present in this meeting and Judas was dead, so actually no more than ten apostles were there.

The two from Emmaus found that the group was already celebrating the good news that Jesus had risen. He had appeared to Peter. The other Gospel accounts do not mention this appearance, but Paul lists it first among the appearances (1 Corinthians 15:5). It is interesting that the disciples did not believe the women when they reported seeing Jesus, but they based their faith on Peter's report.

This does not necessarily mean the women were considered less trustworthy, but the evidence was piling up. Mary saw Jesus; other women saw Him at another time and place; Peter saw Him. It was hard to think all of these were mistaken.

Finally the two from Emmaus got a chance to tell their story. Their report must have intensified the emotions of that hour. All of Jesus' followers had begun that momentous day overwhelmed with sorrow and disappointment. The hopes that had begun three years before and had grown month by month had suddenly been crushed by Jesus' death. But now in a complete reversal, the disciples were experiencing unbelievable joy. Later Peter attempted to give verbal expression to this joy: "Praise be to the God and Father of our Lord Jesus Christ! In his great mercy he has given us new birth into a living hope through the resurrection of Jesus Christ" (1 Peter 1:3).

Jesus Appears to the Group
Luke 24:36-53

Even as the two were still telling about their Emmaus experience, Jesus appeared among them. John 20:19 tell us that the disciples had locked the door to the room "for fear of the Jews." We are left with the conclusion that Jesus' appearance was miraculous. His first words were to assure them: "Peace be with you." He knew their first response would be fear, and He tried to allay this with His greeting. But they were still frightened, supposing that they were seeing a ghost. It seems a bit surprising that they should react in this fashion. They had just been saying that He has arisen. Perhaps the suddenness of His appearance and the fact that He appeared in the room in spite of the locked doors contributed to their shock. But it seems that unbelief was still struggling with their belief. It was not easy to believe that one who had died was alive again.

Jesus met their doubts with calm assurance and visible evidence. He showed them His hands and feet, where the ugly scars were still quite visible. John informs us that He also showed them the wound in His side. He invited them to touch Him. This certainly showed that He was not just a ghost, for ghosts do not have flesh and bones. Yet their attitude was one of disbelief for joy—the news was just too good to be true. And so He made one further effort to reassure them. "Do you have anything to eat?" He asked. When they offered Him a piece of broiled fish that had been left over from the supper, He proceeded to eat it. This action proved to be conclusive, and they traded their doubts for joy.

In this frame of mind, they were in a position to be more receptive to further teaching from Jesus. He began to review the things He had taught them earlier. As He had done for the two on the road to Emmaus, He showed them that everything that had happened was according to the Scriptures. The three portions He mentioned—the Law of Moses, the Prophets, and the Psalms—were the three divisions that the Jews made in the Old Testament. All of these major divisions of the Old Testament bore testimony concerning the work and the office of the Messiah. But the Jews, including the disciples, had not understood all of the testimony. Jesus opened their minds so that they could understand just what the Scriptures did teach about the suffering, death, and resurrection of the Messiah. Luke gives us only an abbreviated account. Undoubtedly Jesus spent considerable time in going over the various Scriptures that pointed to Him. Thus He opened their minds to truths they had not seen before. There is certainly a lesson for us here. There is much more truth in the Scriptures than we have fully comprehended, and this truth becomes available to us when we lay aside our prejudices and open our minds.

But Jesus did not stop with simply expounding for them the various Messianic teachings of the Old Testament. These teachings laid the groundwork for the new and, for them, revolutionary teachings He was ready to present. Repentance and forgiveness of sins would be preached to all nations, beginning right there in Jerusalem. Further, they were to be the witnesses, the heralds, of this exciting new revelation. It was one thing to have the Old Testament opened up to them; it was quite another thing to be told that this message must be carried beyond the boundaries of Judaism to the whole world. It is not likely that they fully comprehended just how revolutionary these teachings were, for at the moment they raised no objection to them. Later they showed some reluctance to go to the Gentiles, as we see in the tenth chapter of Acts.

They were not to face this task alone. Jesus would send them what the Father had promised—that is, the Holy Spirit. John also reports this same scene (John 20:22) and tells how Jesus dramatized His promise as He breathed on them and said, "Receive the Holy Spirit." Yet they did not receive the full measure of the Spirit at that moment. They were to remain in the city until they had "been clothed with power from on high." Many things happened before that occurred at Pentecost seven weeks later. There were other appearance of Jesus— to the eleven, including Thomas, the following Sunday (John 20:24-

29); to seven by the Sea of Galilee (John 21); to more than five hundred and to James (1 Corinthians 15:6, 7); and to the eleven in Galilee where Jesus gave them the Great Commission (Matthew 28:16-20).

Luke then concludes his Gospel with a brief account of Jesus' ascension to Heaven. In the first chapter of Acts he supplies us with further details of this. While the disciples awaited the "power from on high," they spent their time in the temple rejoicing and praising God.

Chronology of Acts

The book of Acts records events of more than thirty years. The exact time of some events cannot be fixed with certainty, but the following approximate dates give a general idea of the time covered.

Chapter in this book	Reference in Acts	Date A.D.
19. Beginning at Jerusalem	1:1—2:47	30
20. The Church Faces Problems	3:1—6:7	30-33
21. Persecution and Expansion	6:8—8:40	33-38
22. The Conversion of Saul	9:1-31	35
23. The Beginning of the Mission to the Gentiles	9:32—11:18	40
24. Paul's First Missionary Journey	11:19—14:28	45-49
25. The Jerusalem Conference and Its Aftermath	15:1—18:22	50-53
26. Paul's Third Missionary Journey and Trip to Rome	18:23—28:31	54-63

Beginning at Jerusalem

Acts 1:1—2:47

The Gospel of Luke ends with the ascension of Jesus. The story is continued in Second Luke—the Acts of the Apostles, or simply Acts, as the book is commonly called. It is almost universally acknowledged that Luke is the author of both volumes. He is "the beloved physician" (Colossians 4:14), or "our dear friend Luke, the doctor," as the *New International Version* has it. He was Paul's companion on many of his missionary travels.

Both Luke and Acts are addressed to Theophilus (Luke 1:3; Acts 1:1), and the writing style of the two is similar. The book of Acts was written near the end of Paul's first Roman imprisonment, which is usually dated A.D. 61-63. Luke did not give this book its title, and in a sense the name "Acts" or "Acts of the Apostles" is something of a misnomer. A more appropriate title might be "A Few of the Acts of a Few of the Apostles," since the book tells of only a limited number of activities of some of the apostles. While the twelve are mentioned at the beginning of the book, Peter increasingly occupies the center of the stage. Then, beginning with the ninth chapter, the apostle Paul increasingly becomes the center of attention.

The narrative is played out on the vast stage of the first-century Roman Empire. It begins in Jerusalem, moves to Judea and Samaria, then to Syria and Asia Minor, on to Macedonia and Greece, and finally to Rome itself. This particular time in history afforded many advantages. Rome provided a stable government, good roads, and sea lanes safe from pirates. Koine Greek was spoken throughout the empire, which meant that the gospel could spread without much hindrance by language barriers. People were able to travel with relative ease, and messengers within a few years carried the word across the empire and beyond. By this time the pagan religions and philosophies were largely bankrupt, so men were more receptive to the Christian message when they heard it. This, then, was the world into which a dozen unlettered men were sent, armed only with faith in the risen Lord and His assurance that He would be with them. Who would dare dream that such an insignificant beginning could produce the world's greatest revolution?

A Commission and a Farewell
Acts 1:1-11

Following His resurrection, Jesus appeared to several different individuals and groups over a period of forty days, giving "many convincing proofs that he was alive" (Acts 1:3). At the end of this period Jesus met with the apostles for the last time to give them their final instructions. They were to remain in Jerusalem until they were baptized with the Holy Spirit. This was a fulfillment of the promise that John the Baptist made before the beginning of Jesus' ministry (Mark 1:8). The word *baptism* means immersion. In this verse it indicates that the apostles would be immersed, buried, overwhelmed in the Holy Spirit. They would receive His power and guidance to an unusual degree. The "few days" that Jesus mentioned turned out to be the ten days till Pentecost, when the apostles did receive the special blessing and power of the Spirit.

The situation and Jesus' promise of the Holy Spirit led the apostles to raise an interesting question: "Lord, are you at this time going to restore the kingdom to Israel?" How disappointing this question must have been to the Lord! For three years He had carefully and patiently tried to show that His kingdom was spiritual in nature. Yet after all this teaching, the apostles failed the final examination. They still had not outgrown their Jewish expectation that the Messiah was coming to reestablish a physical kingdom. This should serve as a warning to us that opinions long held and frequently reinforced are not easy to outgrow, even if they are mistaken.

Jesus responded patiently to their question, not by arguing with them or berating them for their ignorance, but by pointing out that some features of God's plan were not really any of their business.

Instead of talking about when and how certain events would take place in the future, Jesus directed their attention to some immediate duties that lay before them. One wonders if this would not be fitting advice for persons today who seem overly concerned about when and how our Lord will return. Will we not be better off if we give our attention to the immediate duties that the Scriptures set before us?

Jesus summed up the apostles' duties in one simple but all-encompassing statement: "You will be my witnesses in Jerusalem, and in all Judea and Samaria, and to the ends of the earth." Here we have the Acts version of the Great Commission that had been stated previously under different circumstances and is recorded in each of the Gospels (Matthew 28:18-20; Mark 16:15, 16; Luke 24:45-48; John 20:21-23). Jesus could scarcely have made His intent plainer. The teachings of Jesus were not to be limited to a small handful of Jews, but were to be carried across every barrier—national, racial, linguistic—until they had penetrated the distant regions of the globe. We can rejoice that the gospel has been proclaimed in many distant lands about the world. Yet we must hang our heads in shame because even after two thousand years there are still vast areas that remain untouched by the message of salvation.

Following this meeting with the apostles, Jesus led them out of Jerusalem and up the slopes of the Mount of Olives to a place near the town of Bethany (Luke 24:50). There Jesus paused to bless them, and then as they watched He was taken up. As He arose, a cloud intervened to hide Him from their sight.

Just as it was important that there were adequate witnesses to the resurrection, so it was important that the ascension be properly witnessed. Because He left the world in this manner, the apostles were able to testify to what they had seen. Since it occurred in the open and in broad daylight, their testimony was valid.

Since the ascension was unexpected, the apostles were amazed by it and stood gazing up even after the cloud hid Jesus from sight. Perhaps they thought He might reappear. As they stood looking up into the sky and not knowing what to expect next, two men dressed in white stood beside them. Obviously these were angels. Their question, "Why do you stand here looking into the sky?" was designed to turn the apostles' attention from the miraculous ascension to the task that was before them. The apostles were also informed that Jesus would return on the clouds in the same manner that He had just left, a teaching that is found elsewhere in the Scriptures also (Matthew 24:30; Revelation 1:7).

Choosing a Replacement for Judas
Acts 1:12-26

The message of the angels moved the apostles to leave the Mount of Olives and return to Jerusalem, to their temporary quarters in an upper room. This may very well have been the upper room in which the last supper was held. The location of this room is unknown, although some think it was in the southwest section of Jerusalem. Luke then calls the roll of the apostles for us. This corresponds to the lists found in the Gospels (Matthew 10:2-4; Mark 3:16-19; Luke 6:14-16) with, of course, the notable exception of Judas. In the upper room they engaged constantly in prayer, in which they were joined by the mother of Jesus and some of the other women who had accompanied them from Galilee. Interestingly, Jesus' brothers also met with this group. Four brothers of Jesus are mentioned in Matthew 13:55—James, Joseph, Simon, and Judas. Prior to the resurrection, Jesus' brothers were not believers (John 7:5), but the resurrection changed their minds completely. In all, at least twenty people must have been involved, which required a rather large room.

At times the apostles met with a larger group of Jesus' followers. Since there were about a hundred twenty in this group, it is not likely that the upper room was large enough to hold them. They may have met in a room in the temple complex.

As on other occasions, Peter spoke up in the group. The immediate issue was the selection of a replacement for Judas, the traitor. Peter called the whole group to consider it.

It seems that Acts 1:18, 19 are not what Peter said, but a note inserted by Luke to tell of the demise of Judas. At first thought it may appear that this account is at variance with that found in Matthew 27:5, which states that Judas hanged himself. However, it may well be that Judas chose a desolate place where his body hung for some time, and then the rope broke, allowing the body to fall to the ground. In an advanced stage of putrefaction, the body would have burst open as Luke described. Before his death Judas attempted to return the money he had received for betraying Jesus, but the chief priests refused to put it into the treasury because it was blood money. They used it to purchase a potter's field, a place where clay had been dug by potters. This otherwise useless piece of ground then became a burial place for strangers and indigents. The place came to be called *Akeldama*, an Aramaic term meaning "Field of Blood." Judas was dead before it was bought; but it was bought with his money, and so it may properly be said that he bought it.

Peter quoted two passages from the book of Psalms (69:25 and 109:8) as a basis for selecting another to take the place of Judas. The first passage dealt with the removal of Judas from his position and the other with choosing his successor. The basic requirement for this person was that he must have been a follower of Jesus from the time of John's baptism until the ascension. Judas' successor would be a witness along with the other eleven. One can hardly be a witness unless he has seen the events about which he is going to bear testimony. There may have been several persons who met this requirement, but only two names were proposed: one was Joseph called Barsabbas, who was also called Justus; the other was Matthias. After these two had been proposed, the group entered into prayer that the Lord would show which one was to receive the office. The choice was indicated to them by the drawing of lots.

Sometimes this was done by writing each person's name on a piece of wood or broken pottery, which was placed in a vessel. The vessel was then violently shaken, and whichever name fell out first received the office. The practice of casting lots is mentioned in the Old Testament. For example, Canaan was divided by lot after the conquest (Joshua 18:8-10). Achan was discovered by lot (Joshua 7:14-18), as was Jonah (Jonah 1:7). However, the New Testament records only this one time when Christians made a decision by lot. This suggests that God did not intend the practice to be widely used.

The lot fell to Matthias, and he was added to the eleven. This is the last time he is mentioned by name in the New Testament. In fact, this is the last time any of the twelve apostles except Peter, James, and John are mentioned by name in the New Testament.

The Gathering on Pentecost
Acts 2:1-13

Ten days after Jesus' ascension came the Day of Pentecost. This was one of the three great Jewish feasts. The others were Passover and Tabernacles. Sometimes Pentecost was called the Feast of Weeks because it came seven weeks after Passover. It celebrated the grain harvest, and the Jews came to use it also to commemorate the giving of the law on Sinai.

Acts 2:1 says, "They were all together in one place." Does this mean the apostles, or the one-hundred-twenty believers? This is disputed, but most students suppose the larger group was together in some building of the temple complex, close to the big courtyard where uncounted thousands could gather.

Their meeting was suddenly interrupted by a sound coming from heaven and filling the house. It was like the sound of a violent wind, but no wind was felt. Clearly this was a miracle designed to focus attention on what was going to happen next. Then came a second sign of God's presence in their midst. Tongues that looked like fire appeared, then divided and came to rest on each of them. The word here translated *tongue* can have any of three meanings: (1) the physical member of taste and speech, (2) a language, or (3) almost anything shaped somewhat like a tongue. Flames have such a shape. The shape of tongues suggests also the miracle of speaking in foreign languages that was soon to follow.

Did the tongues like flame rest on everyone present, or only the apostles? This is the subject of debate. In verse 14 we are told that Peter stood up with the eleven. This leads us to conclude that only Peter and the other eleven apostles had been speaking in various languages, and that they alone were designated by the flames.

The next miraculous sign came when they were filled with the Holy Spirit and began to speak in other tongues. Speaking thus in tongues is sometimes called the Pentecostal experience, or glossolalia. It has become a controversial or even divisive issue in many churches of our time. Persons who claim to have the gift of speaking in tongues or other miraculous gifts from the Holy Spirit are sometimes referred to as charismatics. Many charismatics use the second chapter of Acts as a basis for their experience. An examination of this chapter may provide some illumination in this matter.

First of all, let us see who heard the apostles speak in tongues. Verse 5 informs us that "God-fearing Jews from every nation of the world" were gathered in Jerusalem to observe the feast of Pentecost. We take this statement to be a hyperbole, an exaggerated statement used for emphasis. The travelers did not come from literally every nation of the whole globe. Yet more than a dozen nations are mentioned in verses 9-11. Most of these areas were within the Roman Empire, but some were outside of its boundaries. Parthia, for example, was a sizeable empire extending from the Tigris to India. At times the Parthians offered a formidable threat to Rome. Jews had lived in this area from the eighth century B.C., when many had been deported from Israel by the Assyrians. Near the Parthians were the Medes. The Medes had united with the Persians in the sixth century B.C. to form a vast empire that ruled much of southwestern Asia until the time of Alexander the Great. The Elamites came from the same general area. They lived north of the Tigris River and east of ancient Babylon. Mesopotamia was the area between the Tigris and Euphrates Rivers. Cappadocia, Pontus, Asia, Phrygia, and Pamphylia were all areas in what we now call Asia Minor. There were many Jewish communities in these areas. Egypt and Libya were in northern Africa. Egypt especially had large Jewish communities. Rome was included in the list, as was Crete, a large island located in the eastern Mediterranean. Arabia was the desert area east of Palestine.

The wind-like sound drew all these people together, probably in the temple area. Once they were assembled, each national group heard the apostles speaking in its own tongue. Various attempts have been made to explain how this happened. Some say that each apostle spoke a different language and addressed only one national group. Since there were more than a dozen national groups, some of the apostles had to speak to more than one group. Others say the apostles took turns speaking to the whole group. This raises an interesting question: did the miracle occur on the lips of the speaker or on the ears of the listener? Since it was clearly a miracle, there is no adequate explanation. We simply believe that it happened and are willing to leave the how to God.

Many of these visitors undoubtedly spoke Greek or Aramaic as well as their national tongues. It was not strictly necessary for the apostles to speak the languages of these various nations in order to communicate. It seems logical to conclude that the miracle of speaking in tongues was intended to authenticate the message the apostles brought. The visiting Jews recognized that the apostles were simple Galileans who could hardly be expected to know all the languages that were heard. This made it easier for the hearers to believe that the Holy Spirit was guiding the speakers.

This leads to another important observation. The languages at Pentecost were known languages spoken by recognized national groups. By contrast, the experience of tongues in the Corinthian church involved utterances in unknown languages (1 Corinthians 14:2). Modern charismatic practice usually follows the Corinthian pattern rather than the Pentecostal. Would it not be more appropriate to speak of modern charismatics as Corinthians rather than Pentecostals?

Whatever else may be said about the sound like wind, the tongues like fire, and the many languages, they were amazing. Everywhere in the growing crowd, puzzled people were asking each other, "What does this mean?" Simon Peter was the one who answered that question for them.

Peter's Sermon
Acts 2:14-41

In every crowd there are likely to be some hecklers, and this crowd was no exception. They made fun of the tongue-speaking phenomena by charging the apostles with being drunk. This was, of course, a most ridiculous charge. Alcohol slurs one's speech; it does not enhance one's linguistic ability. Peter's reply turned away the remarks in a rather humorous fashion, indicating that he took the remark more as a jest than as a serious charge. "How could we be drunk?" he asked. "It is only nine A.M. We haven't had time to get drunk yet!" Peter knew very well that what he was going to say was too serious and too intense for anyone to mistake him for a drunk.

Peter first provided a Scriptural basis for what was happening. The events of that day had been prophesied by the prophet Joel (2:28-32). Joel had predicted that in "the last days" God would pour out His Spirit on all people, causing them to prophesy, see visions, and dream dreams. The point Peter made was that the "last days" had arrived; this prophecy was being fulfilled. Verses 19 and 20 describe wonders and signs that were to take place in these "last days." Some suggest that these signs were seen when Jesus was crucified. However, the expression "last days" does not refer to a brief period of a few days or months. Rather, it refers to a whole new age, the Christian age, the age of grace, that will precede the "coming of the great and glorious day of the Lord," at which time God will bring His final judgment upon the world. The speaking in tongues initiated this new age, and these wonders and signs will signal its end (Matthew 24:29-31). Already nearly two thousand years have passed since the beginning of the Christian age, and no one knows how much time remains until the end.

Peter was now ready for the main thrust of his message—the proclamation of Jesus as the promised Messiah. First of all, Peter identified Him: "Jesus of Nazareth." Some who were visiting in Jerusalem may have needed this identification, for there were other men named Jesus. Jesus of Nazareth was accredited by God through wonders and signs that God had worked through Him. Many of the people had seen some of those miracles. Yet the people had employed the help of wicked men—the Romans—to crucify Jesus. This had not surprised God, however; it was according to His "set purpose and foreknowledge." The resurrection that followed was also a part of God's plan and had been predicted by David (Psalm 16:8-11). The risen Christ has now been exalted to the right hand of God.

In ringing words, Peter brought his message to its climax: "God has made this Jesus, whom you crucified, both Lord and Christ." Peter's conclusion was no gentle homily to soothe his hearers' feelings. It was a slashing indictment for their guilt in sending Jesus to the cross. The fact that this was a part of God's eternal plan did not mitigate their guilt one iota. They stood condemned, and Peter made sure that no one misunderstood this.

The hearers got the point all right. Peter's information convinced them in their minds, and his indictment cut them to the heart. This, by the way, is an excellent formula for effective preaching that works even in our sophisticated age. Their sense of guilt caused them to cry out in anguish, "Brothers, what shall we do?" They realized that their situation was desperate and they appealed to the only source that could help them.

Peter's response was concise and to the point. His message had moved them to faith in Christ as the risen Lord. Now they must repent of their sins. Repentance means a change in allegiance, a complete reversal of the direction of one's life commitment. A person is running from God or fighting Him. Then he repents. Now he is running to God and renouncing all the things that kept him from God. His mind is changed, and his whole way of life is changed to match his renewed mind.

Next, the repentant renegade must be baptized. Most persons in Peter's audience probably knew about John's baptism and understood that Peter was talking about immersion in water. But more was involved in Christian baptism than in John's baptism. Both required repentance and both were for the forgiveness of sins (Mark 1:4); but Christian baptism brought with it the "gift of the Holy Spirit," something not promised by John. Baptism alone does not bring the forgiveness of sins nor the gift of the Holy Spirit. Faith and repentance must necessarily precede baptism. Yet baptism must not be dismissed as unimportant. The idea that one can be a Christian and not be baptized is foreign to the New Testament.

The *gift* of the Holy Spirit must be distinguished from the *gifts* of the Holy Spirit. The gift of the Holy Spirit is the Spirit himself, who lives within the Christian (1 Corinthians 6:19) and helps in many ways as he strives to live a Christlike life. The gifts of the Holy Spirit, on the other hand, include a variety of powers and abilities helpful in the growth and edification of the church (1 Corinthians 12). Every baptized believer receives the gift of the Holy Spirit, but each Christian is endowed with only a few of the gifts of the Holy Spirit.

The promise of forgiveness and the gift of the Spirit were available not only to the hearers but also to their children and, what is more, even to those who were far away. Some hearers may have thought this referred only to Jews who were not then in Jerusalem; but Peter said "all who are far off," and certainly that included Gentiles as well.

The response to Peter's message was overwhelming. About three thousand accepted the divine terms of pardon and were baptized that day. Such a response may have been beyond the wildest expectations of the disciples, but by this time they had seen so many unusual and miraculous happenings that they were able to cope with it.

Continuing Fellowship
Acts 2:42-47

Pentecost was not a one-day evangelistic meeting without any follow-up. Effective efforts were immediately begun to insure the continued growth of these new Christians. We are told that "they devoted themselves to the apostles' teaching and to the fellowship, to the breaking of bread and to prayer."

They continued to be filled with awe both by the joy of God's grace and by the miraculous wonders and signs performed by the apostles. They shared their possessions to meet the needs of all in the group. Every day they met in the temple for worship and teaching, and in smaller groups they ate together in homes. A sense of joy and purpose permeated their lives, and this was recognized by those outside the church. Is it any wonder that the church continued to grow?

The Church Faces Problems

Acts 3:1—6:7

The church was born on Pentecost with three thousand members. Like any normal, healthy newborn baby, the church continued to grow. The three thousand members soon became five thousand (Acts 4:4), and then Luke apparently gave up trying to keep count and simply recorded that "more and more men and women believed in the Lord and were added to their number" (Acts 5:14). Those were exhilarating days—church growth always brings excitement. But growth also usually brings problems, and the early church in Jerusalem did not escape its share. Some of its problems arose because the rapid growth of the church aroused the jealousy and fear of the Jewish religious authorities. Other problems developed from within the church because of sins that crept into the life of church members.

Some of these problems were so serious that, had they not been solved, the growth of the church would have been stifled. Even the very life of the church might have been threatened. Solving the problems was not easy, nor did the solutions come without pain; there rarely are simple, painless solutions to serious problems. The actions the Jerusalem church took to meet these threats give us some examples of how we today can meet similar problems.

Some may argue that the conditions in the first century were so different from ours that we really can't learn anything from them. It is true that there are many differences, especially in technology. Yet in spite of all this material progress, some things have not changed. Man is still a sinner, and the cure for that sin remains the same—the blood of Jesus Christ.

Some may also argue that the means of meeting these problems have changed. After all, the first-century church was led by the divinely-inspired apostles, an advantage we no longer enjoy. True, the twelve no longer live and walk among us, but we have an advantage that the church did not share in the beginning. We have the New Testament, the divinely-inspired testimony of the apostles and other men chosen by the Holy Spirit to reveal God's truth to us. In many ways this is a far greater advantage. An apostle, for example, could be in only one place at a time, whereas the written Word has spread around the world, bringing its message of salvation into many situations the apostles never reached.

Peter and John Face Persecution
Acts 3:1—4:31

The first serious problem the church had to face was persecution. The first instance of this came as the result of a healing. One day Peter and John entered the temple for the afternoon prayer. There at the temple gate called Beautiful lay a beggar, a cripple who had never been able to walk. When he saw the two apostles, he cried out for alms. They had no money to give the man, but Peter gave him something far more valuable. In the name of Jesus he gave strength to the man's feet and ankles so that he could walk. The man lost no time in letting others know what had happened. He went leaping and shouting into the temple courts, giving praise to God.

The people recognized him as the beggar who always sat at the gate, and so a crowd soon gathered. Peter, who rarely passed up an opportunity to preach, began to explain what had happened. The theme was the same as that of his sermon on the Day of Pentecost. God had sent Jesus to them, but they had rejected Him and killed Him. Though they had killed the author of life, God had raised Him up and glorified Him. It was in His name that the man had been healed. The conclusion also was the same as on Pentecost: they were to repent and turn to God so that their sins might be wiped out (Acts 3:19).

The excitement caused by the healing and the sermon did not long escape the attention of the authorities. The priests and temple guards, greatly disturbed because Peter and John were proclaiming

Jesus' resurrection from the dead, seized them and put them in jail overnight. The next day they were brought before Annas and Caiaphas and others who were responsible for Jesus' death. These, of all men, could not bear to hear the resurrection proclaimed.

No doubt they thought they could intimidate these simple Galilean fishermen, but they were quite wrong. The Peter who had denied His Lord in such cowardly fashion was no more. The man who stood before the Jewish leaders lived up to his name—the Rock. With unflinching courage, he accused them of murdering Jesus. But God raised Him from the dead, and it was in His name that the lame man was healed. Peter clinched his argument by quoting Psalm 118:22: Christ is "the stone you builders rejected, which has become the capstone." Peter's conclusion must have completely infuriated the priests: "Salvation is found in no one else, for there is no other name under heaven given to men by which we must be saved" (Acts 4:12). It is this claim above all others that makes Christianity unique. Salvation is not found in Mohammed or Buddha or any of the Hindu gods. It is available only in Jesus Christ.

The religious leaders were enraged, but they were also perplexed. To admit Peter's claim would be to admit that they had been wrong in opposing and killing Jesus. Yet the miracle could not be denied. Besides that, they feared the people, who continued to praise God because of the miracle. Unwilling to risk angering the crowd by harming Peter and John, they sternly forbade them to teach or speak in Jesus' name. But threats had no effect on Peter and John, who flung their threats right back into their faces. "Judge for yourselves," they said, "whether it is right in God's sight to obey you rather than God. For we cannot help speaking about what we have seen and heard" (Acts 4:19, 20). For two thousand years these words have echoed down the corridors of time, inspiring every Christian who has been threatened by some mighty king or petty tyrant.

The Church Meets Physical Needs
Acts 4:32-37

In the days and weeks immediately following Pentecost, members of the church shared their possessions so that no one was in need. This practice began in a unity of heart and mind among the members. This kind of singleness of heart and mind has been exceedingly rare in the history of the church. The lack of it is one reason that the modern church is not able to have the impact on its unbelieving neighbors that the Jerusalem church did. The sharing was based also on a concept of stewardship that recognized that all things ultimately belong to God. The Christians were entrusted with certain possessions, but they realized that these were theirs only to use for the good of God's kingdom. Because of this idea of stewardship, no one among them was in need of food and shelter.

There was a special reason for need among these first Christians. They met every day to hear the apostles teach (Acts 2:46). Their jobs and businesses must have been neglected or abandoned. Many of them were soon out of money; but those who had money were willing to share, and many sold property so they would have something to share. The love and concern shown by these Christians undoubtedly made an impression on unbelievers around them. The apostles continued to preach the resurrection of Christ with great power, but this power was enhanced by the witness of generous, loving lives.

At this point the apostles were in charge of the benevolent program of the church. As needs rose, Christians sold their houses or lands and brought the money to them. They in turn distributed this money to those who had needs. While the church was relatively small, the apostles could handle these matters and still have time for their preaching. The time would soon come, however, when they no longer had time to care for both jobs, as we shall see in the sixth chapter of Acts.

At this point Luke singles out one of the Jerusalem Christians for special mention. Joseph, a Levite from Cyprus, sold a field that he owned and brought the money to the apostles. The special mention suggests that his action was especially generous. Joseph soon was given the nickname Barnabas, which means "Son of Encouragement." This name stuck and apparently became the only name Joseph was called.

There has been much discussion about this practice of the Jerusalem church members in sharing their possessions. Some have called it a form of communism, and by some definitions of the term it was. But it certainly was not Marxian communism! First of all, we need to note that the sharing was voluntary and not achieved by force as is the practice of Marxism. More importantly, Marxism is atheistic and materialistic. It is quite impossible for a person to embrace Marxist philosophy and be a Christian at the same time.

It is worth noting that the practice of the Jerusalem church was not followed by other churches. Looking back on the history of that church, we can conclude that God himself guided its members into extraordinary sharing, even though all of them became poor. Within a short time they faced severe persecution, and many were driven out of Jerusalem (Acts 8:1). If they had clung to their possessions they would have lost them then, or would have been tempted to compromise their convictions in order to retain them. But with their possessions gone, they had no encumbrances to burden them when they had to flee. Furthermore, the intensive teaching in the daily meetings (Acts 2:46) had prepared them to be able preachers of the gospel (Acts 8:4). Thus the church began its marvelous spread outside of Jerusalem.

The practice of sharing possessions with one another was clearly not enjoined upon the whole church for every age. Each Christian was expected to earn his living if he could (2 Thessalonians 3:11, 12; 1 Timothy 5:8). Still the Christians everywhere continued to provide for those who could not provide for themselves (Ephesians 4:28), even for those in distant places (Romans 15:26). The example of concern for others demonstrated by the Jerusalem church should be a model for Christians in every age. Today the church has largely surrendered its benevolent responsibilities to government agencies. In so doing it has also surrendered the powerful witness the Jerusalem church was able to set forth in its community.

Liars in the Church
Acts 5:1-11

Even the Jerusalem church was not a perfect society. True piety and generosity invariably bring forth counterfeits. There have always been some who have wanted the credit for spiritual attainments without being willing to pay the price for them. Such were Ananias and Sapphira. It is rather ironic that Ananias' name means "Jehovah has graciously given."

The couple sold a piece of property and kept part of the money for themselves. Their little scheme was to give only part of the money to the apostles and take credit for giving the whole sum. This was no fleeting temptation that just happened to ensnare them. This was a deliberate and carefully planned plot to deceive the church.

But the scheme didn't work. Ananias had not counted on Peter's being able by divine power to read his heart. Why hadn't this possibility occurred to Ananias? He had certainly seen other miracles worked by the apostles. Peter gives us the answer. Satan had filled his heart. One of his favorite tricks is to deceive us as to the seriousness of our sins and then to deceive us as to their consequences.

Ananias was under no obligation to sell the property in the first place, nor was he obligated to give any part of it to the church. His sin was not in keeping the money, but in pretending that he had given more generously than he really had. In so doing he had lied, not just to the apostles or the church, but to the Holy Spirit (verse 3) and to God (verse 4). Confronted by his sin, he died on the spot. Those who heard about this were filled with fear.

Some of the younger men in the congregation wrapped him in grave clothes, carried him out, and buried him immediately. By custom and by necessity burial followed quickly after death. But still we may wonder why the burial was carried out even before Sapphira was notified. Learning of her husband's death, she might have repented. The only fair conclusion is that God knew her heart and knew that she would not truly repent even at the death of her husband.

Three hours later Sapphira arrived. Peter gave her an opportunity to tell the truth. His question was worded in such a way as to prick her conscience, but she was completely involved with her husband in the plot and brazenly lied to keep up the pretense. When Peter confronted her with her lie and the news that her husband was dead, she too died on the spot. The result in the church and in the community was predictable: "Great fear seized the whole church and all who heard about these events." Yet what followed shortly after was not so predictable. We might reasonably suppose that such an outpouring of God's judgment would have frightened off many members and certainly would have killed off any evangelistic efforts. But such was not the case. As the apostles continued to preach and work wonders among the people, "more and more men and women believed in the Lord and were added to their number" (Acts 5:14). As someone has put it, the subtraction of two led to the addition of many.

The Apostles Persecuted
Acts 5:12-42

The apostles continued to preach and perform miracles of healing, using Solomon's colonnade as a convenient meeting place for the large and growing crowds. This colonnade was along the east wall of the temple's outer court. The activities there could not escape the notice of the religious leaders. They watched, gnashed their teeth, and finally acted by throwing the apostles into jail. Imagine the surprise of the high priest and his associates the next morning when they found the apostles once more preaching to the crowds. Of course, at the time they had no way of knowing that an angel of the Lord had opened the doors of the jail and set them free.

The high priest called together the Sanhedrin, the full assembly of the elders of Israel, determined to put an end to this nonsense once and for all. The apostles were brought in from the temple court where they were preaching. Immediately they were accused of violating the high priest's orders not to teach in Jesus' name. Peter and the other apostles didn't deny the accusation for a minute. "We must obey God rather than men!" they said. Then they accused the Jewish leaders of killing Jesus, but declared that God raised Him up and exalted Him as Prince and Savior.

At these words the leaders became even more enraged. They might very well have killed the apostles right then had it not been for Gamaliel. Gamaliel was a Pharisee and a teacher highly esteemed by the people. Asking that the apostles be taken out of hearing of the discussion, Gamaliel gave his fellow rulers sound advice. He reminded them of a couple of earlier revolutionaries, Theudas and Judas of Galilee, each of whom had led followers in an uprising. Each movement had fallen apart after the death of its leader. Gamaliel advised restraint in persecuting the apostles, arguing that if their movement was human in origin, nothing would come of it. On the other hand, if it turned out that the movement was from God, then the Sanhedrin would find itself fighting against God. His argument was so persuasive that the Sanhedrin decided to let the apostles go. But before they released them, they beat them severely and ordered them not to speak in Jesus' name.

Such an experience might have left the apostles frightened and discouraged. Instead it had just exactly the opposite effect. They returned to their fellow Christians, "rejoicing because they had been counted worthy of suffering disgrace for the Name." Refusing to be intimidated by the threats and beatings of the Jewish leaders, they continued to teach daily in the temple and from house to house.

Meeting the Problem of Neglected Widows
Acts 6:1-7

Even a growing, dynamic church can have problems, and the church at Jerusalem was no exception. In this case the problem developed in the benevolent program. Through centuries before Jesus came, Jews had been scattered across the Roman Empire. Some had been transported by conquerors; some had gone volun-

193

tarily for business reasons. By the first century, many Jews had been born outside of Palestine and spoke Greek or some tribal tongue as their native language. They also picked up some of the other customs of their native lands. Many such Jews came to Jerusalem on Pentecost and became Christians. Because of their different culture, tensions developed between them and the Aramaic-speaking Jews of Palestine. (Aramaic was a Semitic language similar to Hebrew.) Similar tensions exist today between Jews who have immigrated to Israel from Western Europe and the United States and those who have come from Eastern Europe and Arab countries.

No doubt these tensions existed in many areas, but the problem came to a head in the daily distribution of food to the widows. This food was provided by generous Christians for the poor, and the widows were usually among the poor. The Grecian widows, those from foreign countries, complained that they were being neglected. Whether this neglect was real or only imagined, it needed immediate attention, and the apostles acted with dispatch. Wisely they chose not to handle the problem themselves, but to turn it over to others. It would have been poor stewardship of time for them to neglect preaching to do tasks that others could do just as well. There were other good reasons for turning the problem over to the people. For one thing, it gave the people some experience in decision-making. A church will not really grow spiritually unless its members are involved in making decisions as well as carrying them out. This situation gave seven men an opportunity to gain experience as leaders, and with that experience they soon became capable of larger tasks.

In turning the matter over to the congregation, the apostles' only stipulation was that the seven men selected be "full of the Spirit and wisdom." This is still good advice for congregations to follow when they select leaders. The congregation accepted this challenge and chose seven men. Interestingly, all seven bore Grecian names. This does not prove that they were all Grecian Jews, but it does show that they came from families that were not prejudiced against everything Greek. This suggests something about the sensitivity of the congregation. They put the solution of the problem in the hands of those who felt themselves being cheated—or who at least were sympathetic with the complainers. How quickly most of our church fights would evaporate if we could only learn to act so magnanimously!

The men selected were then presented to the apostles, who ordained them by praying and laying their hands upon them. There is nothing at this point in the narrative to indicate that this action imparted any special powers to the seven, though it may have done so. At least it indicated to all concerned that these men were set apart for a special service. It is quite appropriate that we follow this example today in ordaining officers of the congregation. These seven who were selected are sometimes referred to as "deacons." They are not called that in this passage, but the Greek word translated "wait on" in Acts 6:2 comes from the same root as does the word we translate "deacon."

With this problem settled, the "word of God spread" and new members were added rapidly to the congregation. Even a large number of priests became Christians, a fact that must have infuriated the high priest and his cronies. This may have been one of the factors that so aroused them that they were ready for violence, an example of which is treated in the next chapter.

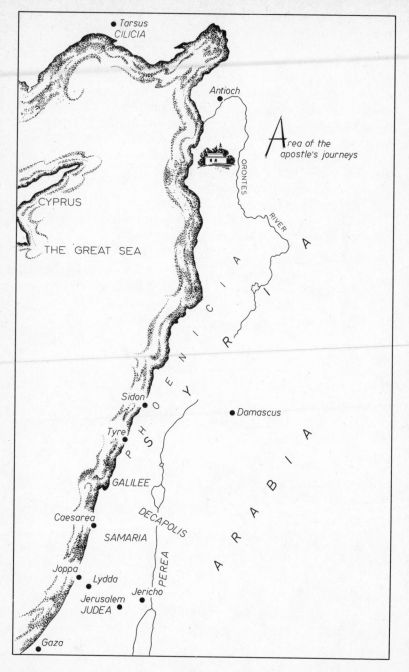

Tarsus
CILICIA

Antioch

ORONTES

RIVER

_Area of the
apostle's journeys_

CYPRUS

THE GREAT SEA

PHOENICIA

ARABIA

Sidon

Damascus

Tyre

GALILEE

DECAPOLIS

Caesarea

SAMARIA

PEREA

Joppa

Lydda

Jericho

Jerusalem
JUDEA

Gaza

ARABIA

Persecution and Expansion
Acts 6:8—8:40

The first five chapters of Acts are devoted mainly to the activities of the apostles as they led the church in Jerusalem. The sixth chapter records that seven men were chosen to manage the care of the poor. Soon two of these men, Stephen and Philip, became actively involved in other ministries. Stephen's preaching so aroused the anger of unbelieving Jews that he was murdered. In the persecutions that followed, Christians were forced to flee Jerusalem. Wherever they went, they proclaimed the gospel. Luke tells us of the experience of Philip, who went to Samaria to preach.

Stephen's Preaching Arouses Opposition
Acts 6:8-11

We are not told how long Stephen's ministry was confined to benevolent work, but certainly before very long he was actively involved in preaching. Accompanying his preaching were great wonders and miraculous signs. We do not know when or how he received the power to perform miracles. Some think the apostles imparted this power to him when they ordained him for service in the benevolent program (Acts 6:6). Philip, who was ordained at the same time, also had this power (Acts 8:6). Five others were ordained along with these two, and we are not told whether they received miraculous power or not.

Before very long Stephen's preaching aroused opposition. This came first from members of the Synagogue of the Freedmen rather than from the high priest and his comrades. There were many synagogues in Jerusalem, each appealing to its own constituency. The name *Freedmen* suggests that the members of this particular synagogue were slaves who had been freed by the Romans. Some think this one synagogue had members from different areas—Cyrene, Alexandria, Cilicia, and Asia. Others think men from these areas belonged to other synagogues, but joined the freedmen in opposing Stephen. In either case we see that Stephen was opposed by Greek-speaking Jews who had come from countries outside Palestine. It seems likely that Stephen had been preaching in Greek in their synagogue or synagogues. This explains why they attacked him rather than the apostles who taught in Aramaic. This was the native language of the Hebrews in Palestine of that time. It is called Hebrew in some versions of the Bible (John 5:2; 19:20; Acts 21:90), but it was somewhat different from the Hebrew of the Old Testament.

For a time Stephen's opponents tried to debate with him, but they could not match "his wisdom or the Spirit by which he spoke." Guided by the Holy Spirit, Stephen was wise in showing how Jesus fulfilled the Old Testament prophecies of the Christ. He did this so convincingly that the opponents could not answer him, but they were not willing to accept a Christ who would not establish an independent kingdom of Israel. Unable to best Stephen in fair debate, they soon resorted to underhanded methods. They persuaded some men to say he had blasphemed against Moses and against God. Probably they twisted some of his words to make them sound blasphemous. Similar tactics were used against Jesus at His trial (Matthew 26:59-61).

Stephen Before the Sanhedrin
Acts 6:12-15

Stephen's opponents played their hand well. Spreading the charge of blasphemy, they soon aroused the people, along with elders and teachers of the law, to take action. They seized Stephen and took him to the Sanhedrin. There the false witness made two charges against him.

First, they said he kept attacking the temple. Stephen's defense before the Sanhedrin may reveal the basis for that charge. He argued that God does not live in houses built by men (Acts 7:48). If he had been saying that before, we can see why the people of Jerusalem were angry. They had both a patriotic and an economic interest in the temple. It was at the center of their national pride and their pride was hurt when Stephen spoke lightly of it. Also, the tourist trade would be hurt if people from all over the empire no longer felt the necessity of coming to Jerusalem for the great Jewish feasts. Thus business interests combined with national pride to make the people of Jerusalem resent anything that might be taken to be disrespectful towards the temple.

The second charge was that Jesus of Nazareth would change the customs Moses handed down. At this point the Christians were continuing to meet in the temple for worship, and undoubtedly they were still observing the laws of Moses. There is no evidence that they ever urged Jews to abandon those customs, though they did insist that Gentiles who became Christians did not have to become Jews. But Christians taught that obeying Moses' law was not enough. Even Pharisees needed to be born again (John 3:1-5). Even Jews in good standing needed to repent and be baptized so their sins would be forgiven (Acts 2:38). An enemy would think this was reason enough to charge them with changing the customs Moses established.

Apparently Stephen was not given a chance to speak until the witnesses had finished their testimony. He sat through the proceedings with a certain calmness that even his enemies noted. His face was like that of an angel. There was in his countenance the visual evidence that he had put his life in the hands of God, and so with serenity and assurance he could face whatever might come. When the witnesses had finished giving their testimony against him, Stephen was allowed to speak in his own defense.

Stephen's Defense Before the Sanhedrin
Acts 7:1-50

Stephen's speech is one of the longest recorded in the book of Acts, which suggests something about its importance. In it Stephen did much more than defend himself against the charges of his opponents. By basing his speech on Israel's long history, he was at first able to get a sympathetic hearing from the Sanhedrin. After all, who doesn't enjoy hearing his glorious history repeated? But more than that, he was laying out a philosophy of history that placed God at the very heart of it, watching over His people and intervening when necessary to rescue them. Stephen also pointed out that the people often had been stiff-necked and rebellious. Even that was quite acceptable to his hearers. They freely acknowledged the sins of their ancestors. They listened calmly, even approvingly, till Stephen came to the climax of his speech and charged his hearers with the same kind of rebelliousness. Before coming to that point, the body of this speech falls into three parts: the period of the patriarchs (Acts 7:2-16); the period of Moses (Acts 7:17-43); and the period of the tabernacle and the temple (Acts 7:44-50).

Quite appropriately, Stephen began with Abraham. God called him while he still lived in Mesopotamia, challenging him to leave his home and traditions and follow where God would lead. Stephen may have been suggesting that his hearers should display a similar willingness to leave behind their old traditions and follow God's leading in Christ, but the suggestion was too subtle for them to see it yet.

After mentioning Isaac and Jacob, Stephen introduced Joseph. Though Joseph was rejected by his brothers, it was he who saved them. In this he was similar to Jesus. Jesus too was rejected by His Jewish brothers, yet He alone could bring them salvation. The many mistakes of God's people in ancient times ought to warn the people of Stephen's time and ours to avoid similar mistakes.

Moses also was a savior of his people, although they rejected him time and again and "in their hearts turned back to Egypt." Stephen referred to Deuteronomy 18:15 to show that Moses predicted the coming of a prophet like himself (Acts 7:37). That prophet was Jesus Christ.

Stephen then reminded them of the tabernacle that had been made according to God's pattern. Eventually the tabernacle was replaced by the temple, which was planned by David but actually built by Solomon. Then came Stephen's bombshell: "The Most High does not live in houses made by men." He quoted Scripture (Isaiah 66:1, 2) to prove that God has Heaven as His throne and earth as His footstool. Since God made the whole universe, what need has He for a building man makes with his own hands?

This issue may not seem especially pertinent to us, now that the temple is long gone. But Stephen's thought has wider applications. God cannot be localized or confined. There are always subtle temptations to suppose that God is somehow locked into a particular socioeconomic class, or a particular denomination, or a favored nation. Of course we deny ever harboring such an idea, but our actions sometimes betray our inmost thoughts.

Stephen's Application
Acts 7:51-53

Until the final few sentences of Stephen's argument, the audience was with him. He reminded them of their long history, a story they loved to hear even though it was familiar. He sounded completely orthodox, and may even have garnered a few amens. Thus his audience was hardly prepared for the jarring conclusion of his sermon. "You stiff-necked people," he charged, "with uncircumcised hearts and ears! You are just like your fathers: you always resist the Holy Spirit!" Their fathers had persecuted the prophets. Now they in turn had murdered the Righteous One whom the prophets had looked forward to. They had not learned at all from the mistakes of their forefathers who had persecuted God's spokesman. They had made the very same mistake. But the one they had crucified was more than just another spokesman, He was the Son of God.

The Stoning of Stephen
Acts 7:54—8:1

This was more than the rulers could stand. Stephen had been brought before them charged with blasphemy; but instead of denying the charge and defending himself, he had charged them with murdering the Christ. As their rage reached the boiling point, Stephen showed no fear. He looked up into Heaven and reported what he saw. "Look," he said, "I see heaven open and the Son of Man standing at the right hand of God" (Acts 7:56).

On this same spot Jesus had stood and made a similar statement. When the high priest had demanded that Jesus tell him whether He was the Messiah, He had replied, "I am." Then He had gone on to state that they would see the Son of Man sitting at the right hand of God and coming on the clouds (Mark 14:62). This statement was all the evidence the Sanhedrin needed to convict Jesus of blasphemy. Stephen's statement they took to be equally blasphemous.

The staid members of the Sanhedrin completely lost control of themselves, and legal formalities were cast to the wind. Those who started out to conduct a proper judicial hearing ended by becoming a howling lynch mob. They dragged the helpless Stephen outside the city, where they stoned him.

A question arises at this point. This same Sanhedrin had not dared to kill Jesus without the approval of the Roman governor, Pilate (John 18:31). How did they dare to kill Stephen? Obviously they were so carried away by their anger that they gave no thought to such a legal nicety. Pilate himself probably was in Caesarea rather than Jerusalem. He had troops stationed in Jerusalem to control rioters, but in this case perhaps the murder was done and the mob dispersed before the soldiers could get into action.

At this point Luke introduces Saul of Tarsus, who is later to play an important role in the book of Acts. At first glance, he may appear to be only a bystander. However, he was custodian of the coats of those who began the stoning, he approved what was being done, and he took a leading part in the persecution that followed (Acts 7:58; 8:1, 3). These facts suggest that he was acting in some official capacity, even though the stoning was supposedly unofficial.

Even as the stones struck Stephen, he prayed that the Lord would receive him. Then as he fell to his knees, his last words were for the forgiveness of his persecutors (Acts 7:59, 60). Thus in his death he became the model for the long line of martyrs from his time right up to this very day. From that day to this, men have gone to meet Jesus with a song in their hearts and a prayer on their lips for the forgiveness of their persecutors. Yet after nearly two thousand years the tyrants have not learned that, in the words of Tertullian, "the blood of the martyrs is the seed of the church." And even as the executions continue, the church survives and grows.

Not only did Stephen set an example for future martyrs; there is little doubt that the way he died had a profound effect on Saul. Saul immediately unleashed a wave of suffering upon the church, but the very violence of his actions suggests that the terrible seed of self-doubt was beginning to take root in his heart. He was the more furious because he was fighting his own misgivings as well as the Lord's disciples. When finally the Lord confronted him on the road to Damascus, Saul's heart was prepared to listen.

The Church Scattered
Acts 8:1-3

Devout men buried Stephen, but the antagonism against Christians was not buried with him. His death sparked a terrible new wave of persecution for the church. The leader in this new campaign of violence was Saul. Though he had been a student of Gamaliel, he was quite unwilling to follow his teacher's more tolerant advice about how to deal with Christians. The "wait and see" attitude of Gamaliel (Acts 5:33-39) did not satisfy the impatient Saul. He wanted action right now. He was not content just to prevent Christians from worshiping in public; he went from house to house, dragging men and women off to prison. The Sanhedrin was undoubtedly pleased to have such a zealot carry out their work for them, and they probably provided enough temple guards for him to do the job effectively.

Philip in Samaria
Acts 8:4-25

Since Christians were no longer safe in Jerusalem even in their own homes, they had little choice but to leave the capital city. We in the twentieth century who have seen so many political and religious refugees know something about how terrible this can be. But God can use even terrible persecutions for His glory, and He did in this case. Those who fled Jerusalem "preached the word wherever they went." Paul's efforts to stamp out the church only led to its more rapid spread.

Philip, one of the seven chosen to care for the poor, was one of those forced to leave Jerusalem. He may have gone to Samaria because it offered a safe refuge. Since the Jews and the Samaritans mutually despised one another, Philip had good reason to think the Samaritans would not be eager to cooperate with Saul. Another reason for going to Samaria was that Jesus had commanded it (Acts 1:8). It was unfortunate that it took persecution to make the Christians carry out this part of the Great Commission. There was still another reason for going to Samaria. Jesus had worked there to prepare the soil for the coming of the gospel (John 4:1-42; Luke 17:11-19).

We do not know exactly where Philip worked in Samaria. The *King James Version* says it was the city of Samaria, but several modern translations have "a city in Samaria." The ancient city of Samaria, the capital of Israel, had been destroyed more than a hundred years earlier. Later it had been rebuilt by Herod the Great, who renamed it Sebaste.

Philip performed many miracles among the Samaritans, including the healing of cripples and the casting out of demons. As a result many responded to the gospel and were baptized.

One of those who were greatly impressed by Philip's miracles was Simon the sorcerer. He himself had enjoyed quite a following among the people as a wonder worker, but he quickly recognized that his powers were limited in comparison to those demonstrated by Philip. Finally Simon himself believed and was baptized (Acts 8:13).

When word of the evangelistic campaign in Samaria reached Jerusalem, Peter and John were sent to Samaria. The purpose of their visit is not stated. Perhaps they went to investigate, to be sure all was in order. Perhaps they went to help and encourage, to assure the new Christians of support and fellowship. Perhaps they went to do what they did do, as recorded in the next verse.

When the two apostles arrived, they found that none of the Samaritan Christians had received the Holy Spirit. Does that mean they had not received the gift of the Holy Spirit mentioned in Acts 2:38—the gift received by Jerusalem Christians and twentieth-century Christians upon baptism? If that is the meaning, several questions arise. (1) Why did they not receive that gift when they were baptized? (2) How did anyone know they had not received it? (3) After the apostles prayed and laid hands on them, how could anyone know they had received the gift? (4) Specifically, how could Simon see that the Spirit was given? (5) Why did Simon attach any monetary value to the ability to give that invisible gift?

These questions are hard to answer. It seems more probable that we are to understand that the Samaritan Christians had not received the Holy Spirit with miraculous power, as the apostles and Philip had. It could readily be seen that they had no such power. After the apostles prayed and laid hands on them, it could readily be seen that they did have, and Simon could see the monetary value of such power. We conclude that Peter and John, by prayer and the laying on of their hands, were able to convey to others the power to perform miracles.

Simon immediately saw the economic potential of this power possessed by Peter and John. He wanted the power to give others the ability to work miracles. He could envision himself a wealthy man if he could have such power at his command. There was nothing subtle about Simon's approach. Like many in our day, he mistakenly thought that everything had a price tag on it. Peter's answer was short and to the point: "May your money perish with you, because you thought you could buy the gift of God with money!" The Phillips translation puts it even more bluntly: "To hell with you and your money! How dare you think you could buy the gift of God?" Peter then admonished him to repent of this wickedness. Simon, shocked by Peter's words, asked the apostles to pray for him that he might escape the dreadful punishment that was in store for him. Commentators debate whether this request was sincere or not. Later traditions—and these are only traditions—tell us that Simon became a great apostate. But the Scriptures are silent about his later years. His name is the source of the word *simony,* which means the buying and selling of religious offices.

Philip Converts an Ethiopian
Acts 8:26-40

In the midst of a highly successful evangelistic campaign, Philip was called to a new ministry. But this was not the call of a pulpit committee from a larger church offering financial inducements. An angel of the Lord came with a message from the throne of God. "Go south to the road—the desert road—that goes down from Jerusalem to Gaza," he said. With such a call, Philip didn't waste any time starting south, even though he had no idea what he would do when he reached that road.

On the Gaza road, Philip saw a chariot approaching. At that time he had no way of knowing that the chariot carried a high official over the treasury of Queen Candace of Ethiopia. *Ethiopia* here refers to the modern Sudan, the area immediately south of Egypt, rather than the area we today call Ethiopia. All kinds of speculation have arisen about the man from there. Was he black or white? Was he a Jew by birth, or a Gentile convert to the Jewish faith? There is simply no way that we can answer these questions with assurance. It is entirely possible that the man was born a Jew. The lives of Joseph, Daniel, and Nehemiah give us examples of Jews who gained prominent places in foreign governments. Further, many Jews settled in southern Egypt following the destruction of the temple by the Babylonians.

In any event, the Ethiopian was returning from Jerusalem, where he had gone to worship, probably at one of the great feasts. This indicates that his faith was Jewish, whatever his ancestry was. As he rode along in his chariot, he was reading aloud from Isaiah 53. Philip, who had been directed by the Spirit to approach the chariot, heard the man reading. This prompted him to ask the man if he understood what he was reading. The man was baffled by the passage, as were most Jews of that day. This passage describes the Messiah as a suffering servant, and it really is hard to understand unless one sees that Jesus is that suffering servant.

This provided a perfect opening for Philip, who proceeded to use Isaiah's words as a starting point to tell the good news about Jesus. The Ethiopian was a very receptive listener, and as they came to a stream, he asked to be baptized. We gather from this that Philip's preaching of the good news included some mention of baptism. Since the man had been led to believe that Jesus was the Christ and was willing to commit his life to Him, there was no good reason why he should not be baptized. The Ethiopian ordered the chariot stopped, and he and Philip went down into the stream, where Philip baptized him. Once they had come up out of the water, the Spirit suddenly took Philip away. But that did not keep the man from rejoicing as he went on his way. We would like very much to know what happened to him when he got back home. We would like to believe that he became an active evangelist, but while we know that Christianity in Ethiopia dates backs to an early date, there is no historic evidence to connect it to this treasurer of the queen.

Philip next appeared in Azotus, the Philistine city of Ashdod in the Old Testament. From there he moved up the coast, preaching as he went, until he came to Caesarea. There he is mentioned for the last time in the New Testament (Acts 21:8, 9).

The Conversion of Saul

Acts 9:1-31

In chapter 9 of Acts, Luke begins to shift his focus of attention from the twelve apostles and Jerusalem with its surrounding territory to Saul of Tarsus and the whole Roman Empire. As Saul (soon to be called Paul) and his companions are mentioned more and more frequently, Peter and the other apostles are mentioned less and less. We often say that all men are equal before God, and of course that is true in a way. But some men, because of their greater dedication, their greater skills, and their available opportunities, are able to make far greater contributions to the kingdom of God. Saul of Tarsus was one of those dedicated, gifted men who was in the right place at the right time to serve God in an outstanding way. There is no doubt that in time the church could have spread across the Roman Empire without him. At the same time, there is no doubt that the evangelistic sweep was more rapid and more effective because of him.

Saul's Conversion
Acts 9:1-19a

Saul didn't start out as a great preacher of the gospel. After doing his best to stamp out the church in Jerusalem, he was determined to seek out Christians in other areas. We have difficulty dating the events of this time. Scholars generally accept the fact that the church began on Pentecost in A.D. 30. But after that, there are few references to contemporaneous events in the secular world to give us precise dates for this period. Later in Saul's ministry we do have some such references, but not here. As a result, scholars are not in agreement about when these events occurred. Some, F. F. Bruce, for example, date Saul's conversion as early as A.D. 33. Others date it as late as A.D. 36.

Once the members of the Jerusalem church were either scattered or driven underground, Saul went to the high priest and asked for authority to go to Damascus to ferret out Christians there. Apparently some of the Jerusalem Christians had fled to Damascus to escape persecution, but Saul was determined that they would find no refuge there. The letters he received gave him authority to go into the synagogues and find those who belonged to "the Way," an interesting term used to designate Christians (Acts 19:9, 23; 24:14, 22). The city of Damascus, one of the oldest cities in the world, lay east of the Anti-Lebanon Mountains, and about a hundred thirty-five miles north-northeast of Jerusalem.

Armed with the letters and accompanied by a body of soldiers or temple guards, Saul set out for Damascus, about a week's journey away. As he neared the city, suddenly a brilliant burst of light surrounded him. From shock or from reverence before the supernatural, he fell to the ground. Then he heard a voice calling, "Saul, Saul, why do you persecute me?" Of course Saul had not directly persecuted Jesus; but he had persecuted Jesus' followers, and this amounted to the same thing. See Matthew 25:41-46.

"Who are you, Lord?" asked Saul. The term *Lord* sometimes is a term of respect similar to our *Sir.* Sometimes it is used of God. We cannot tell just how much respect or reverence Saul meant to express at the time. However, the light was brighter than the noonday sun (Acts 26:13). Certainly it was more than natural, and anyone who spoke from such a light must be more than human. Saul did not yet know who it was, but he responded with respect.

Then the speaker identified himself: "I am Jesus, whom you are persecuting." These words, like a sharpened sword, must have slashed through to the very heart of Saul. Suddenly he was faced with the realization that he had given himself totally to a cause that was completely wrong. Yet there is a suggestion that in the depths of his heart he had been undergoing a struggle. When Paul later related this experience before Agrippa, he included a further statement of the Lord: "It is hard for you to kick against the goads" (Acts 26:14). This is a reference to the long goads used to drive oxen.

These sticks had a sharp point that was used to direct the ox. If he stubbornly refused to obey, he felt the sharp point. The more he resisted, the worse the pain. This leads us to believe that deep down Saul had some misgivings about his mission to Damascus, some pricking of conscience that became more painful as he resisted it and concealed his misgivings with ever more violent action. Now in one dramatic, explosive moment the whole thing came to a head.

We can only imagine the thoughts that raced through Saul's mind. The men who traveled with him were of little help. They had seen the bright light and heard the sound, but they had no idea what was going on. Finally Saul staggered to his feet; but when he opened his eyes, he discovered to his horror that he could not see. Now his companions could help. Helpless as a baby, he had to be led by the hand into Damascus. There he was taken to the house of Judas on Straight Street, where he remained for three days without food or drink. Those certainly must have been the longest days in his whole life. Not only was he helpless, but all his future dreams and ambitions had suddenly collapsed about him.

As he remained in this state, the Lord was at work. He spoke to a man by the name of Ananias, a disciple living in Damascus. The Lord told him to go to the house where he would find Saul in prayer. But Saul's reputation had preceded him, and Ananias had some misgivings about getting that close to such a terrible enemy. Ananias knew that Saul had come to Damascus for the express purpose of persecuting Christians, and he had no wish to be first on the list.

The Lord reassured Ananias, informing him that Saul was God's chosen instrument to carry the message of salvation to the Gentile world. Laying aside his fears, Ananias then made his way to the house where Saul was staying. When he entered the room, he immediately placed his hands on Saul and greeted him in a manner that broke down any barriers: "Brother Saul," he said. Might not we also be able to defuse many tense situations by a similar attitude of openness and brotherliness?

Then Ananias informed Saul that Jesus had sent him that he might see again and receive the Holy Spirit. Immediately something like scales fell from Saul's eyes, and he was able to see again. After informing Saul that he was to become God's chosen vessel to carry the message to the Gentile world, Ananias said to him, "What are you waiting for? Get up, be baptized and wash your sins away, calling on his name" (Acts 22:16). Saul obeyed without question, and after taking food he began to regain his strength.

Saul's Early Ministry
Acts 9:19b-25

Luke gives us only an abbreviated account of what happened after that, and so we need to consult Paul's letter to the Galatians to fill in some of the other details. See Galatians 1:13-24. Immediately after his baptism, Saul began to preach in the synagogues of Damascus. His message, that Jesus is the Son of God, brought surprise to all who heard him. They recognized that he was the one who had created such havoc among Christians in Jerusalem, and they knew that he had come to Damascus for the same purpose. They could not understand the complete change they now saw in him. Many challenged the message he was preaching, and many debates must have followed. But the challengers were no match for Saul, who was a scholar of the Old Testament and who now had further enlightenment from the Holy Spirit. The Old Testament that he knew so well now became the basis for proof that Jesus was the long-awaited Messiah.

After a short time in Damascus, Saul left the city for an extended stay in Arabia. This was probably not the Saudi Arabia that we know, but the Nabataean kingdom, which held a large area east of Palestine and at this time ruled Damascus. Its king was Aretas. It is often said that Saul spent this time in prayer and quiet meditation, and certainly it took some thinking to bring his earlier education in line with what he now knew about Jesus. But during the rest of his life he was a human dynamo, constantly busy and on the go. The only quiet periods he had came when he was locked up in jail. It is likely that in Arabia he continued to preach that Jesus was the Messiah, the Son of God, but we have no record of his preaching or its results.

After a time, he returned to Damascus, where once more he engaged in preaching. This time the opposition became so bitter that his life was endangered. When Saul learned of the plot to assassinate him, he sought once more to leave Damascus; but the assassins enlisted government help and watched the gates of the city so doggedly that he could not escape (2 Corinthians 11:32). As long as he remained in the city, his life was in danger. Saul and his friends realized that before long the assassins would find a way to get to him. Therefore a plan was devised to get him safely out of the city. Although his enemies could maintain a constant watch on the gates, they could not keep all the walls under surveillance. Through an opening in the wall, Saul's friends lowered him to the ground in a basket. Probably friends awaited outside the wall to escort him to safety. This was but the first of many brushes Saul had with death—already he was beginning to experience how much he must suffer for Christ's name (Acts 9:16).

Saul in Jerusalem
Acts 9:26-31

From Damascus, Saul made his way back to Jerusalem, whence he had come some three years earlier (Galatians 1:18). (Actually the time may have been somewhat less than three full years, since it was a common practice to count any part of a year as a whole year.) His stay in Jerusalem was brief. He was, to use a term employed by modern diplomats, *persona non grata*. His former companions had certainly heard of his conversion, and they wanted nothing to do with him. Knowing Saul, we have a feeling that he tried to reach them with the gospel, but with no success. On the other hand, the disciples were suspicious of him. After all, some of them probably bore on their bodies the scars that Saul's efforts had inflicted. They too had heard reports of his conversion, but they were discreetly cautious lest this be some kind of a trap set by Saul's vicious mind.

It was Barnabas, good old Barnabas the big-hearted, who finally broke the ice. Barnabas was willing to listen to Saul's story and immediately was convinced that it was true. He took Saul to the apostles so that they too could hear his story. Actually, most of the apostles were absent from Jerusalem at the time; but Saul conferred with Peter and with James, the Lord's brother, who had become an outstanding leader among the Christians (Galatians 1:18, 19).

Almost as soon as Saul arrived in Jerusalem, he began to proclaim Jesus as the Messiah. He centered his attention on the Grecian Jews, the same group who had reacted so violently to the preaching of Stephen. They responded no less violently to Saul, seeking some way to kill him. Saul seemed unconcerned about his own physical danger and might very well have stayed there had he not received orders from on high. One day while praying in the temple, he fell into a trance and heard the Lord saying, "Quick! Leave Jerusalem immediately, because they will not accept your testimony about me." When Saul argued that he ought to be permitted to stay, the Lord responded, "Go; I will send you far away to the Gentiles" (Acts 22:17-21). Finally convinced that he must leave Jerusalem, Saul was escorted down to Caesarea by some of the brothers and put on a ship to Tarsus, his hometown.

Following Saul's departure from Jerusalem, the church enjoyed a period of peace. The persecutions directed by him had scattered the Christians in all directions. Courageously the apostles had stayed in Jerusalem for a time (Acts 8:1), but it seems that in time most of them went to minister in other places so that Saul saw only Peter (Galatians 1:19). With much of the leadership absent from Jerusalem and Saul no longer whipping up antagonism against the believers, this wave of persecution ebbed away. A zeal for persecution is hard to maintain at a white heat without available victims and without the single-minded leadership that Saul supplied. Whatever the reasons for this brief period of peace, the church enjoyed it and took advantage of it to grow both in numbers and in spiritual maturity.

The Significance of Saul's Conversion

The conversion of Saul must be considered one of the most significant events in the history of the early church. The missionary thrust was dramatically advanced by Saul's efforts. The thrust that broke out of the narrow confines of Judaism began when Peter converted Cornelius and convinced his fellow Christians that the gospel was not for Jews alone (Acts 10, 11). It continued when unnamed brethren preached to Gentiles in Antioch (Acts 11:20). Persons unknown to us also planted the gospel in Rome, North Africa, and other places. But God powerfully used Saul of Tarsus to establish churches in the population centers of Asia Minor and Greece, and to convince Jewish Christians for the second time that in Christ there is no wall between Jews and Gentiles (Acts 15).

Saul's change was complete. He had been a bitter persecutor of Christ's disciples. Now he was one of them. How can this dramatic change be explained? Clearly it did not occur because Saul sought honor or prestige. He had these already as a leader among the Jews. He lost them when he became a Christian. Nor could he have turned to Christianity in search of wealth. The Christians were as a group quite poor, and anyone who joined them could hardly expect to escape the same poverty.

Some may argue that Saul suffered some kind of an emotional breakdown. Most of us have seen persons whose personality changed completely as a result of such a breakdown. Usually these people are either in institutions or are incapable of functioning powerfully in the real world. Saul's change does not fit this pattern. No one, not even his worst enemies, could accuse him of being incapacitated by his experience. He was an efficient missionary, an able administrator, and a remarkable writer. Such a busy and fruitful life can hardly be expected from one who is emotionally unstable.

If any should doubt Saul's sincerity, a glance at the sacrifices he made and the suffering he willingly faced should dispel all doubt. He was willing to face any kind of suffering—beatings, stonings, imprisonment, and even martyrdom. Nor did strenuous labor, perils on land, or perils at sea deter him. These are the marks of a sincere man.

All of these things point to one fact. Saul was sincere and his conversion was real. This kind of evidence has, through the centuries, convinced men of the truth of Christianity. It still continues to convince men, and will so long as the ninth chapter of Acts remains in our Bible.

The Beginning of the Mission to the Gentiles

Acts 9:32—11:18

The tenth chapter of Acts tells of a most important event in the life of the church—the conversion of Cornelius. This marks the first long step in proclaiming the gospel to people outside of the Jewish nation and those closely related to the Jews. Philip had evangelized among the Samaritans, but they were akin to the Jews both racially and religiously. Philip also had baptized a man of Ethiopia, but he must have been a Jew either by birth or by conversion. Otherwise he would not have gone to Jerusalem to worship.

Cornelius was clearly different. He was a Gentile. He and his family had become believers in the true God, but there is nothing to indicate that he had become obedient to the law of Moses. Many Jewish Christians were less than enthusiastic about accepting Gentiles into the church; but with the conversion of Cornelius the door was opened, and it could never again be closed.

Peter Ministers in Lydda and Joppa
Acts 9:32-43

Peace came upon the church when the bitter persecution of Saul was ended. In that time of calm Peter could leave Jerusalem and visit congregations at some distance. We find him at Lydda, a town west of Jerusalem and about a dozen miles from the Mediterranean. Luke refers to the Christians living there as "saints," a designation that

Paul uses often in his epistles. It then meant "holy" or "set apart." Across the centuries the word has acquired other meanings. Today we are likely to think of a saint as one who has reached a high level of moral attainment. Only a few ever reach this exalted status. But this is not what the word means in the New Testament. A saint was one who was set aside or dedicated to God. A new Christian struggling to escape the clutches of the world and a mature Christian with years of service behind him were both called saints. The mature Christian with years of practice might live up to his dedication better than the beginner did; but both were dedicated to Christ, and so both were saints.

At Lydda, Peter found a paralytic named Aeneas. There is nothing to indicate that the man was a believer, but his healing opened the area for the preaching of the gospel. Peter was careful to point out that Aeneas was healed by the power of Jesus, not by any power of Peter's own. The healing was instantaneous, and the man was told to get up and make his bed. The effect on Lydda and the surrounding area was dramatic. Many came to the Lord following this miracle.

Word of Peter's activities soon spread to nearby Joppa, located on the coast. There was already a community of believers there, possibly the result of Philip's preaching (Acts 8:40). One of the disciples, a woman named Tabitha (Dorcas in the Greek, Gazelle in the English), became ill and died. Instead of being buried promptly, her body was placed in an upper room. Then the disciples sent for Peter.

Peter hastened to Joppa. He was greeted by several widows who, even as they mourned, showed him some of the clothing Dorcas had made for them. Though no one voiced the sentiment, yet they must have hoped that Peter might in some way be able to restore her. Without giving any indication of his intentions, he sent everyone out of the room. This reminds us of Jesus' action when He raised Jairus' daughter (Mark 5:40). With the mourners out of the room, Peter knelt down and prayed and then spoke to her: "Tabitha, get up." Immediately she opened her eyes and sat up. Peter took her hand and helped her to her feet.

Then came the happy moment when Peter called the people back into the room. They could hardly contain their joy when they saw their beloved Dorcas standing once more before them alive. This good news spread quickly, and before long the whole town knew about it. It should not surprise us that a revival meeting followed and many were won to the Lord.

Cornelius Calls for Peter
Acts 10:1-8

The scene now shifts from Peter in Joppa to Cornelius in Caesarea. This city was situated on the coast about thirty miles north of Joppa. It was a relatively new city, having been founded about 12 B.C. by Herod the Great, who named it in honor of Caesar Augustus. It quickly became an important city both as a seaport and later as a center of government. Some of the most impressive Roman ruins in Palestine may be found there today.

Luke identifies Cornelius in some detail because he played such an important part in the history of the early church. We learn that he was a centurion in the Roman army of occupation. Ordinarily a centurion commanded a group of one hundred men. He was responsible for training them, drilling them, and leading them in battle. However, it was not uncommon for a centurion to be detached from his troops and given a special assignment, so we do not know what Cornelius' duty was in Caesarea. Cornelius, along with his family, was devout and God-fearing. While he had not become a full proselyte to the Jewish faith—he was uncircumcised (Acts 11:3)—yet he was a believer in the true God. Perhaps he read the Hebrew Scriptures and attended the synagogue services. Such a person was sometimes referred to as a "proselyte of the gate." Cornelius reminds us of the centurion of Capernaum who was commended by Jesus for his faith (Luke 7:1-10). Cornelius' deeds matched his avowed convictions: he gave generously to the poor and prayed diligently.

At three o'clock one afternoon, Cornelius was observing his usual prayer period. This was the time of the afternoon prayer in Jerusalem, and devout Jews who lived at a distance from Jerusalem usually observed it. His prayer period was suddenly interrupted by the appearance of an angel. Although God at times does speak through dreams, this was not a dream. Cornelius was wide awake and in complete possession of all of his faculties. The angel stood before him and called him distinctly by name. As a Roman soldier, Cornelius had been trained to cope with hazardous situations, but nothing in his training had prepared him for this. It comes as no surprise that he was afraid.

The angel's first words reassured him. God had heard his prayers, and his good works had given indication of the sincerity of his prayers. Of course we do not know the content of Cornelius' prayers, but it is reasonable to suppose that he prayed for further enlightenment and direction for his life. No doubt many others had prayed similar prayers, but God chose to act upon Cornelius' prayer. Why God chose Cornelius above all others we do not know. We can only speculate that his character and reputation, his spiritual openness, and his position made him an appropriate person to lead the way as the doors of the church were opened to Gentiles. While Luke uses only a few words to describe Cornelius, everything he tells us increases our admiration for this man. He deserves the more credit because he remained admirable in spite of the many temptations that face a military man.

To Cornelius, the angel gave specific instructions. He was to send to Joppa for Peter, who was staying there at the home of Simon the tanner. As soon as the angel disappeared, Cornelius acted. Calling in two of his servants and a soldier, he told them of his vision and sent them on their way to Joppa. We are told that the soldier was a devout man, which was probably the reason he was chosen for this mission. The faith of the soldier under Cornelius' command seems to suggest that the centurion's influence extended beyond his own family.

Peter's Housetop Vision
Acts 10:9-23a

About noon the next day the messengers were already approaching Joppa. They must have left immediately after Cornelius' vision and walked most of the night to arrive so soon. Of course it is possible that they rode horseback. Peter had gone up on the top of the house to pray. On a typical Palestinian house the flat roof afforded an excellent place for fresh air, privacy, and prayer. As Peter waited for a meal to be prepared, he entered into a time of prayer. Before long, he fell into a trance. The word translated "trance" (ekstasis) is the word from which comes "ecstasy." It conveys the idea of existing outside of oneself, a state in which one is less conscious of things around him and more open to revelation from God. Apparently this was somewhat different from the wide-awake condition of Cornelius when the angel came to him.

Peter had an important lesson to learn, and God chose to teach that lesson in a dramatic fashion. Peter must have had all the typical Jewish prejudices against Gentiles. All of Jesus' teaching and even His final order to go into all the world probably had not shaken these prejudices. But in Peter's trance he saw heaven open up and a large sheet descend. This most unusual sheet contained all kinds of four-footed animals, reptiles, and birds. It is worth noting that God's revelation came to Peter while he was in prayer and in a most receptive attitude. Some have suggested that Peter's hunger and the presence of a cloth canopy over the roof may have given shape to his vision. If so, that in no way diminishes the divine nature of the message. Peter saw and heard what God wanted him to see and hear.

A most unusual command came: "Get up, Peter. Kill and eat." Peter did not ask how he was going to accomplish this without tools or equipment. Rather, his concern was about obedience to the Old Testament dietary laws. Not all animals could be used for food (Leviticus 11). Animals that had split hooves and chewed the cud were considered edible. Many birds were forbidden, especially birds of prey and carrion eaters. So were snakes, lizards, and other creeping things. And animals that were used for food must be carefully butchered and drained of blood (Leviticus 17:13, 14). With these regulations in mind Peter protested against the command. He had never eaten anything impure or unclean, and he did not intend to start now. But the voice reproved him for his objection: "Do not call anything impure that God has made clean." Apparently Peter was hard to convince, for the action was repeated two more times. He must have been quite perplexed about what the experience meant, but he did not have long to mull over the matter.

At that very moment the three men sent by Cornelius were at the gate, inquiring for Peter. Since Peter was no longer in a trance, the Spirit spoke to him. Whether He spoke audibly or silently, His message was plain. He told Peter to go downstairs and greet the men. Since the men were Gentiles, Peter may have had some problem with this; but the Spirit assured him that He had sent them. Still Peter's greeting does not sound very cordial: "I'm the one you're looking for. Why have you come?"

The men explained why they had come, and gave Peter the invitation to go with them to Cornelius' house. A day earlier Peter might have refused, but his bias was swept aside by the nature of their message along with the experience he had just gone through. Peter even invited the messengers to be his guests, an action that would have been unthinkable to an orthodox Jew.

Some have suggested that Peter had already compromised his orthodoxy by dwelling with a tanner. According to the Jewish tradition of that day, a tanner was considered unclean because he often worked with dead carcasses and with the skins of unclean animals. For that reason and because of the foul odors from the tanning process, tanners were required to live outside of town. Gradually Peter's narrow Jewish view was widening. He had entered into cordial fellowship with Samaritans (Acts 8:14-17). He had become a guest in the house of a tanner. Now he invited Gentiles to share that hospitality. But there was more to come.

Peter at the House of Cornelius
Acts 10:23b-48

The visitors spent the night at the house of Simon the tanner. The next day they set out for Caesarea, along with Peter and six of the brothers from Joppa (Acts 11:12). Cornelius anticipated their arrival and invited some of his relatives and friends to be there for the occasion. He wanted to share whatever message was to be brought by this man whom a shining angel had recommended. When Peter came in, Cornelius fell before him in reverence. The Greek word that is here translated "reverence" is translated "worship" in the *King James Version*. This must have been quite embarrassing to Peter. He said to Cornelius, "Stand up. I am only a man myself." God's human messengers make it plain that they are no more than human. Worship is to be offered to God only.

A good-sized audience was waiting, and probably it was composed entirely of Gentiles. Peter reminded them of the Jewish law that prohibited a Jew from associating with a Gentile. He explained that he was violating that prohibition because God had taught him not to call any people unclean. Peter did not reveal what a struggle it was for him to abandon the prejudice of a lifetime. God gave him a vision to help him, and the Holy Spirit plainly told him to go with the messengers; but even so it could not have been easy. Peter knew he would face criticism from his fellow Jews in the church in Jerusalem. He certainly is to be commended for his courage.

To explain why he had sent for Peter, Cornelius told of the angel who had comes to him four days earlier. Surely that helped bring Peter another step along the way as he left the accumulated prejudices of centuries and moved toward the truth. Jehovah God is the God of all nations and all races. He had blessed the Israelites in a special way, but these blessings were designed to prepare them to become the channel of God's blessing for all people. Now the time had arrived to tell the whole world that good news. God accepts all men who fear Him and do what is right. We have accepted this truism for so long that we fail to realize how revolutionary it was in the first century.

Starting with the ministry of John the Baptist, Peter then began to tell about Jesus. This was not entirely new to Cornelius and his friends, for everyone in that area had at least heard about the sensational ministry of Jesus. At the very heart of His story were the crucifixion and resurrection, facts attested to by many witnesses, including Peter himself. The climax of the message was that forgiveness of sin is available to any who are willing to believe in Him.

At that dramatic moment the Holy Spirit came upon those who heard the message. While no sound of a rushing wind was heard and no tongues like fire as at Pentecost, no one doubted the presence of the Holy Spirit. Cornelius and his friends were speaking in tongues as the apostles had done on Pentecost. The brothers from Joppa were amazed, not just that the Holy Spirit had come, but that He had come to Gentiles—and Peter may have been no less amazed.

There are several differences between what happened here in Caesarea and what happened in Jerusalem at Pentecost. At Pentecost the Spirit came upon the apostles, but not upon the hearers. At Caesarea He came upon the hearers but not upon the speaker. At Pentecost the apostles spoke in languages that visitors in Jerusalem understood. At Caesarea it is not clear what languages were spoken, nor whether anyone understood what was said.

Likewise the purpose of the Spirit's coming was similar, but different. At Pentecost the Spirit came to the apostles to show the hearers that those apostles were God's accredited spokesmen. At Caesarea the Spirit came to the hearers to show the speaker that those hearers were acceptable to God even though they were not Jews.

The unmistakable manifestations of the Holy Spirit prompted Peter to take the next logical step. Clearly God had made known His will that Cornelius and his household be received into the church, and Peter had no intention of trying to thwart the will of God. He ordered that they be baptized, and so the first Gentile members were added to the church.

The new Christians asked Peter to remain with them a few days. This allowed Peter to do further teaching, something that both he and Cornelius deemed necessary. The church today can well learn a lesson from this. Far too many are born into the kingdom and then are abandoned by the church that helped them gain the new life. Church rolls are filled with the names of babes in Christ who have died of spiritual starvation because they have been neglected by their more mature Christian brothers.

Peter Explains His Actions
Acts 11:1-18

When Peter admitted Gentiles to the church, the news spread swiftly "throughout Judea." This is another indication that it was truly revolutionary. Jewish Christians who heard about it were shocked, and lost no time in passing on the news. As a result, the Jewish Christians at Jerusalem were ready for Peter when he arrived. It is interesting that they did not charge Peter with baptizing Gentiles. Instead they were concerned about what certainly was a lesser offense—he was accused of entering into the home of a Gentile and eating with him. That was a clear violation of a well-established tradition.

Peter did not attempt to defend his position with theological arguments. Instead he simply told what had happened. When he had completed his story, especially the part about the outpouring of the Holy Spirit, the critics had three options open to them.

First, they could reject the whole thing either as an outright lie or as a figment of Peter's imagination. But Peter was very well known, and he was not known either for falsehood or for fantastic imagination. Besides, six brothers from Joppa could confirm his story of what happened at Caesarea. No doubt Peter had that in mind when he asked them to go with him.

The second choice was to accept the facts Peter presented, but to reject his conclusion that Gentiles should be welcomed into the church. But that too would be unreasonable. How could Christians bar anyone who had received the Holy Spirit?

Happily, the Christians chose the third option. They accepted both the facts and the action that resulted. Peter concluded his presentation with the statement that he did not want to be found opposing God. The Jewish Christians agreed. They dismissed their jealousy and praised God that He had granted the Gentiles repentance unto life.

We wish we could conclude this incident with "and they lived lived happily ever after," but it did not quite work out that way. The Jewish Christians were willing to accept this conclusion in theory, especially when it involved only an isolated case some distance from Jerusalem. Many began to have second thoughts, however, when Gentile converts became numerous. If we have trouble understanding why this later posed a problem, we have only to look at what has occurred in American churches in recent years. Few American Christians ever denied that the gospel is for all races. Many willingly gave money to send missionaries to work in Africa and Japan and Southeast Asia. But when a Black or Japanese or Cambodian showed up in their congregation—well, that was different!

Long after Cornelius and his friends became Christians, there was continuing controversy over admitting Gentiles into the church. Many Christians had trouble in overcoming their Jewish prejudices, but we can be thankful that most of them did overcome. If we are troubled because some Christians today still cling to prejudices, let us rejoice that so many have overcome them.

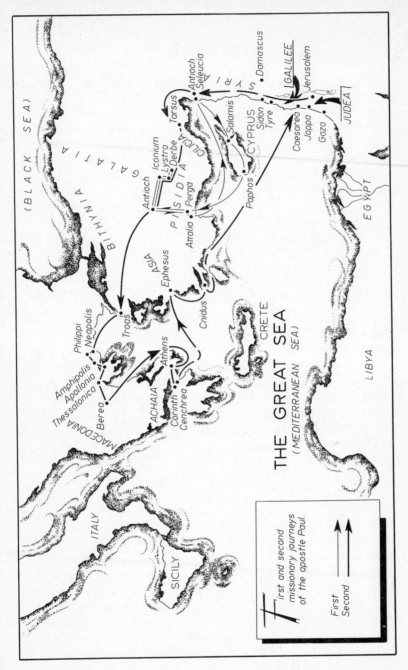

THE GREAT SEA
(MEDITERRANEAN SEA)

First and second missionary journeys of the apostle Paul.

First
Second

Paul's First Missionary Journey

Acts 11:19—14:28

After recording the conversion of Cornelius and the discussion that followed in the Jerusalem church, Luke turns to an exciting new phase of the expansion of the church. This phase began in Antioch, a city on the Orontes River about fifteen miles from the Mediterranean Sea. Antioch was the capital of Syria and the third largest city in the Roman Empire. Its population had reached five hundred thousand by the middle of the first century. More than a dozen cities bore the same name, and this city is usually referred to as Antioch of Syria to distinguish it from others.

Success in Antioch
Acts 11:19-30

Following Stephen's death and the ensuing persecution, Christians were scattered to Phoenicia, Cyprus, and Antioch, where they attempted to reach their fellow Jews with the gospel. But some of these scattered Jewish Christians were men of Cyprus and Cyrene. In those places they had lived among Gentiles before they went to Jerusalem and became Christians there. To them the gulf between Jews and Gentiles did not seem so wide as it did to Jews of Jerusalem. In Antioch they began to preach the gospel to Gentiles as well as to Jews. The results were dramatic—"The Lord's hand was with them, and a great number of people believed and turned to the

Lord" (Acts 11:21). Apparently there was no great objection from the Jews in Antioch, either from those who had become Christians or from those who had not. So, for the first time, there was a local church in which Jews and Gentiles mingled together happily as followers of Christ.

Before long, news of this great evangelistic effort came to Jerusalem. Earlier they had sent men to visit the first church among the Samaritans (Acts 8:14). So now they sent one of their members to visit the first church that included many Gentiles. The choice of an emissary was crucial. Had they sent someone who thought the Gentile Christians must become Jews, probably the evangelistic effort would have been killed or a serious division would have resulted in the church. Fortunately they chose Barnabas, who had already shown both his generosity and his openness to God's leading.

When Barnabas saw what was happening in Antioch, he became enthusiastically involved in it. Realizing the importance of the work in that great city, he soon saw that he needed help, and he knew where he could find it. Although he had not seen Saul for several years, he knew Saul could provide the kind of leadership needed in this great and growing church. And so he personally went to Tarsus to find Saul and bring him to Antioch.

The Scriptures provide us little information about Saul during this period of his life. Did his devoted Jewish family reject him because he had become a Christian? We are not told. Knowing Saul, we also feel sure he labored hard to win his family and others in Tarsus to Christ. But if his efforts had led to spectacular results, wouldn't Luke have recorded it? At least it seems that Saul was not totally estranged from his family. Years later a nephew did him a great favor that may have saved his life (Acts 23:12-24).

In Antioch, Barnabas and Saul labored together for a year with continued success. It was at this time that the disciples first came to be called Christians (Acts 11:26). During this period some prophets came to Antioch from Jerusalem. One of their number, Agabus, predicted that a severe famine would soon come. This would be especially hard on the Christians in Jerusalem. They were already impoverished for two reasons. First, they had left their jobs and businesses to listen to the apostles teach every day (Acts 2:46). Second, the great persecution had resulted in suffering and increased poverty (Acts 8:1-3). Therefore the Christians in Antioch took a collection for their brethren in Jerusalem. Barnabas and Saul were chosen to deliver it to the elders of the Jerusalem church.

Persecution in Palestine
Acts 12:1-25

At about this same time, King Herod unleashed a terrible persecution upon the church. This was Herod Agrippa I, grandson of the Herod who had killed the babies of Bethlehem at the time of Jesus' birth, and nephew of Herod Antipas, who had murdered John the Baptist. Agrippa now held sway over the same territory his grandfather had ruled. He was trying hard to win the favor of the Jewish leaders who hated the Christians. For that purpose Agrippa executed the apostle James, brother of John. Seeing that the Jews were pleased, the king arrested Peter, planning to deal with him when the week-long feast of unleavened bread was over. His plan failed when an angel set Peter free. After this, Herod returned to Caesarea, where God struck him down for his arrogance. Through all of this the "word of God continued to increase and spread" (Acts 12:24).

Barnabas and Saul Set Apart for Service
Acts 13:1-3

When Barnabas and Saul returned from Jerusalem to Antioch, they brought with them Barnabas' cousin, John Mark. (Some versions call him a nephew.) By this time several men in addition to Barnabas and Saul were providing leadership for the church. It is interesting to note that one of these leaders was Manaen, who had been brought up with Herod Antipas, the tetrarch. If he was about the same age as that Herod, who was born in 20 B.C., then he must have been in his sixties when he was leading in the church at Antioch. The presence of such a prominent person makes it clear that Christianity was not restricted to slaves and lower classes. People of all kinds can be saved.

On one occasion as the church worshiped and fasted, the Holy Spirit revealed His will to them. The time had come for the good news to be carried to more distant places, and the Spirit made it clear that Barnabas and Saul had been chosen for this mission. They were not selected by the church nor were they self-appointed. We are not told how the Holy Spirit made known His will in this matter, but it must have been clear enough that no one questioned it. The church then entered into a season of fasting and prayer in which the two were set apart for this ministry. The early church often fasted on occasions such as this, and the practice is still followed in ordaining Christians to a special ministry. While fasting is not specifically commanded, it lends solemnity and seriousness to the occasion.

226

First to Cyprus
Acts 13:4-12

Barnabas and Saul, sent on their way by the Spirit, traveled to Seleucia, the seaport of Antioch, and there took a ship to Cyprus, the original home of Barnabas. John Mark, the cousin or nephew of Barnabas (Colossians 4:10) accompanied them on this part of the journey. Though they were not the first to preach the gospel on this island, it seemed a reasonable place for them to begin. Barnabas knew the territory and was known there, which meant that it was likely to be easier for him to get a hearing.

Arriving at Salamis, they went first to the Jewish synagogues, a practice they were to follow during the rest of this journey. We are told nothing about the results of these efforts. Neither are we told whether they preached at other places on their way across the island. But we know they traveled some ninety miles to the capital, Paphos. Their preaching soon attracted the attention of Sergius Paulus, the proconsul, who sent for them in order to hear them. But Bar-Jesus (also known as Elymas), a Jewish sorcerer attached to the court of Sergius Paulus, did not share this enthusiasm for the word of God. In that day the Romans were quite superstitious, and even an intelligent Roman such as the proconsul often kept a sorcerer in his court. Bar-Jesus was determined to prevent Barnabas and Saul from getting a fair hearing. He knew that if Sergius Paulus accepted the gospel, his freeloading days in the court would be numbered.

Saul, who now for the first time was called Paul, was not inclined to tolerate any of the sorcerer's interference. Looking him straight in the eye, Paul minced no words in denouncing the man: "You are a child of the devil and an enemy of everything that is right!" Then Paul announced that the Lord would strike him blind for a season. Immediately the man was struck blind and had to seek someone to lead him about. It would be interesting to know how long he remained blind and what he did afterward. Was he convinced of the truth of the gospel, or did he just think Paul was a more powerful sorcerer? But Luke goes on with his story without pausing to give us any such information.

Sergius Paulus was tremendously impressed. He gave an attentive ear to the teaching brought by Paul and Barnabas. Luke succinctly records his response: "He believed." Scholars debate whether his faith was purely intellectual or whether he was baptized and became a Christian. Although Luke does not say Sergius Paulus was baptized, that seems to be the clear implication of the passage. In other passages "believed" seems to mean "became Christian" (Acts 13:48; 14:1; 17:34) and Christians are called "believers" or "those who believe" (Acts 2:44; 4:32; 5:14). Luke gives a most abbreviated report of the work of Barnabas and Paul in Cyprus. He does not mention any baptisms at all as they made their way through the island, yet it is hard to believe that no conversions resulted from their efforts.

From Cyprus to Pisidia
Acts 13:13-52

Luke gives no indication of how long Paul and Barnabas remained on the island of Cyprus; but once it was obvious that their work there was done, they sailed from Paphos to Perga in Pamphylia in Asia Minor. At this point John Mark left them and returned to Jerusalem. Since Luke suggests no reason for his departure, commentators have been free to offer a variety of motives. Some suggest that he was homesick; others believe that he was fearful of traveling into the interior of Asia Minor, where robbers might be hiding in the hills. Whatever his reason, Paul considered it less than honorable and refused to take him along on a later journey (Acts 15:36-40).

The two missionaries did not tarry long in Perga, but traveled directly on to Pisidian Antioch. Luke used this designation to distinguish it from Antioch of Syria, where they had begun this missionary journey. Antioch lay thirty-six hundred feet above sea level, giving it a more healthful climate than the coastal regions. Caesar Augustus had made it a Roman colony. There were a number of Jews living in Antioch, and also a number of Gentiles who had been attracted to the faith and joined in the synagogue worship.

On the first Sabbath following their arrival, Paul and Barnabas attended the synagogue service. They were at once recognized as visitors and were extended the courtesy of speaking to the group if they wished. That was exactly the invitation they were waiting for. On this occasion Paul became the spokesman. As he stood up, he motioned with his hand. This must have been a characteristic gesture of his. It is mentioned on other occasions (Acts 21:40; 26:1).

This is the first sermon of Paul that Luke records for us. He addressed the hearers as "men of Israel and you Gentiles who worship God," realizing that both Jews and Gentiles were present. What we read here is certainly not a verbatim record of all that Paul said, but a condensation of his message. At many points it parallels the speech Stephen presented before the Sanhedrin (Acts 7:1-53, discussed in chapter 21 of this book). Paul began by tracing the long history of God's dealings with the Israelites. The faith of Israel was grounded in history, and they never tired of hearing this history rehearsed.

The culmination of God's actions for Israel came when God brought the Savior Jesus, a descendant of King David. Paul's purpose was to show that Jesus did not come on the scene in some accidental fashion, but was the climax of all that God had done for His people. The tragedy came when the Jewish leaders at Jerusalem refused to recognize that Jesus was the Savior. Instead, they rejected Him and without any proper legal basis had Him executed. But the grave could not hold Him, for God raised Him from the dead. For many days He was seen by numerous witnesses.

Paul showed that because of the death and resurrection of Jesus the promises made to David and his generation were now available to the present generation. The promise was that their sins might be forgiven through faith in Jesus, a promise that could not be fulfilled earlier because man could not be justified through the law of Moses. After presenting God's plan for human redemption through Jesus Christ, Paul concluded with an appeal that they heed the message and not harden their hearts to it as their fathers had done in olden times.

The sermon was enthusiastically received, and Paul and Barnabas were invited to speak again about these matters the following Sabbath. Many, however, were not willing to wait until the next Sabbath. They followed the two men and continued the discussion. Word of this sermon spread quickly through the city. When the next Sabbath came, the synagogue was packed with eager listeners. The implication is that many of those who came were Gentiles. The Jews were upset by the response. Filled with jealousy by the popularity of this new message, they began to speak disparagingly about it.

Paul and Barnabas did not retreat from the challenge, but boldly defended the word they had proclaimed. Paul pointed out that his first obligation was to offer God's new terms of pardon to the Jews. When Jesus called Paul and commissioned him, he was called to be the apostle to the Gentiles. Yet even as he was given a special mission to the Gentiles, he was also to carry Christ's name "before the people of Israel" (Acts 9:15). In the Roman epistle he points out that the message was "first for the Jew" (1:16). Paul never wavered in his faithfulness to that commission. Everywhere he went, he tried first to reach the Jews. Only when they rejected the message of salvation, as some of them did here, did he turn to the Gentiles. Paul was careful to point out that in turning from the Jews his motive was not revenge. From the beginning God had planned to save Gentiles as well as Jews. He had made the Jews a light to the Gentiles so that salvation might be proclaimed to the ends of the earth.

The message that the Jews rejected so vehemently was the same message that gladdened the hearts of the Gentiles, and many of them became believers. The word of the Lord spread quickly through the entire area, but its growing power was met by growing opposition. The Jews, unable to meet Paul's arguments in open debate, resorted to other methods. They prevailed on some of the God-fearing women to use their influence with their husbands to arouse persecution against Paul and Barnabas. Luke does not give us any details of this persecution. From other sources we can glean some hints about it. In 2 Timothy 3:11 Paul writes of persecutions that befell him in Antioch, Iconium, and Lystra. In 2 Corinthians 11:25 he mentions being beaten three times with rods. Since this form of punishment was meted out by the Romans, it probably happened in Roman colonies such as Antioch. This may have been one of the occasions. In the face of such persecutions it was no longer possible for Paul and Barnabas to work effectively in Antioch. Shaking off the dust from their feet as a testimony against the Jews of that city, they made their way to Iconium. They left behind a group of disciples filled both by joy and by the Holy Spirit.

On to Iconium
Acts 14:1-7

In Iconium, in the province of Galatia about ninety miles east of Antioch, Paul and Barnabas went "as usual" to the synagogue. They refused to change their method of operation even though the Jews in Antioch had created problems for them. The pattern in Iconium followed that in Antioch. Probably Paul preached the same message, and at first a great number of the Jews and Gentiles believed. But some Jews refused to accept the message and began to stir up opposition among the Gentiles by poisoning their minds against the preachers. However, it took longer for the Jews to arouse strong opposition, and Paul and Barnabas were able to stay longer in Iconium. During this time, which may have been several weeks or even several months, their ministry was enhanced by "miraculous signs and wonders." But even this evidence of the blessing of the Lord did not convince everyone, especially many of the Jews. Once more those enemies resorted to underhanded tactics. This time they plotted to stone them, but Paul and Barnabas learned about the plot and quickly left for Lystra and Derbe.

In Lystra and Derbe
Acts 14:8-20

Lystra was about twenty-five miles south of Iconium. It is entirely possible that some people there had already heard of Paul and Barnabas, but Luke makes no mention of that. Neither does he mention the synagogue in Lystra, though Paul may have taught there first. Apparently he was speaking in a street or public square, to heathen rather than to Jews and Gentiles who believed in the real God, when Paul noticed a lifelong cripple. Realizing that the cripple accepted the message and believed that he might be healed, Paul looked directly at him and ordered him to stand up. Immediately the man responded and began to walk.

This reminds us of the incident at the temple gate involving Peter and John (Acts 3:1-10). There too a crippled man was healed, but the subsequent events were quite different. In Jerusalem Peter and John were arrested and ordered not to preach anymore. In Lystra, by contrast, Paul and Barnabas were acclaimed as gods. The *King James Version* tells us that Barnabas was thought to be the Roman god Jupiter and Paul was thought to be Mercury, but most modern translations give the Greek names, Zeus and Hermes. There was an ancient myth that at one time those gods had visited Lystra in the guise of men. The city had a temple of Zeus just outside the gate.

Seeing the miracle worked on the cripple, the crowd became excited, thinking that their patron gods were visiting them again. Led by the priest of Zeus, they began to prepare an elaborate sacrifice at the temple of Zeus. As they made these preparations, they were speaking in their native Lycaonian tongue. Perhaps neither Paul nor Barnabas understood that language, and so they did not at first realize what was taking place. Once they understood what was happening, they immediately took steps to halt it. Shouting for attention, they rushed in among the crowd. Then Paul was able to inform them that these missionaries were not gods but only men.

Once the crowd quieted, they were able to tell the reason for their mission. They were the messengers of the one true and living God, who had sent them to proclaim the good news that He cares and provides for people on earth, even people who do not know about Him. But even after they delivered this message, it was hard to keep the people from offering the sacrifice to them.

Following this dramatic incident, Paul and Barnabas may have spent some time in Lystra, sharing the gospel. They remained long enough to win some converts, for there were disciples there when the missionaries came back a little later (Acts 14:21). Lystra was the home of Timothy. It seems likely that Timothy was converted during this first visit of Paul and Barnabas. Later, when Paul visited Lystra on his second missionary journey, Timothy joined Paul's party and traveled with him (Acts 16:1-3).

Luke does not tell us how long Paul and Barnabas were able to remain in Lystra, but before long their work was interrupted by Jews who came from Antioch. The Jews were able to convince many of the people that Paul was a dangerous threat to the community, and so they stoned him and dragged him out of the city, leaving him for dead. What a striking change in attitude! When Paul arrived, he was hailed as a god. Now he was brutally set upon by a lynch mob. But did not our Lord experience something similar? After all, only five days separated the triumphal entry from the crucifixion. It is difficult for us to imagine the kind of hatred that Paul's preaching engendered among many of the Jews. Unable to answer his arguments logically, they turned to violence to silence him.

But Paul was not to be silenced yet. As the disciples gathered around him mourning his apparent death and planning his burial, Paul regained consciousness. Some students think he actually died and was restored to life. Luke does not indicate this, however, and so we conclude that Paul was only knocked unconscious by a stone. This led his enemies to believe he was dead. If there was no miracle, then it was painfully and with help that he got to his feet and returned to the city. The next day he and Barnabas left for Derbe. Every step must have brought him agony from the cuts and bruises that covered his body. Later on, in writing to the church at Corinth, Paul mentions this experience (2 Corinthians 11:25).

Back Home to Antioch
Acts 14:21-28

Derbe, located about thirty-five miles southeast of Lystra, provided fertile soil for the preaching of Paul and Barnabas. A large number of disciples were won to Christ. This city marked the limit of the first missionary journey; now it was time to return home. The shortest route home was overland, through the Cilician Gates, the famous pass through the Taurus Mountains. This route would have taken them through Tarsus, Paul's hometown. Instead they chose to return the way they had come—and for a good reason. In each of the cities where they had preached, they had left a group of followers. These people, young in the faith and faced by strong opposition, needed the encouragement that a visit from Paul and Barnabas would provide.

To return to those cities where they had so recently been expelled took some courage on the part of these two missionaries, but they were up to the challenge. In each city they visited, they appointed elders to lead the flock.

After visiting the churches in Lystra, Iconium, and Antioch, they went down to Attalia on the Mediterranean coast, where they took a ship back to Antioch of Syria, where this first missionary journey had begun. Apparently they bypassed the island of Cyprus on this return trip. Once they were at home, they called the whole congregation together and reported what God had done through them. Especially they told how He had opened a door of faith to Gentiles.

The Jerusalem Conference and Its Aftermath

Acts 15:1—18:22

It is obvious that Luke attaches great importance to the Jerusalem conference. Even though he wrote only a dozen or so years after the event, he was a historian competent enough to realize that this conference was one of the major turning points in the history of the church during the first century. Under the guidance of the Holy Spirit, he has given us an inspired account of this crucial event. Although some scholars think otherwise, it seems likely that Paul was describing the same meeting in Galatians 2. While there are differences between the two accounts, these can readily be explained by the fact that the two men are writing from different viewpoints and for different purposes. Although there is no universal agreement concerning the date of this conference, it must have occurred about A.D. 50.

The Calling of the Conference
Acts 15:1-4

After returning from their first missionary journey, Paul and Barnabas continued to teach for some time in the church in Antioch. Their teaching was disrupted by some brethren who came from Judea declaring that Gentiles who became Christians must also be circumcised according to the law of Moses. It would be reasonable to suppose this issue had been settled earlier when Peter had baptized

Cornelius, a Gentile (Acts 10, 11; chapter 23 of this book). Some in the Jerusalem church had been upset because he had had dealings with Gentiles. Peter had explained that God had directed him and that the Holy Spirit had been poured out upon Cornelius and others at his house. The objectors then had been willing to accept these Gentiles. Perhaps they had felt that Cornelius' conversion was only an isolated case, an exception to the rule. But probably in Antioch and certainly in the churches begun by Paul and Barnabas in Galatia, Gentiles formed the majority. The narrower Jews could tolerate an occasional Cornelius, but the prospect of Gentiles outnumbering Jews in the church frightened them. Old prejudices die slowly, as we who have been through the racial strife of the past three decades can well attest.

The objection now was a little different. These Jews from Jerusalem did not say it was wrong to go to Gentiles with the gospel and win them to Christ, but they insisted that the Gentiles could not be saved unless they became Jews as well as Christians.

Paul and Barnabas were not inclined to allow the results of their successful missionary work to be rejected in such a fashion. The Holy Spirit had sent them on their mission and had directed them, and He had not indicated that Gentile Christians must become Jews. Paul and Barnabas therefore took issue with the Jerusalem brethren. When this debate was not quickly resolved, Paul and Barnabas along with others were sent to Jerusalem to confer with the apostles and elders. Paul was no less inspired than the apostles in Jerusalem; but this trip would make it clear whether or not this doctrine of the original church was correctly represented by the teachers who had come recently from Jerusalem.

On the way to Jerusalem, the group of travelers passed through Phoenicia and Samaria. They paused to visit with the brethren in various places, telling them of the great work that had been accomplished. On every hand their report brought rejoicing. At Jerusalem they received a similar welcome by the church and its leaders.

The Discussion During the Conference
Acts 15:5-21

There were some in Jerusalem who agreed with those who had opposed Paul and Barnabas in Antioch. Luke calls them the party of the Pharisees. Though they had become Christians, they still had the legalistic mind-set that was characteristic of many of the Pharisees whom Jesus encountered during His ministry. Hearing of the many

Gentiles who had turned to Christ, they remained unmoved. They declared those Gentiles who became Christians must become Jews also.

After much discussion, Peter took the floor to present his argument. He reminded the hearers of his experience in the house of Cornelius, which he had reported to them some time earlier. In that situation God had given the Holy Spirit to Gentiles to demonstrate that they were acceptable to Him. Peter said therefore that God is no respecter of persons, but accepts all who come to Him in faith. He then made his argument a bit more personal by reminding the Jewish brethren that neither they nor their fathers had been able to live up to the law. Then why did they want to put this unbearable yoke upon the necks of the Gentiles?

Apparently Peter did not enjoy the complete authority that some Christians later ascribed to him. His pronouncement did not settle the issue, and the debate went on.

Barnabas and Paul next took the floor. The whole church listened attentively as they told how God had blessed their efforts among the Gentiles by miraculous signs and wonders. These were sure signs that He approved what they were doing as they received Gentiles into the church without making Jews of them.

Then James, the brother of the Lord, spoke up. Although he had not been a believer in Jesus until after His resurrection, he had by this time become a recognized and respected leader in the church at Jerusalem. He is the author of the book that bears his name. Later sources say that he came to be called James the Just as a tribute to his virtuous leadership.

Because James had not traveled widely beyond Judea, we would naturally expect him to be conservative on this issue. Indeed, some of the Judaizers looked to him as their leader (Galatians 2:12). When he arose to speak, they may have expected him to defend their position. But if James had any inclination to do so, he laid it aside. Not only did he refer to Peter's report, but he quoted Amos 9:11, 12 to support his position. Since God had made it known that He would accept Gentiles, and since He had foretold this centuries before, Jewish Christians should not make it difficult for Gentiles to come to God. Rather, they should throw open wide the doors to the church.

James left no doubt about where he stood on that basic principle. Submission to the Mosaic law could not be imposed on the Gentiles as a condition of salvation. Yet James was a practical man (his epistle

236

shows this quality well), and he knew that problems would arise in churches where Jews and Gentiles worked side by side. And so he made certain suggestions that, if observed, would certainly lead to more cordial relations between Jewish and Gentile Christians. His plan was to write a letter to the Antioch church (and it would circulate to other churches) outlining these suggestions. Certain things acceptable to heathen Gentiles and probably even some Gentile Christians were highly offensive to Jews. James lists four of these: food offered to idols, sexual immorality, meat of strangled animals, and blood. This list was not to be construed as a moral catalog or a Gentile version of the Ten Commandments, but it gave practical admonitions that would help prevent misunderstanding and strife between Jews and Gentiles.

In his speech James dealt with two issues. The first question was whether Gentile Christians should have to obey the law of Moses. This had to do with the basis of salvation. Are men saved by obeying the law, or by grace? James accepted the position that Peter presented: salvation is by grace. The leaders and the whole church in Jerusalem endorsed this position.

The second issue James discussed was the practical one of how people from diverse backgrounds can worship and work together in the same congregation, an issue that every generation has to face in one form or another. James' solution was that each party must be willing to make some concessions to avoid trampling the delicate sensitivities of the other party. This principle has universal application, and if it were observed it would prevent much strife in our churches today.

For example, a few years later Paul had to deal with the matter of meat sacrificed to idols (1 Corinthians 8). In this case it was not the Jews who were offended, but new Christians who had just come out of paganism. They were still close enough to paganism to be vividly conscious of it, and they thought that eating the meat offered in sacrifice to idols would mean taking part in idol worship. Paul knew the idols were not real gods and could not contaminate the meat offered to them. Yet his solution to the matter exemplified the principle James set forth here. "If what I eat causes my brother to fall into sin," he wrote, "I will never eat meat again" (1 Corinthians 8:13). In other words, Paul would not demand his rights, but would give them up if that would be helpful to a brother in Christ. How many of our difficulties would vanish if more of us were willing to follow his example!

237

A Letter to the Gentiles
Acts 15:22-35

James' solution to the problem met with the approval of the whole church, and so a letter was written and sent to the Gentile believers in Antioch, Syria, and Cilicia. It is important to note that the decision did not originate in the minds of the men. It began with the Holy Spirit and then was accepted by the Jerusalem church: "It seemed good to the Holy Spirit and to us" (Acts 15:28).

Judas (also called Barsabbas) and Silas from the Jerusalem church were sent back to Antioch with Paul and Barnabas when they took the letter. The Christians at Antioch rejoiced when they read the letter. And they were further strengthened by the preaching of Judas and Silas. It was now clear that Jewish law was not to be imposed upon Christians, and this cleared the way for continued energetic preaching of the gospel to all people.

Another Missionary Journey
Acts 15:36—16:8

After a time Paul expressed a wish to revisit the churches that he and Barnabas had founded in Asia Minor. Barnabas agreed, and the two began to lay plans for the trip—and then they disagreed! Barnabas wanted John Mark to accompany them. Paul refused to take a worker who had deserted when the going got tough. They disagreed so sharply that they had to go their separate ways. Barnabas took Mark and went to Cyprus, and Paul took Silas with him and went to visit the churches on the mainland.

Silas proved to be an excellent companion. He, like Paul, was a Roman citizen, which gave him special status anywhere in the empire. In addition, he had the confidence of the Jerusalem church.

Paul and Silas first visited Derbe and then Lystra, where Timothy joined them. Timothy, who as a youth may have witnessed the stoning of Paul, was highly regarded by the brethren of the area. He had been reared in a devout household. Although his father was a Greek, his mother, Eunice, and grandmother, Lois, were pious Jews who had trained him well in the Scriptures.

As Timothy prepared to accompany them, Paul circumcised him so that he would not give offense to Jews along the way. Even though Paul strongly resisted imposing circumcision upon the Gentiles as a condition of salvation, he, in keeping with the spirit of James, was willing to make concessions to the consciences of the Jews.

As the missionary team went through the towns where Paul and Barnabas had preached on their first journey, "the churches were strengthened in the faith and grew daily in numbers." Once these churches had been visited and strengthened, Paul and his party turned their eyes to other horizons. To the west was the Roman province of Asia. Later "a great door for effective work" was opened there (1 Corinthians 16:9). But on this trip the time was not right, and the Holy Spirit forbade them to preach in Asia. Next they looked to the north to Bithynia, but the Spirit of Jesus closed that door also. Paul must have felt thoroughly frustrated by this time, wondering what the Spirit did want him to do. Without stopping to preach, he and his companions went on to the west till they came to the city of Troas on the Aegean Sea.

Entering Europe
Acts 16:9-40

Troas was located near the site of the ancient city of Troy. Caesar Augustus had made it a Roman colony, and it had become prosperous as a trade center. Here Paul had his famous vision that was to change dramatically the course of early church history. In the vision a man of Macedonia stood and pleaded, "Come over to Macedonia and help us!" Feeling sure that God had spoken to him through this vision, Paul wasted no time in seeking passage to Macedonia.

It is at this point that Luke, the author of Acts, enters the account. The story now reads "we," not "they." We wish Luke had told us more about himself, but all we get are a few hints here and there. We can only guess how he became a Christian and how he happened to be in Troas.

From Troas, Paul and his party sailed to Neapolis, the modern Kavalla, in Macedonia. They did not remain in the seaport, however, but moved on to Philippi, ten miles inland. Like Troas, Philippi had been a Roman colony from the time of Octavian, better known as Caesar Augustus. It was the eastern terminus of the famous Egnatian Way, a Roman road across Macedonia from the Aegean to the Adriatic.

The Sabbath found Paul and his companions at a place by the river outside the gate. There they met with some women for worship. From this we conclude that there were not enough Jewish men in the city to form a synagogue.

Paul spoke to the group, which included Lydia, a Gentile worshiper of God. She had come from Thyatira in Asia minor, but now was in business in Philippi. Lydia responded to the gospel message and soon she was baptized, along with her household. Some have seen here a basis for infant baptism. Since no children are mentioned, however, this is a rather weak basis for such an important doctrine. As her first act of Christian helpfulness, this good woman insisted that Paul and his party stay in her home. By profession she was "a dealer in purple cloth." Purple dye was rare and costly, so Lydia probably was a person of some affluence and quite able to provide for the visitors.

We do not know how long Paul remained in Philippi on this first visit. Probably he used the time to teach, perhaps in the streets and marketplaces as well as in Lydia's house and at the meeting place by the river. On one occasion when he was going to the place of prayer, he was met by a slave girl who was possessed by a spirit that enabled her to predict the future. As a result, she was quite profitable for her owners, who were exploiting her affliction. The girl began to follow Paul and the others, shouting, "These men are servants of the Most High God." This was repeated for several days before Paul finally turned and spoke to the spirit, ordering it to leave the girl.

When her owners discovered that they had lost their easy source of revenue, they were furious. To be set free by Christ may be a costly experience. In this case it cost the slave girl the power to predict the future, and it cost the owners their easy profit. No doubt the girl was glad to be free from the tyranny of that spirit, but the owners were not glad to lose part of their income. Angrily they seized Paul and Silas and charged that they were throwing the city into an uproar by advocating illegal practices. Actually the owners themselves were generating the uproar, but the careless crowd in the marketplace was easily caught up in the anti-Jewish demonstration. Apparently the magistrates thought the best way to end the riot was to side with the noisy crowd. They ordered the men stripped, beaten, and thrown into prison, apparently without even giving them a chance to identify themselves or offer any defense. This was a clear violation of the law, but mobs are not noted for paying strict attention to the law. The magistrates were intent on stopping the uproar, for the Roman authorities had little patience with local officials who could not maintain order.

Paul and Silas were turned over to the jailer, who put them into the inner prison and fastened their feet in stocks. These conditions were hardly calculated to enhance congregational singing, but about midnight the pair were singing hymns. In the midst of their concert, an earthquake so shook the prison that the doors were opened and the prisoners' chains came loose. The jailer, waking up and seeing the open doors, thought surely the prisoners had escaped. He drew his sword to commit suicide. Roman law required that a jailer who allowed a prisoner to escape must pay with his own life. This jailer apparently felt that suicide was less humiliating than a public trial and execution.

Paul stopped the man before he could do himself harm. The prisoners were all there, but the poor jailer still was beside himself with fear. He cried out, "What must I do to be saved?" What did this pagan jailer mean by that? Did he want to be saved from execution because of a jail break? Or did he have in mind something more— eternal salvation? Paul took his question to refer to eternal salvation; and since Paul was there when the man asked the question, he was certainly in a better position than we are to know what the man meant.

Paul had been in Philippi for some time. The jailer may have heard him preaching in the marketplace. Or he may have heard reports of his preaching. Obviously this jailer didn't know much about the gospel, but he knew enough to ask the right question. Paul informed him that he should believe in the Lord Jesus, and then he proceeded to speak the word of the Lord to him and others in his household. The jailer believed the message and demonstrated his faith and change of heart by tending to the wounds of Paul and Silas, and then by being baptized along with members of his family who also heard and believed the message.

In the morning the magistrates wanted to forget the whole affair and get the two men out of town as quickly as they could. They sent their officers to the jail with an order to release them, but Paul would have none of that. He demanded that the magistrates themselves come and escort them out. Paul wanted to make sure that it was publicly known that they were not criminals. Along with the demand, he sent word that he and Silas were Roman citizens. It was illegal to punish them without a fair trial, and the magistrates would be in trouble if the two prisoners reported the violation to higher authorities. Quickly and humbly the magistrates came to release them and beg them to leave town. Paul and Silas wanted no trouble. They went to the home of Lydia, and then left for Thessalonica. Now again the record says "they" instead of "we." Apparently Luke stayed in Troas.

241

Moving on in Macedonia
Acts 17:1-15

In Thessalonica, Paul followed his usual custom of visiting the synagogue the first Sabbath he was in town. For three Sabbath days he reasoned with those in the meeting, and some of the Jews along with many of the Gentiles accepted his message. The Jews who rejected the message rounded up some of the town riff-raff and started a riot against Paul and Silas. They sought them at the home of Jason, where they were staying; but the two were not there at the time, so the crowd dragged Jason before the town officials and charged him with harboring subversives.

In this kind of hostile atmosphere it was impossible for Paul to work. As soon as night came, he and Silas were sent to Berea. There they received a warm welcome and made many believers. "The Bereans were of more noble character than the Thessalonians, for they received the message with great eagerness and examined the Scriptures every day to see if what Paul said was true" (Acts 17:11). Who knows how many Sunday-school classes have taken the name Berean? And, for that matter, what finer name could a class find? But this happy situation was not to last for long. Word soon got back to Thessalonica, and the Jews there sent some agitators to Berea to stir up trouble.

Paul in Greece
Acts 17:16—18:17

Once more Paul thought it best to leave town in a hurry. This time some of the brethren accompanied him to Athens, where he was to remain until Silas and Timothy joined him. As he waited for his companions, Paul's heart became heavy as he saw the great number of idols about the city. In Athens he reasoned not only in the synagogue but in the marketplace. Here his witnessing soon attracted the attention of some of the philosophers, who liked nothing better than to dispute about such matters. They seem to have been especially intrigued by his preaching about the resurrection. Finally they brought him to the Areopagus (or Mars Hill), where he was invited to speak.

In Athens Paul had seen an altar to an unknown god, and this became the starting point for his sermon. He said the God unknown in Athens was the true God who had created all men. Now God required that all men repent, for a day of judgment was coming. God had given assurance of this by raising Jesus from the dead.

Some sneered at his teaching about the resurrection, but some wanted to hear more. Paul's efforts did not win so many people in Athens as they did in some other places, but at least a few became believers. Intellectuals, secure in scholarly pride, have often been the most difficult to win to the Lord.

It seems that Timothy at least, and possibly Silas, caught up with Paul at Athens as planned. Paul then sent Timothy to encourage the Christians in Thessalonica, where the preachers had stayed only a short time (1 Thessalonians 3:1-3). Nothing is said about what Silas did at the time. Perhaps he went back to Philippi, or stayed a longer time in Berea, while Paul went on to Corinth alone.

In Corinth Paul met a Jewish couple, Aquila and Priscilla, who had recently come from Rome because Emperor Claudius had expelled all Jews from that city. As usual, Paul went first to the synagogue. He taught there every Sabbath, and through the week he worked as a tentmaker to earn his living.

When Silas and Timothy joined Paul there, they probably brought offerings from the Christians in Philippi, Thessalonica, and Berea. Now Paul could stop his tentmaking, and the three of them could teach full-time.

More vigorous teaching brought more hostile opposition. Some of the Jews became so abusive that Paul turned to the Gentiles, and great numbers of them became Christians. In a vision the Lord assured Paul that he was to continue his ministry in Corinth in spite of persecution. After a year and a half, the Jews stirred up trouble for Paul and brought him before Gallio, the proconsul. But Gallio threw the case out and drove the Jews from his court. Paul remained in Corinth a while longer, strengthening the growing church.

It is interesting to contrast the progress of the gospel in Athens and in Corinth. In the great cultural center of the ancient world, the word received only a modest response; in the worldly and wicked seaport town of Corinth, the church grew rapidly.

Journey's End
Acts 18:18-22

When Paul was ready to move on, again we read nothing about Silas and Timothy. Perhaps they went back a second time to encourage the churches they had left behind. Paul took Aquila and Priscilla with him as he sailed across the Aegean Sea to Ephesus. That was in Asia, where he had been forbidden to teach at an earlier time. Now he found a willing audience in the synagogue, but he was determined to push on to Palestine. Leaving Aquila and Priscilla in Ephesus to work among the people, he promised to return. Again taking ship, he landed at Caesarea in Palestine, went up to Jerusalem to greet the church, and then returned to Antioch of Syria. So ended his second missionary journey.

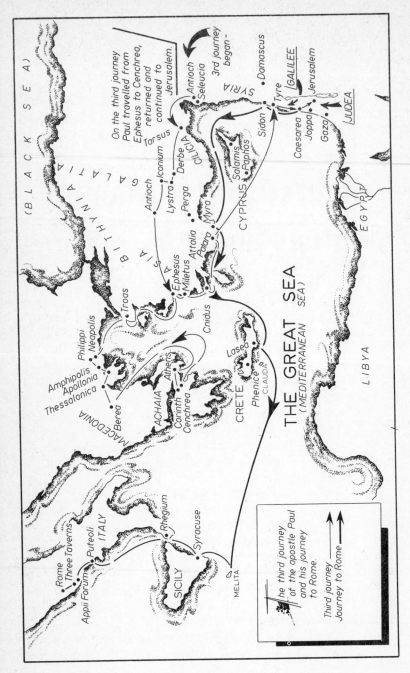

On the third journey Paul travelled from Ephesus to Cenchrea, returned and continued to Jerusalem.

(BLACK SEA)

GALATIA

BITHYNIA

ASIA

SYRIA

3rd journey began-

Antioch
Seleucia

Damascus

GALILEE
Jerusalem

JUDEA

Tarsus

Antioch

Iconium
Lystra
Derbe
CILICIA

Perga
Attalia
Patara
Myra

Sidon

Tyre

Caesarea

Joppa

Gaza

Salamis
Paphos

CYPRUS

Ephesus
Miletus

Cnidus

Troas

Philippi
Neapolis

Amphipolis
Apollonia
Thessalonica

Berea

MACEDONIA

ACHAIA

Athens

Corinth
Cenchrea

Lasea

Phenice
CLAUDA

CRETE

THE GREAT SEA
(MEDITERRANEAN SEA)

LIBYA

EGYPT

Rome
Three Taverns

Appii Forum
Puteoli
ITALY

Rhegium

Syracuse

SICILY

MELITA

The third journey of the apostle Paul and his journey to Rome.

Third journey
Journey to Rome

Paul's Third Missionary Journey and Trip to Rome

Acts 18:23—28:31

After his second missionary journey, Paul spent some time in Antioch. No doubt he needed a rest, but probably he was active in teaching even while he rested. But Paul's great aim was to preach the gospel where it had not been heard before (Romans 15:20). Soon he set out on a third journey.

The first part of this trip took him through the familiar territories of Galatia and Phrygia where he had worked twice before. Derbe, Lystra, Iconium, and Pisidian Antioch were there. Paul spent some time among the Christians in those towns, strengthening them spiritually rather than engaging in extensive evangelistic activities.

Victories in Ephesus
Acts 18:23—19:41

From Galatia, Paul took the road westward through the province of Asia, a route that the Holy Spirit had closed on his second missionary journey. So he came to Ephesus, where he had stopped briefly near the end of his second tour.

Between Paul's first visit to Ephesus and his return, a strong witness had been maintained in the synagogue, thanks to Aquila and Priscilla. Their efforts had been strengthened by the appearance of Apollos, a Jew from Alexandria. Though his knowledge of Christianity was incomplete, he spoke eloquently in the synagogue. Priscilla and Aquila "explained to him the way of God more adequately"—that is, showed him the difference between John's baptism and Christian baptism. He then became even more effective. Before Paul arrived back in Ephesus, Apollos had left for Achaia. There he was active in Corinth, and Paul later commended his work (1 Corinthians 3:5, 6).

Among the disciples that Paul found in Ephesus were a dozen who knew only John's baptism and knew nothing of the Holy Spirit. How they came to be in Ephesus, we can only guess. Some students suppose they had been converted by Apollos before he received the adequate teaching from Aquila and Priscilla. If that is the case, it seems strange that Apollos had not also shared his improved knowledge with them. Now under Paul's teaching they were baptized into Christ and received the Holy Spirit.

The opportunity was open for Paul to speak in the synagogue, and he was able to continue this for three months before Jewish antagonism forced him out. He soon found a place of meeting in the lecture hall of Tyrannus, where he was able to teach daily for a period of two years. During this time Paul worked many mighty miracles by the power of God. Sick people were healed and demons were driven from persons they had possessed. Some Jewish exorcists, the seven sons of Sceva, observed the power Paul had through the name of Jesus. Seeing that Paul's exorcism was better than theirs, they tried to drive out a demon by the name of Jesus, but with painful and embarrassing results. The demon knew Jesus and Paul, but not these pretenders. The possessed man viciously attacked them and drove them out naked and bleeding.

Word of this incident spread quickly through the city, causing many who practiced black magic to have some second thoughts about it. Great numbers brought their books or scrolls of black magic and burned them publicly. It must have been quite a bonfire, because the value of the books came to fifty thousand drachmas. (A drachma was a workman's pay for a day.) These events led to the spread of Christianity, not only in Ephesus but to other cities in the province of Asia.

Paul's stay at Ephesus was long and fruitful. From there he wrote his first letter to the church of Corinth, which desperately needed his inspired guidance before he was ready to leave Ephesus (1 Corinthians 16:8). But after nearly three years he planned to move on. Timothy was with him now, and another helper named Erastus. He sent the two of them ahead of him to Macedonia. They could arrange meetings of Christians so Paul could give them his help and encouragement without staying there very long, and Paul could go on with his work in Ephesus while they were making those arrangements.

That delay in departing from Ephesus almost proved fatal. Paul's preaching had won multitudes to the faith, and they were having an impact on the community. Some who made their living from idolatry were dismayed. Their business was hurting.

Ephesus, with a good harbor and connecting overland trade routes, was the most important commercial center in western Asia Minor. It was also the center for the worship of Artemis. The *King James Version* uses the Roman name, Diana, but the Ephesian idea of the goddess was different from the Roman. Artemis was thought to be the mother goddess of the earth. At Ephesus was her magnificent temple, considered one of the seven wonders of the ancient world. The presence of such an outstanding tourist attraction brought substantial economic blessings to the city, and especially to those who made and sold the shrines or images of the goddess. Tourists would pay high prices for those little silver items that could be not only beautiful souvenirs but also home worship centers. But now people all over the province were becoming Christians, and Christians bought no souvenirs of Artemis.

Demetrius was an activist. Energetically he organized a demonstration. "Great is Artemis of the Ephesians" was a popular cry. When the silversmiths began it, loafers in the street and market were quick to join in, and the group swiftly became a mob. Failing to find Paul, they seized two of his friends and took them to the theater, a huge arena where thousands could gather. When Paul learned what was happening he rather rashly wanted to go and reason with the mob, but the Christians and some officials of the city joined in restraining him. Cautiously the officials let the demonstration go on for a couple of hours. By that time perhaps the people were feeling a little foolish and tired of shouting. The town clerk was able to get their attention and speak reasonably. He said: (1) Everybody knows Artemis is great, so what is the shouting about? (2) The men you have seized are not guilty of any crime. (3) We have regular courts to handle any charges. (4) We have a legal assembly to take care of any matters that do not require court action. Further, he reminded the people, the Roman authorities were likely to take a dim view of such unprovoked violence. This quieted the people, and the crowd was dismissed.

Through Macedonia and Greece
Acts 20:1-6

Once the uproar had quieted, Paul took leave of the disciples and left for Macedonia. He encouraged the brethren there and moved on to Greece, where he remained for three months. He might have remained longer, but Jewish opposition grew. A Jewish plot against his life caused him to travel overland back through Macedonia rather than go by ship. From Philippi, they sailed over to Troas. Luke joined the party at Philippi, and once more the narrative says "we."

The Journey to Jerusalem
Acts 20:7—21:16

Arriving in Troas, Paul and his companions remained seven days, apparently waiting until the first day of the week so that they could meet with the whole congregation. The practice of the church was to meet on the first day of the week for the breaking of bread (the Lord's Supper), and at their meeting Paul had an opportunity to speak to them. Not programmed for twenty-minute sermonettes, he preached until midnight. This was apparently past the bedtime of one of his listeners, a young man by the name of Eutychus, who fell fast asleep. Apparently the room was quite crowded, for he had unwisely taken a seat in the third-story window. Falling to the ground below, he was taken up for dead. But Paul threw himself upon the lifeless body and put his arms around it and then pronounced the young man alive. We can well imagine that the communion service that followed was filled with wonder and rejoicing.

Paul's party had sailed on ahead, and he joined them down the coast at Assos. From here they sailed to Miletus, where Paul asked the elders of the Ephesian church to meet him. What follows is one of the most poignant scenes in the New Testament. He rehearsed for them the highlights of his ministry among them, recalling how he had faithfully proclaimed the good news in the face of hardships and threats. Compelled by the Spirit, he was now going to Jerusalem. Although he did not know in detail what the future held, he knew that he would suffer imprisonment. He also knew that he would never again see all of them face to face. With his final words to them as leaders, he urged them to guard the flock carefully. He warned that savage wolves would threaten the flock. Even within the church false teachers would arise and draw away followers after them. Across the centuries, countless heresies and divisions in the church have demonstrated the accuracy of this prophecy.

In this farewell to the elders Paul gives us a statement of Jesus that is not recorded in the Gospels: "It is more blessed to give than to receive" (Acts 20:35). This is an important truth for anyone who would be a leader. After they knelt down and prayed together, the elders embraced Paul and kissed him good-bye.

Paul and his companions continued their trip by sea until they came to Caesarea. There Paul stayed in the home of Philip the evangelist. While he was there, Agabus, a prophet, came down from Judea. He brought the same disturbing message that Paul had heard before. Great danger awaited him in Jerusalem. Agabus dramatically made his point by taking Paul's belt and tying his own hands and feet to illustrate his prophecy that Paul would be made a prisoner of the Roman authorities. Hearing this, the members of Paul's traveling party as well as the disciples in Caesarea urged him not to go to Jerusalem. But neither their fears nor their pleadings could change his mind.

Paul in Jerusalem
Acts 21:17-26

Upon his arrival in Jerusalem, Paul was warmly greeted by the brethren. And well they might welcome him, for Paul and his companions brought relief from the churches for the benefit of the brethren. Offerings had been gathered from several congregations (Romans 15:25-27). Paul had given those churches to understand that he personally would go with their messengers to take those offerings to Jerusalem (1 Corinthians 16:3, 4). Perhaps that was why he insisted on going in spite of warnings of danger.

At first there was no sign of the predicted trouble. The brethren in Jerusalem were concerned, however, because word had gotten back that Paul had been teaching the Jews to turn away from the law of Moses. Leaders in Jerusalem knew that thousands of Jewish Christians, hearing these false rumors, would be disturbed when they learned that Paul had arrived.

They had a plan that they hoped would silence criticism. Four men had taken a vow. Details of the vow are not given, but evidently it involved rites of purification in which sacrifices would be offered. Afterward the men would have their hair cut. Since the sacrifices were costly, sometimes a patron would pay the expenses for those being purified. James and the elders of the Jerusalem church were urging Paul to become the patron for these four. His participation in the public service would be observed, and it would give the lie to the rumors that Paul had turned away from Jewish laws and customs. Paul was quite willing to do this. It was in keeping with his practice to "become all things to all men so that by all possible means I might save some" (1 Corinthians 9:22). That passage deals specifically with evangelism, but it seems equally applicable in this effort to maintain peace among the brethren.

The next day Paul went with the men to the temple to give notification about the time when offerings would be made. But this effort to conciliate the Jewish Christians almost proved fatal for reasons the elders had not anticipated.

Paul Arrested
Acts 21:27—22:29

It seems that seven days were involved in the rites of purification. All went well till the week was nearly over. Then some non-Christian Jews from Asia saw Paul and immediately set up a clamor against him. They charged him with teaching men to reject the law, and worse, they charged that he had defiled the temple by bringing a Gentile into it. Neither charge was true, but in the excitement they created, no one bothered to ask about that.

Hearing the noise of shouting, the whole city came running to see what was happening. The agitated crowd seized Paul and dragged him from the temple, intending to kill him. But before they could carry out their terrible deed, word reached the commander of the Roman troops that were quartered close by the temple to deal with just such riots as this. The troops came running on the scene just in time to keep Paul from being beaten to death by the angry mob. Seeing that Paul was the center of the activity, the commander ordered him put in chains. He tried to learn the cause of the violence, but the mob was so excited that some shouted one thing and some another until it was impossible to get at the truth. There seemed to be nothing to do but to take Paul back to the barracks in protective custody.

As he was being led away, Paul asked permission to speak to the crowd. When he started to speak to them in their own language, the people became quiet and listened as he told them about his earlier life. He told how as a zealous Jew he persecuted Christians, even causing some to be put to death. Then he started to Damascus to arrest Christians who had fled there. But before he reached his destination, he met Jesus of Nazareth. Overwhelmed and blinded by the confrontation, he readily obeyed the Lord and went on to

251

Damascus. There Ananias, a respected Jewish Christian, was sent to minister to him. He received his sight and was baptized, washing away his sins. After this he returned to Jerusalem. While he was praying in the temple, the Lord told him to leave Jerusalem and carry the message of salvation to the Gentiles.

The crowd listened until he mentioned Gentiles. That sent them into a rage again. At this, the commander sent Paul into the barracks with orders for the soldiers to flog him and make him tell what he had done to anger the people. As they were about to beat him, Paul informed them that he was a Roman citizen. To beat him without a trial was illegal. This got the immediate attention of the commander, who was quite alarmed because he had put a Roman in chains.

Paul Before the Sanhedrin
Acts 22:30—23:11

To get to the bottom of the affair, the commander ordered the chief priests and the Sanhedrin to assemble the next day. Paul knew very well that he would get no justice from that prejudiced tribunal, so he resorted to a stratagem. Some of the judges were Sadducees and some were Pharisees. Paul identified himself as a Pharisee. Then he said, "I stand on trial because of my hope in the resurrection of the dead." That was quite true. That very doctrine had brought the beginning of persecution years before (Acts 4:1-3). Nevertheless, this split the Sanhedrin. The Pharisees now defended Paul, while the Sadducees attacked him more violently, because they did not believe in any resurrection. The dispute became so violent that the commander feared for Paul's life and ordered him back to the barracks. That night the Lord stood near and once more encouraged him: "Take courage! As you have testified about me in Jerusalem, so you must also testify in Rome."

Paul's Escape From Jerusalem
Acts 23:12-35

Thwarted in their efforts to do away with Paul, some of the fanatical Jews formed a conspiracy to assassinate him. But Paul's nephew heard of the plot and brought word to Paul and the commander. The commander lost no time in making his prisoner secure. He ordered Paul sent to Caesarea under a heavy guard. Felix the governor had his headquarters there, and the commander sent him a letter explaining the situation. Upon receiving Paul and the letter, Felix ordered him kept under guard until his accusers arrived.

The Trial Before Felix
Acts 24:1-27

Five days later the high priest Ananias arrived in Caesarea along with some of the elders and a lawyer named Tertullus. Tertullus presented the Jews' case before Felix. Paul was accused of being a troublemaker and a ringleader of the Nazarene sect, that is, the Christians. He was also accused of desecrating the temple.

Paul then was allowed to defend himself. He denied that he was a rabble-rouser or that he had profaned the temple. He went on to point out that he had not come to Jerusalem to stir up trouble, but to bring alms for the poor. The troublemakers were some Jews from Asia. If they had any complaint against him, said Paul, they ought to be there to testify.

Felix had a reputation for being corrupt, but he was no fool. He readily saw that Paul was no dangerous criminal, but he didn't want to antagonize the Jews by releasing him. So he postponed the case till he could hear from the commander in Jerusalem. In the meantime Paul was kept in lenient custody. Friends were free to visit. Luke was there to help him. Others had come to bring funds to Jerusalem (Acts 20:4), and perhaps they also stayed for some time. Philip the evangelist probably was a frequent visitor, along with other disciples who lived in Caesarea.

Felix had more than a passing knowledge of the Jewish faith. His wife, Drusilla, was Jewish, the sister of Herod Agrippa II. So the governor often found time to talk with Paul the prisoner. Paul used these opportunities to speak to the governor about righteousness, self-control, and judgment to come. That kind of preaching was aimed right at the governor's sins, and it frightened him. One reason, and perhaps the main reason, for talking to Paul was that he hoped Paul would offer him a bribe. But this Paul never did, and so for two years Paul was left in prison.

Paul Before Festus and Agrippa
Acts 25:1—26:32

After two years Felix was succeeded by Porcius Festus, who soon traveled to Jerusalem and met with the Jewish authorities. They had not forgotten Paul even after two years, and they urged Festus to send him to Jerusalem for trial. What they really hoped was that his trip to Jerusalem would give them a chance to ambush and assassinate him. But Paul guessed what they were plotting. He evaded them by appealing to the emperor at Rome, as any Roman citizen had the privilege of doing. Festus then had no choice. He had to send the prisoner to Rome.

It is obvious that Festus was not greatly impressed by the Jews' case against Paul. As a newcomer in the country, he knew little of the frantic feuding among the Jews. This put him in a difficult spot. He had to send a prisoner to Rome, but he had no substantial charge to send with him, no valid reason for his being a prisoner. He had a chance to get some information when King Herod Agrippa arrived for a state visit. This king's family had been ruling Jews for five generations. Agrippa himself now ruled a territory north and east of Galilee.

Readers of the New Testament are likely to have trouble keeping the Herods straight. This Agrippa was Herod Agrippa II. His father was Herod Agrippa I, who had the apostle James killed (Acts 12:1, 2). His grandfather had no place in New Testament history, but his grandfather's brother was Herod Antipas, who killed John the Baptist. And his great-grandfather was the infamous Herod who killed the babies of Bethlehem.

Festus hoped to get some advice from Agrippa. Agrippa, with a wide and deep knowledge of all things Jewish, knew about Paul and was eager to hear him. So the prisoner was brought before the visiting king.

Before Agrippa, Paul recounted his devout, even fanatic life as a Pharisee. Then he told of his experience on the road to Damascus. He summed up his later life in these words: "So then, King Agrippa, I was not disobedient to the vision from heaven." He pointed out that the gospel he preached was in perfect harmony with the Old Testament prophecies known to the king. Agrippa turned aside the personal appeal, but he was deeply impressed. He agreed with Festus that Paul had done nothing worthy of imprisonment and could have been set free if he had not appealed to Caesar.

Paul's Trip to Rome
Acts 27:1—28:31

Paul had appealed to Caesar, and so to Rome he must go. Paul had long wanted to visit Rome and even the regions beyond (Romans 15:23-28). It is not likely that he had planned to arrive in chains, but God was answering his prayer in a way he had not hoped for. Chapter 27 relates in some detail the voyage that began in Caesarea. Late in the season their ship arrived in Crete, where Paul advised the sailors to remain for the winter. But ignoring Paul's advice, they set out, only to be caught in a terrible storm that drove the ship helplessly before it. Finally the ship went aground on the island of Malta.

On Malta, Paul and his companions spent the winter. But the time was not wasted, for Paul was able to carry on a healing ministry there. In the spring they resumed their trip to Rome. Word of Paul's coming preceded him, and some of the brethren came down the Appian Way to meet him.

Once Paul got to Rome, he was turned over to the proper authorities. Instead of being kept in prison, he was allowed to live in his own quarters, guarded by a soldier. There he had many visitors and many opportunities to teach. The Jews in Rome had not received any word from Jerusalem about him, and so they were willing to listen to him. As in most other Jewish communities that Paul visited, some accepted his message and some rejected it.

For at least two years Paul remained in Rome under these conditions. In addition to his teaching and preaching, he found time to write. It is generally believed that Ephesians, Philippians, Colossians, and Philemon were written during this period. Luke closes the book of Acts at this point, leaving us in suspense about what happened at Paul's trial. This strongly suggests that he finished the book while Paul was still in prison, about A.D. 63.

Many scholars believe that the charges were dropped or he was acquitted. Apparently upon his release he traveled again in the regions north of the Mediteranean. Then about A.D. 67, in the fanatical persecution by Emperor Nero, he was arrested a second time, tried, and executed.